Lingo!

Tab Julius

New Riders

New Riders Publishing, Indianapolis, IN

Lingo!

By Tab Julius

Published by:
New Riders Publishing
201 West 103rd Street
Indianapolis, IN 46290 USA

Printed in the United States of America 1 2 3 4 5 6 7 8 9 0

Library of Congress Cataloging-in-Publication Data

```
Julius, Tab, 1962-

     Lingo! / Tab Julius.

          p.    cm.

     Includes index.

     ISBN 1-56205-592-5

     1. Lingo (Computer program language)   I. Title.
QA76.73.L22J85   1996                        96-14085
006.6--dc20                                  CIP
```

Warning and Disclaimer

This book is designed to provide information about Lingo. Every effort has been made to make this book as complete and as accurate as possible, but no warranty or fitness is implied.

The information is provided on an "as is" basis. The author(s) and New Riders Publishing shall have neither liability nor responsibility to any person or entity with respect to any loss or damages arising from the information contained in this book or from the use of the disks or programs that may accompany it.

Publisher	*Don Fowley*
Publishing Manager	*David Dwyer*
Marketing Manager	*Mary Foote*
Managing Editor	*Carla Hall*

Development Editor
John Kane

Project Editor
Laura Frey

Copy Editor
Phil Worthington

Technical Editor
Clarence Lamb

Associate Marketing Manager
Tamara Apple

Acquisitions Coordinator
Stacey Beheler

Publisher's Assistant
Karen Opal

Cover Designer
Aren Howell

Cover Production
Aren Howell

Book Designer
Sandra Schroeder

Production Manager
Kelly Dobbs

Production Team Supervisor
Laurie Casey

Graphics Image Specialists
Stephen Adams, Dan Harris, Clint Lahnen, Laura Robbins

Production Analysts
Jason Hand
Bobbi Satterfield

Production Team
Kim Cofer, Tricia Flodder, Aleata Howard, Krena Lanham, Beth Rago, Erich J. Richter, Megan Wade, Christy Wagner, Karen Walsh

Indexer
Cheryl Dietsch
Debra Myers

About the Author

Tab Julius is president of Penworks Corporation, a multimedia software development company. He is also the publisher of the *Lingo User's Journal,* a monthly publication dedicated to Lingo and xobject/xtra programming. In addition to *Lingo!,* he is a contributing author of *More Tricks of the Game Programming Gurus* (1995, Sams Publishing) and *PC Techniques C/C++ Power Tools* (1992, Bantam Books). He has been writing software since 1976. Some commercial credits include Express Publisher v3.0, an award-winning desktop publisher, CD-ROM and Windows versions of many children's educational software games for The Learning Company, and enhanced CDs for various bands in the music industry.

Trademark Acknowledgments

All terms mentioned in this book that are known to be trademarks or service marks have been appropriately capitalized. New Riders Publishing cannot attest to the accuracy of this information. Use of a term in this book should not be regarded as affecting the validity of any trademark or service mark.

Dedication

To my wife, Lori, and my sons, André and Spencer.

Acknowledgments

I'd first like to thank my wife, Lori, for putting up with my writing project, even though she thinks I already have plenty to do. My editors, John Kane and Laura Frey, deserve awards not only for making my writing understandable, but for tolerating my penchant to flagrantly ignore traditional rules of English. Of course, there are many others at New Riders who had an equal, if not as visible (to me), role in this project; it takes everyone to make it come together. The folks at Macromedia were very helpful with access and information about Director 5.0, so thanks go to them, too. And, of course, the readers of this book. A book isn't much good unless there's someone to read it; I hope this one has helped to take some of the mystery out of programming in Lingo.

Contents at a Glance

Table of Contents

Introduction

What We Intend to Accomplish Here

Welcome! This book is something I've wanted to do for a long time. Lingo is a very powerful language, but many people who use Macromedia Director shy away from Lingo. With Director you can create multimedia titles using just the score, with as little Lingo as possible, or you can do it all in Lingo and never go near the score.

Some of the users of Director are artists, producers, or designers and view Director as a tool to help their ideas come to life. Others are programmers who have come to Director hoping to make their lives easier. Of course, there are those who are in both categories (and probably a few in neither). And, finally, there are those who are using Director because their company told them to do so.

As one might expect, the programmers gravitate toward Lingo and the non-programming-inclined gravitate toward the score. Sometimes the Lingo-only people jump through hoops to do something that's actually very easy using the score, and sometimes the score-only people create these big elaborate scores in order to accomplish something that's very easy using Lingo.

There just comes a point, though, where the score doesn't cut it. Certain things you want to do, certain ways you want to make your title behave, just need Lingo to make it happen. This is where the magic line is. Who will cross over?

Lingo itself is not hard, as far as programming languages go. The problem that most non-programmers face is that for them, there's not one learning curve to Lingo, but many. Certainly there's the syntax—what command, what format, how to type it, and so on. A programmer trained in some other language who comes to Lingo has to deal with the syntax, and some other quirks specific to the Director environment, but that's about the extent of it.

The non-programmer, however, also is faced with converting his concept of what he *wants to do* into getting Lingo to *do* it. This isn't merely the syntax. In fact, the syntax is the least part of it. Most of it is learning programming concepts and approaches to problem solving.

As an alternative to banging your head against the wall trying to figure something out by trial and error, I intend, through this book, to take you into advanced programming concepts with Lingo. If you decide to work in another language after Lingo you will find that the theory of what you learn here applies to many other programming languages as well.

Should you already develop in another language but want to or need to start working in Lingo, you can use this book to quickly convert the concepts you know from your other languages into their Lingo equivalents.

In other words, I intend to help you become a Lingo developer.

This book assumes you have read the manuals. I'm not going to explain every last thing about Director, and I'm not going to relist every single Lingo command. You already have manuals that do that. The intention here is to get into things that the manuals do *not* cover, but which are critical to a true understanding of Lingo and developing with it.

Something about Who You Are

So, which one are you? Programmer or non-programmer? Let me explain how I prefer to break it down.

Non-Programmers

The non-programmers break down into Those Who Want To Program and Those Who Do Not.

If the thought of programming concerns you, and for that reason you are one of Those Who Do Not, you might find through reading this book that it is actually easier than you thought, if only someone explains the concepts to you (as we will do here).

If you are one of Those Who Do Not because the thought of programming actually *offends* you, you probably shouldn't be reading this book. Actually, you probably *aren't* reading this book, so we won't waste any more time on this paragraph.

On the other hand, if the thought of programming interests you, intrigues you, or maybe even excites you—that is, if you are one of Those Who Want To Program—but you have never really done much with it, this book will be very good for you in that it will reveal many programming concepts and perhaps will help take you from the position of non-programmer to one of the programming levels. I would suggest however, that you supplement this book with one of the introductory Lingo books that are available. With both in hand, you should be set.

Programmers

Programmers I would break down into Those Who Want To Program, and Those Who Actually Do Program. In other words, you don't need to program to be a programmer, you just need the programming mentality—a compelling desire to learn or do as much programming as possible. More than anything else though, to be a programmer at heart you need to have decided that programming is *fun*. And it really is (at least I think so).

The ones in the Those Who Want To Program group are those who, regardless of origin, have decided that programming is fun but need to learn more. If you're in this group then this book is perfect for you. I'll teach you all sorts of things.

Those who fall into the Those Who Actually Do Program category have some subgroupings:

The Beginners

The beginners have dabbled with it, but need many basic concepts cleared up. Concepts such as how handlers work, what parameters are and how *they* work, the ideas behind global variables, and so on. We'll cover a lot of this, and hopefully turn the beginners into intermediates, if not advanced.

Intermediates

Intermediates understand the basic theory behind handlers and variables and such, and are ready to become advanced. By this point the adage of "the more you learn, the less you know" starts to ring true. Having gotten through the preliminaries, things like lists, objects, MIAWs, and xtras or xobjects beckon to be learned.

Although I will show you all this stuff in the effort to move you on to advanced, it would be in your best interest to still read the chapters on things you think you might already know. You might find that I explain some little points that make it all seem clear, or that I fill in some missing pieces that perhaps you didn't even know were missing. It won't hurt—it might even help, and you don't have to tell anyone that you read them if you don't want to.

Advanced Programmers

Advanced programmers I would say have enough of a background that they could work professionally if they want to (some do). They work with lists, objects, and MIAWs without flinching, and might even be flirting with writing xtras.

Professional Programmers

The professionals are those who *do* make their living through software engineering. Most likely they have a college-level degree in computer science, and they program in a variety of languages, such as C. I would also place those who have a computer science degree, but haven't been in the work force yet, in this category too, because they have a solid foundation in programming concepts and undoubtedly have done programming in at least a few different languages (I suspect BASIC, Pascal, and C, and perhaps assembly).

Professionals get used to acquiring a variety of information sources and gleaning what they can from each of them. I'm expecting that this book will be used for the same purpose. You will find that Lingo is surprisingly advanced for a "scripting" language, as it is modeled somewhat after SmallTalk, and has object-oriented features for the OOPers among you. It is a very loosely typed language, too, which can be good or bad depending on what you're used to. If you like to compile your C code with the STRICT settings on, and run your programs through Lint in your spare time, you might be a little offended at the informality of the language, but I think you'll overcome that quickly.

You should find the language relatively easy to pick up. You'll probably be held back more by the idiosyncrasies of Director than by anything else. And, yes, you can extend it with C. You can write xtras (formerly known as xobjects) that can be called from Lingo, so essentially anything that you can't accomplish through Lingo you can do yourself in C. This is one of the things that particularly attracted me to Lingo.

Something about Who I Am

Depending on where you are on the Lingo learning curve, my viewpoint and background may or may not be of interest, but I'll explain them anyway. It helps to put the things I say, and why I say them, into perspective.

I personally think programming is fun, at least while things are working the way I want them to. A bug that goes on for weeks or months and starts to screw up my work schedule ceases to be fun and starts to be a frustration. That aside, though, I enjoy what I do.

My first contact with a computer was a demonstration machine that was at the Ontario Science Center that played Tic-Tac-Toe. I was 9 or 10 at the time. When I played it, I made a move that should have let me win. Instead, the computer recorded a *different* move that let *it* win. I came away with the following impressions:

- ✤ Computers are fun and can be used to play games

- ✤ They can be made to cheat, or they can have bugs in them

- ✤ As a result, a computer shouldn't be taken too seriously

This would have been around 1972.

By 1976 I had an account on Dartmouth College's computer via my high school. There were chat/talk programs where we could try to pick up Dartmouth girls (until they figured out we were dialing in from a high school), cookie programs (that give you a saying), games, and other things that were just plain *fun*. Because I grew up in Vermont, I had very few things around that were as interesting as the world the computer opened up. I started writing my first program.

Because, in 1976, high schools didn't have computer classes (most didn't even have computers), there was no one to teach programming. Anything I learned, I managed to learn from reading other people's programs, or through total trial and error. There weren't even any books available to me.

It wasn't until I got to college that I had access to books and classes that started to explain things I wished I had known years ago. Having been so used to scrounging for the slightest bit of information and fitting it into the puzzle, I suddenly had a surfeit of resources and, basically, just pigged out learning about computers.

Remembering those first four years looking for the slightest crumb of knowledge, I am very understanding of what it is like not to have the information you need. Many books *assume* you know certain aspects, when those aspects are in fact the missing links you need to put it all together. I well recall being mystified by loops, parameters, and other similar things, and no longer take for granted that other novices understand these things either.

When I first started to work with Lingo, I was frustrated by the lack of information that existed outside of the manuals. I also realized that others would be struggling with the concepts more than just the syntax, just as I did twenty years ago. After a point I decided to start publishing the *Lingo User's Journal,* which is a monthly publication dedicated to Lingo and xtras (information on the journal is in the back of this book), but there are some subjects that you just can't cover in a twenty page monthly newsletter. And that's where this book comes in, and that's why I organized it the way I did.

Why This Book Is Organized the Way It Is

My intent is for you to approach this book in step with how you would naturally approach Lingo and programming concepts. The stuff at the end won't do you much good unless you've got a grip on the stuff at the beginning. This means basic fundamentals, like a good solid understanding of variables, handlers, loops, and lists.

Often when these things will be discussed I'll try to shed some light on how they work internally. Knowing how the computer implements something gives you the ability to wield that feature in exactly the way you want it. For this reason it's important that you try to read those chapters anyway, even if you think you "know that stuff already." You might be surprised. And, as I know from years of putting together the pieces, every little piece helps make a picture.

I'll also be covering the debugger, and other debugging techniques. Although not technically "Lingo," it's foolish to ignore or gloss over the debugger. *The debugger is your friend!* Often, 50 percent (or more!) of programming time is spent debugging. So many books and articles give short shrift to debugging, but the mark of a good programmer is how quickly he can move beyond the bugs and get some work done. And to move beyond the bugs, you need to know how to *de*bug.

I'm also going to speak from the point of view of developing a commercial-quality program. I doubt if many (or any) of you spent all that money on an authoring tool like Director just to play around with it at home. On the assumption that you intend to create a professional-looking title, I will attempt to address those issues when appropriate.

Finally, I assume you've got the manuals and have read them. I'm not going to waste time re-explaining something that you already have books on. The intent is to take over where the manuals left off.

The *Lingo!* CD-ROM

The CD-ROM included with *Lingo!* contains various materials to help increase your productivity when creating with Lingo. You'll find scripts that were created in the examples in this book, Director files used as starting points for the book's examples, and several helpful utilities. The CD is arranged in two categories:

☘ **Chapters.** The Chapters folder/directory contains the project files and scripts mentioned in the chapters listed.

☘ **Software.** The Software directory/folder contains software for use with both PC and Macintosh computers, including Macromedia's Knowledge Base for Director.

Breakdowns, Tips, and Pitfalls

Lingo! features many special sidebars, which are set apart from the normal text by icons. This book includes three distinct types of sidebars: Breakdowns, Tips, and Pitfalls. These passages have been given special treatment so that you can instantly recognize their significance and easily find them for future reference.

A *Breakdown* includes extra information you should find useful or interesting. Breakdowns might explain programming concepts to help you understand the current discussion, provide in-depth help or information on a topic, or point you to other areas of reference outside of the current discussion. Breakdowns will also provide definitions of terms or topics new to the discussion.

A *Tip* provides quick instructions for maximizing your productivity when using Lingo. A Tip might show you how to speed up a procedure or how to perform time-saving and system-enhancing features.

 A *Pitfall* generally tells you how to avoid problems or describes the steps you can take to remedy them. Pitfalls will help you understand common programming errors and why they happen, show you why your scripts don't work out the way you think they should, and point out Lingo and Director features to keep in mind as you work.

As well as the sidebar icons, you'll also see this *Director 5.0* icon from time to time. This icon points out Lingo topics that are new to Director 5.0.

There's More Where This Came From

Hopefully the words in this book will not be the last that I write on this subject (in book form, that is). Director is an ongoing, evolving product, Lingo is an ongoing, evolving language, and this is an ongoing, evolving book.

Please contact me and let me know what you liked or didn't like about the book, and what you'd like to see in the next edition. I want to make this a book worth having.

Finally, lots of people helped, but only I made the mistakes. Remember that if you find any, and let me know so that I can fix them.

Enjoy!

Tab Julius
Penworks Corporation
Net: tab@penworks.com
Web: http://www.penworks.com
CIS: 72037,3662

part I

Preliminaries

Why Use Director for Your Development?

Why *should* you use Director for your development? Good question! Before tackling any software development project, it's important to choose the right development tool. With Director, someone else gets to do the dirty work while you do the fun stuff.

No, really! There are two ways I can think that using Director might be an attraction for you:

* You're not familiar with doing behind-the-scenes engineering

* You are, but you're sick of it

Either way, you're a good candidate for Lingo and the Director environment. I personally fall into the second category. I've worked on lots of titles, both commercial and non-commercial, for the PC environment since about 1984, and I've always had to do the behind-the-scenes graphic engines, animation engines, text engines, mouse event routines, video drivers, you name it.

Years ago, I was leading a group that was upgrading a popular desktop publisher, and I recall spending an inordinate amount of time chasing what we called "the jumping mouse bug." I'd be pulling down a menu or something and the mouse would suddenly decide, for no apparent reason at all, to relocate itself somewhere else. If it happened during a button down condition, then accidental deletes, or who knows what, could happen.

I chased that thing over what was probably a four month period. Although intriguing at first, the novelty quickly wore off. I chased it through interrupts and mouse drivers and video drivers, and it was only after a tremendous waste of everyone's time that it finally got nailed.

And although the techno-weenie in me sort of liked it, the rest of me got real tired of it real quick.

And that's what I like about Director—someone else gets to worry about those sorts of problems for a change. I've had my turn.

Not Constantly Learning New Frameworks

Developing effective graphics and audio engines for today's microcomputer platforms has become extremely complicated as of late, and it's only the larger companies that can afford to invest the time to develop their own, particularly an engine that's cross-platform. In order to take full advantage of the latest operating system and processor improvements, not to mention the variety of video drivers available, most developers find themselves obligated to use engines and frameworks developed by others, rather than hope to keep pace with the technology themselves.

Director abstracts you from the final playback destination, and the folks at Macromedia worry about keeping up to date on all the platforms, so you don't have to yourself. *I* certainly find this an attraction. I had just about mastered VAX/VMS system calls and internals when the PC started to get popular. I spent years getting to the point that I started to really know my way around the insides of MS-DOS when Windows got really popular. I finally got to where I was doing high-end work with certain Windows internals when Windows 95 came around. Just on the Windows platform alone, in the past few years, I've seen and worked with WinG, then WinToon, then the Windows 95 Game SDK. And don't forget OWL and MFC. And *then* I bought me a Mac.

In other words, I want to pick just one authoring environment and stick with it. As improvements come along in display and sound technology, I'll gladly let Macromedia bang their heads against the wall over the newest framework technology. I just don't have time for it anymore. I could spend so much time adjusting my bottom-up DIBs for top-down ones that I'd never actually get anything *accomplished*.

I much prefer this way instead.

Someone Else Worries about Patent Infringement

Software Patents are a controversial subject that has come to the fore in the last few years. Just as regular technical discoveries and innovations can be patented, so too, apparently, can software innovations.

Not surprisingly, this has been a touchy topic, because it turns out that certain companies have attempted to patent software concepts that developers have been using for years. The patent office has not traditionally had a lot of experience in evaluating the validity of the patents, and this has made way for lots of lawsuits, ill-will, and attempts to collect royalties from unsuspecting developers.

Granted, I don't stay up at night worrying about patent infringement, but I suspect that a popular enough title would eventually become subject to scrutinization by someone who's patented the technique for putting blue pixels on the screen or whatever. If I'm not doing the behind-the-scenes stuff, it's just one less thing I have to worry about. In a very self-centered sort of way, if Macromedia unknowingly infringes a patent, it's their problem, not mine. By using their engine, it's one less thing that I have to worry about.

Multi-Platform!

Yes, yes, yes! It's not so much that I'm afraid of learning curves, it's just that I've been through so many. And, *now*, with CD-ROM, it's expected that you deliver both a PC *and* a Mac version of your product on the same disk. And one for the Internet, and the Sony PlayStation, and OS/2, and NextStep, and the Amiga, and and and... .

For my company to put all that stuff out gets expensive. For me to learn it myself gets time consuming. And what about all those poor souls who bet their careers over the last few years on OS/2? They bet on a technical winner that was a marketing loser, and now they have to regroup. By having all their eggs in one operating system basket, they tied their fate to that of the success of the operating system itself. With Director, and its "Author Once, Play Anywhere" approach, you are insulated from a dependence on the popularity of any one specific platform. Your potential market is larger, and your risk is smaller.

By working with Director you can abstract yourself from the platform, at least as long as you don't fiddle with xtras and just focus on Lingo. Macromedia has resources to develop engines for all the major platforms, so while they do the back-end stuff, you get to do the front-end stuff. And when you're done, you can release it on all the players that Macromedia has written. I mean, it's really silly not to leverage that sort of technical momentum.

Extensibility

Extensibility is the capability to extend, or add to the functionality, of Director and Lingo. Director is extendible through the use of *Xtras*—plug-in modules that allow fuller, less restricted access to the platform you're targeting, be it Windows, or Macintosh, or whatever.

This is the nice safety net for your choice of a platform. If you're reluctant to use Director because you're not sure if you can do some particular thing in

Lingo, don't worry—it's *not a problem.* If it's really important that you have that functionality, you can extend Lingo via your own custom xtra, which is basically a C-module plug-in (certain other languages can be used too, albeit with a little more effort).

True, when you start writing your own external code, you lose the cross-platformness, but you only have to write the code you need, which means that you only have to port the code you wrote. And, in fact, the MOA (Macromedia Open Architecture—the API behind the xtras) is written to be as cross-platform as possible, so even that problem is kept to a minimum.

That's not to say that there wouldn't be any porting work involved, but it's a heck of a lot easier than writing the whole dang project in C. Trust me.

How to Approach Development within Director

In preparing for battle I have always found that plans are useless, but planning is indispensable.

Dwight D. Eisenhower

When I work on a big project (anything over 5 minutes of work), I rarely just sit down and write code. To do so without giving some thought to the overall structure of the program is to invite trouble.

I'm not talking so much about the specification of the program (which does what and when) as the *structure* of the program. It's important to have the feature specification on paper so that everyone understands what's expected of the program, but the structure is typically up to you, as long as it performs.

Performance is often the focus of structure, because no one's going to appreciate a poorly performing program. When I sit down and try to figure out in my head what the structure is going to be, I have to consider what the environment that the program will run in is going to be.

CD-ROM Considerations

For the developer, the CD-ROM carries some unique programming considerations.

To begin with, it's slow. That is, it's a lot slower than your hard drive. Some people wait until their projects are done before pressing a CD-ROM, at which time they find out just how slow it is, and what sort of impact that delay will have on their final product's performance.

The problem is that a CD-ROM might access and transfer data some ten to thirty times slower than a hard drive. Your animation or load time can scoot right on by when run from your 2 GB SCSI, but stick it on a double-speed CD-ROM and watch it crawl.

Because everybody in the world has double-speed CD-ROMs, you should have one too, for testing. And before you say that many have quad-speed CD-ROMs, I'm telling you that from a developer's point of view, everyone in the market has a double-speed CD-ROM. They also have 486/33s.

Of course, if you're developing for a kiosk, or otherwise want to require higher-level equipment, that's up to you. In a kiosk you have control over the playback platform, and can set your own requirements, so the equipment assumption doesn't apply. But if you're developing general consumer-quality software, you have to assume the worst.

Fortunately, we've moved past the 386/33 and single-speed CD-ROM phase, so you can take a little pleasure in that.

Still, the speed (or lack thereof) of the CD-ROM brings some special considerations. Because data and programs do take extra time to load, you have to plan whether or not you want to have your projector on your hard drive.

I would recommend that you do. However, be aware that most consumers do not care to have some 20 MB of product installed on their disks (though more and more I suspect they're getting resigned to it).

What you'd be better off doing is creating a small projector that puts up a little "hello—wait while I get ready" screen and then loads the real movie off the CD-ROM. This provides instant response to the user, and makes you look a little more professional. Gosh, if there's something a consumer likes, it's instant gratification.

So this has provided your first clue toward your design—it will have a projector with a small launch movie, and the main movie (or movies) will be on the CD.

In other words, you're letting the medium dictate the design.

Because CD-ROM *is* slow, the last thing you want to be doing when a user clicks a button is spending 5 seconds transferring the sprite that does the highlights. This is your second clue—better bone up on your preloading and unloading techniques (I'll discuss these in Chapter 22).

I will also comment that if you plan to play digital video (QuickTime or AVI) at some point in the program, you had darn well better test it from a CD-ROM long before you plan to ship it. This is clue 2.5. It may be that you need to resample the video and make it smaller, or preload it, or *something* to improve the performance.

CD-ROM enables you to play audio direct from the compact disc. You can have CD audio and your program playing at the same time! This is good. It might seem like a great idea to play some audio while your program loads in the next movie. Keep the user entertained with CD audio! Excellent idea!

Unfortunately, there's a bit of a problem with loading your next movie from CD-ROM at the same time you're playing audio from CD-ROM. The CD-ROM is being used for double access, and the suckage level of the performance suddenly goes through the roof. This is bad. So, this is your third clue—don't try to have the CD-ROM do more than one thing at a time. It's slow enough that things that were barely noticeable on your hard drive become a real problem when played back on CD-ROM.

CD-ROM is a read-only medium. This creates a little extra work for you.

It mainly deals with the storage of information. If you want to store what section the user was in so that they can come back to it next time, or record the serial number, or the user's name, or set an expiration date, you can't store it on the CD-ROM. You have to create a directory on the hard drive and store it there. Not impossible, just more work. This is your fourth clue to the design.

The allure of the CD-ROM is its wide-open spaces. 660 megabytes, Wow. Just think of how many *videos* I can put on! And sound? 44 KHz, here I come! Lots of audio, background music, this'll be great!

The problem is, my friend, that because CD-ROM is so slow, to use a 44 KHz 16-bit stereo wavefile instead of a 22 KHz 8-bit mono one means that the size of your wavefile, and thus the transfer time, will be four times greater. Use a 22 KHz/8-bit instead and you've cut your transfer time for the audio by 75%! If you can get yourself a decent 11 KHz/8-bit wavefile audio, then you'll save 87.5% in transfer time. See, you wouldn't really notice this if you waited until the end to test from CD-ROM. Last clue in the CD-ROM department.

CD-ROM is nothing to be scared of—it's just slower and more restricted than the hard drive. I've done fast titles on a CD-ROM, and I'm sure you've seen plenty yourself. It certainly can be done; you just have to take the characteristics of CD-ROMs into account and plan accordingly.

Web Considerations

Designing for the Web using Shockwave technology means that you have to contend with transfer speed problems that are even worse than those that you have with CD-ROM. So, all those comments apply, and more.

Under Shockwave, there's a variety of features that you don't have access to. Some are simply technical limitations, others are intentional, to keep some unscrupulous Shockwaver from wreaking havoc on some poor user's machine. If you're planning for Shockwave you'll need to understand just what features are and aren't available. If you think that you might be releasing on the Web, you should read Chapter 29, "Extending Your Audience with Shockwave," for more information on these limitations.

You'll also have to *really* keep the size down. One day, everyone will have a T1 line coming into their home, or cable modems, but it ain't there yet. Because transfer speed is so awful, you'll have to really pick and choose what features you want, decide how to get the maximum effect for the least size, and keep the screen size down to just a quarter-screen window or so. There's also no writing to the user's hard drive at *all* with Shockwave, which is a very real limitation.

Cross-Platform Considerations

Macromedia has Macintosh and Windows players for Director, and other platforms in the works.

If you're planning to make a cross-platform title, you should make it from the viewpoint of the Mac. That is, you can certainly author on Windows (I do), but make sure that your external files are .AIFs, not .WAVs, .PICs, not .BMPs, and QuickTime video not .AVIs. The Mac resources like .PICs, .AIFs, and Quicktime .MOVs will play back on the Windows platforms under Director, but the reverse is not necessarily true (that is, external Windows resources do not always play back on the Mac).

Xtras and Xobjects are not portable. The MOA architecture, as I mentioned, makes them more portable-ish, but you still need to compile separately for each platform, and if they do any platform-specific code, it's not portable, obviously (otherwise, it wouldn't be platform-specific!).

Projectors

The movies you create are cross-platform, but the projectors are not. You'll have to create separate projectors, which means you need to own both the Mac *and* the Windows versions of Director.

You'll also need to test on both platforms, because each has subtle differences. It's still a lot easier than writing in C, but you can't blow it off until the last minute.

Be aware, too, that even within platforms there are differences in projectors. Windows has both a 16-bit *and* a 32-bit projector, so during install time you're going to have to accommodate that, and you'll also have to create and test both projectors.

The Mac side also has multiple types of projectors. You can compile for all Macs, in 68K, or for PowerMacs. It might seem tempting to compile just for all Macs, but you'll quickly find that an all-Mac projector runs like a sheep-dog on the PowerMac, because the PowerMac executes the 68K code in emulation mode, causing it to be a lot slower. What you need to do is create a separate projector for the PowerMac, which will run in native PowerMac code, just screaming along when compared to the all-Mac code you were just running.

I mention this particularly so that you don't develop on a regular Mac and hear howls of protests from your customers who call you up saying that they go to run it on their PowerMac and that the performance sucks. Likewise, you don't want to just do a PowerMac version and then hear from those customers who can't get it to launch on their non-PowerMac. You need to do it for *both* Mac platforms and *both* Windows platforms.

In theory you can blow off doing a 32-bit Windows version, because the percentage of the market that's actually moving to Windows 95 is still pretty small, and the 16-bit one will run decently under Windows 95. It'd be a shame, though, because the 32-bit version really flies—the performance is *very* impressive.

Projectors, regardless of how you'd like to think otherwise, do cause your movie to behave differently in subtle ways from the way it does when in the authoring environment. Don't wait until the last minute to create your projector. Create one early, and test often.

Palettes

Beginning with Director version 4.04, there was a restriction on the number of palettes in a movie to just 54. This might cause problems for you if you're intending to import 5,000 images, each with its own palette. You might have to import your images on-the-fly (hello, speed problems!), or create a super-palette where no image has an optimal palette, but they all share a fairly decent common palette. (If you do need to create a super-palette, the apparent tool of choice is DeBabelizer, by Equilibrium, which only runs on the Mac, by the way.)

Protected Movies

You can (and should) release your product with the movies "protected," which means that the readable Lingo is stripped out (the compiled Lingo is still intact). You should know, though, that with the right know-how anyone can reverse a protected .DXR back into a loadable .DIR, with everything present except the readable Lingo. The big concern would be if you had any sort of sensitive information in text cast members, or if you had any imported wavefiles or images that you didn't want some unscrupulous character going after.

The score would also be revealed if the .DXR file was reversed to a .DIR file, but I suspect most people wouldn't care much if the score was secret or not. If you write it all in Lingo, though, then this won't be a problem. And that leads us into the next planning consideration:

Lingo-Heavy, Score-Heavy, or Both?

In Director, there are really three ways to create a program. You can work almost entirely within the score, or entirely within Lingo, or you can mix the two.

I assume that you're either planning to be Lingo-heavy, or at least mix the two, otherwise you wouldn't be reading this book.

I'm not going to recommend one technique over the other, nor am I going to make fun of you and call you a score weenie if you decide to use the score instead of going all Lingo, because how you do work is largely a matter of your background and training and what you're comfortable with.

I will tell you a little about going all Lingo, just so you know how it's done, but typically only those with a programming background tend to work this way because it's the most like what they're used to. Even if you mainly use the score, you owe it to yourself to understand what you're doing with whatever Lingo you *do* put in there, which is what this book is for.

On one of the online forums someone commented recently that they had always thought of the single-frame movie as being sort of a holy grail, in that it was hard to achieve, desirable to achieve, and that in order to achieve it you have to be particularly proficient in Lingo. I personally had never thought of it that way, and don't particularly think that it is either desirable or *un*desirable. The one-frame movie is simply the way to extricate yourself from the score and work solely in Lingo.

A One-Frame Movie

Whereas a score-based movie will have hundreds of frames with different sprites in different channels in each frame, a Lingo-based, or one-frame, movie has but one frame in which everything happens, and the movie just loops around on that frame (as opposed to going on to another, different frame).

To pull this off, you would want to just puppet all 48 channels and then manipulate those sprite channels via Lingo as the program progresses.

I will usually put the background screen into channel 1, but in the remainder of the channels I put a dummy sprite, which is just a mini-bitmap (just one pixel), that I position off-screen (say, at -500, -500, or some equally far-off negative location).

I do this because I later want to go back and stick my own cast members in by changing the memberNum of some sprite to be the cast member I want. However, unless you're using Score Generation (which we discuss in Chapter 14), Director only allows you to change the sprite to another member of like type, which means that if you intend to use bitmaps, you must have a number of channels with dummy bitmaps in them. If you intend to use digital video, you must have one channel reserved for each video you intend to have playing simultaneously (which is most likely just one). If you intend to have a text box, you must make a channel with a text box cast member in it, and so on.

In my startMovie handler, because I have all the dummy sprites there, I then loop through and puppet them all, which means they are now officially under Lingo control. Then I set the visible of all the sprites, except the background image if I have one, to FALSE. From that point on, I can swap in cast members and turn on or off the visibility of the sprite as necessary in Lingo.

Finally, to make sure the program keeps running, I have an exitFrame handler that simply does a go to the frame, thus causing a constant loop in that frame (I use quit to stop the projector).

In reality, for best performance, you should have not one frame, but three. Put your background image, if you have one, in each of the three frames' sprite 1 channel, but only load your dummy sprites into the channels of frame 2. Then, in your on startMovie handler you should have as one of the first statements an instruction to go to the frame +1 (or refer to it as frame 2, your choice).

The reason for this is that Director assumes regular score design, and thus places special consideration on the first and last frames of the score, and performs certain housekeeping tasks when entering and exiting those frames.

Now if you've got only one frame in the score, it automatically qualifies as both the first and last frame. This obligates that frame to incur housekeeping overhead on an ongoing basis, thus slowing down your loop and, as a result, your animations. To avoid this, you also need to make dummy intro and exit frames, so as to eliminate any unnecessary overhead.

Multiple Movies

Some of the projects I work on have wholly different "sections," with totally different behavior in each section. I did just this with a program I wrote in Lingo, called Granny's Delicious Morphabet Soup. The game starts from a QTVR kitchen, and you can then go to individual areas where there are special activities. One area, for instance, is an Alphabet Soup game where you try to build words from letters in the soup. Another is a blend game where you try to find letters that go to form phonic blends.

Because each area is actually a whole game, I decided to make each area a movie unto itself. Each has its own cast, its own startup and game code, and so on. I can then easily update a particular game without having to rebuild everything. It also subdivides things enough that I don't feel like I have this huge monster of a program by the time I'm done.

Movies that are launched from other movies, but run simultaneously, are run as what is called a movie in a window (MIAW). This name is so given because you create a separate child window for the movie and then run that movie. Each MIAW has its own `startMovie` handler, its own score, and so on.

An MIAW can be small, or it can take up the whole screen. I usually use them to take up the whole screen, because this best fits the way I keep whole sections in separate movies. However, many people also use them as smaller movies executing on-screen and within a larger one. The choice depends on your needs. For instance, if you wanted to create a floating calculator, you could create one in the form of an MIAW and then position it on the screen wherever you want.

MIAWs can share global variables with other movies—all global variables go into an "inter-movie global pool," making it easy to transfer information back and forth. Further, one movie can tell another movie what to do—run it remotely, as it were. You can give commands to the other movie that it can execute as if from within its own context. This feature is the key to the success of the Services Movies.

Common code, in the Morphabet project, I put into a Services Movie, which is a technique to share Lingo code among various movies. It really is an MIAW that runs in the background and has no visual elements (just code). Because it runs simultaneously with the regular movie, it can provide common functionality to each of the modules. This way, I'm not duplicating code in each of the games, even though they're all individual movies. In Director 5.0, though, the Services Movie becomes less of an important concept because multiple cast files also provide a way to share code without duplication, but it's still an option.

Multiple Casts

Ah, the pleasure of the multiple casts.

This is a new one in 5.0. Up until now, there has only been one cast per movie, plus you could make a special shareable cast to be shared amongst all the movies in a project. The shareable cast would be merged with your regular cast.

Thank goodness that's over. Now you can create individually named and loadable casts.

What are some of the benefits? There are many—the following lists just a few that come to mind:

❖ **Organization:** Keep your audio in one cast, your scripts in another, your artwork in a third, and so on.

❖ **Reusability:** Common art and scripts can be utilized in more than one movie, which just makes project management a lot easier.

❖ **Internationalization:** The language/culture-specific artwork, audio, and text can be in separate casts. If you want to release in a different language, just include the appropriate cast files with your projector. It also makes localization easier because you can keep the audio, graphics, and text cast files separate, so the localization of one doesn't impact the others. Also, you don't have to release your source scripts to anyone.

❖ **Customization:** You can customize the cast and save it back out to disk. What developers do with this remains to be seen, but the potential is great.

Xtras

Xtras are how you extend Director's functionality. Formerly called xobjects, in their new incarnation they are far more powerful, with extensive access to the internals of Director via the Macromedia Open Architecture (MOA) specification.

Xtras are plug-in modules, typically written in C, that have the capability to implement custom transitions, sprites, authoring-time tools, Lingo commands, and other features and functionalities. For instance, if you needed to access a database, you'd probably do it through an xtra. If you needed to interface with a specific device, you'd need an xtra. If you needed to avail yourself of some specific operating system feature, you'd need an xtra.

Some of these xtras might be available publicly—it's possible that someone else has created one to solve the very problem that confronts you. If so, you're in luck. Of course, it might be that no such xtra exists, or perhaps you *want* to write an xtra. If so, you need to look at the Xtra Development Kit (XDK) that was provided with your copy of Director 5.0.

The scope of MOA and xtras really exceeds what we can cover in this book—it really demands a book of its own. However, it's important that you at least understand that Director can be extended. If you can't find the feature you need in Lingo, perhaps you can write an xtra, or have someone write it for you.

part **II**

Fundamentals

Scripts and Events

If you've gone through the tutorials that came with Director, worked with the Director manuals, or just some introductory book, you've undoubtedly written some sort of Lingo in a script, even if it was just a go to the frame in an exitFrame handler. But what actually *is* a script?

When you click on the script button in the cast member or sprite member info dialog box, you often get a script template that looks like figure 3.1.

Figure 3.1

*This is one of the
scripts that Director
automatically starts
you off with.*

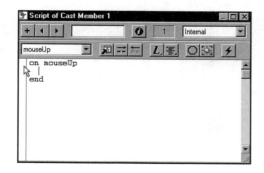

All sorts of questions come to mind. Sure, it's a script, but what kind is it? Where is it kept? What if you want to make other changes? What are you allowed to put in there? What aren't you allowed to put in there?

In order to answer those questions it's necessary to understand that scripts are used for mainly two reasons: to subdivide tasks (break up complex tasks into more manageable portions) and to provide a way to respond to *events*, which are happenings in Director.

There are different kinds of scripts, each with a special purpose, and they'll be described here. But first, I'll describe events and the path that the events travel in the process of being handled, or taken care of. It's necessary to understand event handling in order to make sense of scripts.

Events

Events are any happening you consider to be important, and in the world of Lingo, they are things like a mouse click. A mouse click is an event worth noting. In fact, it can be broken into a mouseDown event and a mouseUp event.

After an event has occurred (say it's the mouseDown event), it becomes necessary to do something with it. This is called *delivering* the event. Director wants to provide as much opportunity as possible for somebody to take responsibility for the event.

By taking responsibility for it, I mean *responding* to it. For instance, the mouse button being pressed (a mouseDown event) is an occurrence that most developers want to be able to respond to. Director will try to deliver that event to some appropriate handler so that the program can respond to the event. If Director can deliver it, great. If not, Director will simply ignore, or *discard*, the event.

You should understand that many of the events are generated *internally* in Director. For instance, `exitFrame`, `idle`, and `stopMovie` are events that Director generated. These are internal events. There are also events like `mouseUp` and `keyDown` that are *external*, which is to say that they were initiated outside of Director (by you or the operating system).

What Director is offering you is not so much an opportunity to totally handle the response to the event, as it is an opportunity to *plug in* to the response of the event. Director has already handled the event in its own particular way. For instance, when it comes time to advance to a new frame in the movie, Director has many things that it needs to do. One of the last things it does is offer *you* the opportunity to perform some tasks as well; in this case, through the `enterFrame` event that it generates.

In an effort to give you both the greatest degree of control, should you want it, and the greatest ease of use, should you prefer it, Director has a hierarchy of ways it attempts to deliver events.

* Sprite
* Cast member
* Frame
* Movie script

Sprite

When a `mouseDown` occurs, Director attempts to figure out what to do with it. First, it sees if it was clicked on a sprite. If so, it's only fair to give the sprite priority, in case the sprite wanted something special done when it was clicked on.

You can tell if the sprite wanted something special done when it was clicked on if you have taken the time to define an on mouseDown handler for it. This means that there needs to be a script attached to that sprite, and that the script needs to contain a handler named on mouseDown. If it does, then it will be invoked, and the event will be delivered.

It's possible that a little investigation shows that no one has bothered to include an on mouseDown handler in the script for the sprite. In fact, it's likely the sprite has no script at all. In either case, you weren't able to deliver it to the sprite.

Because in this example we *did* click on a sprite, but the sprite itself had no handler to handle that click, perhaps at the next level up, which is the cast member, there is a handler for the mouseDown.

Cast Member

Because a cast member resides once in a cast but can beget many sprites, it becomes convenient to attach a script to the cast member itself. That way, if any of its sprites are clicked on, they can all partake of the cast member's script, instead of needing one themselves.

With that thought in mind, because you didn't find the handler for the mouseDown event attached to the sprite, perhaps its mother cast member has one. First, Director needs to determine if the cast member even has a script at all, and if it does, whether that script contains the particular handler it needs to respond to the event.

Should there actually be a script attached to that cast member, and should that script contain a handler for the mouseDown event, then it would be possible to deliver the event to the cast member. This would cause the contents of the on mouseDown handler in the cast member script to be executed, and the event would be delivered.

But what if neither the sprite specifically had a handler, nor the cast of that sprite? What then?

Frame

The third place Director will look is to the frame to see if there's a script in the frame script channel and, if so, if it has a handler for the event that Director is trying to deliver. Should there be a script in the frame channel, and should that script have an on mouseDown handler, then it becomes possible to deliver the event to the on mouseDown handler of the frame script.

Obviously, as we move down the hierarchy, the handlers that receive the events have to be written more and more generically. When you write a mouseDown handler for a sprite you know that if it's invoked it is because the sprite was clicked. If you write one for a cast member, and it gets invoked, you only know that *one* of the cast member's sprites were clicked on, but not which one. (You have to use calls like the clickOn to see specifically which one it was.)

If you have a handler in the frame script and it gets invoked, that means that something in the frame was clicked on, but goodness only knows *what* it was until you start checking. It also means that the click didn't get picked up by any intervening sprites or cast members, so you can take that into account, if appropriate.

Movie Script

Finally, the last refuge is a handler in a movie script. Handlers in a movie script are the last in the hierarchy, because they have dominion over the whole movie. If Director didn't find a preceding handler to take the event, either in a sprite script or a cast script or a frame script, then it tries to see if there's an on mouseDown handler defined for the movie itself. Such a handler would reside in a movie script, which is present in the cast window, but not attached to anything.

If it turns out that there's an on mouseDown handler defined in a movie script somewhere, then Director can deliver the event to that handler (which it does by *invoking*, or calling, the handler, and causing the instructions in it to be performed).

And, of course, there's the question of what to do if you have not defined an on mouseDown script anywhere. Not on the sprite, nor its cast, nor the current frame, nor in the movie. Director will then say the heck with it and forget about it, thus discarding the event.

Overriding the Event Hierarchy

There's an alternative you can use that might be appropriate in instances when you want to override all this hierarchy chasing: provide a single overriding instruction of what Director should do when it receives a mouse click (*any* mouse click, that is). There is a property you can set to contain this instruction, called the mouseDownScript (there are also equivalent ones for mouseUps, keyDowns and keyUps). You use it like so:

```
set the mouseDownScript to "whatchuwannado"
```

What you set it to can be the name of a handler, which will cause that handler to be invoked, or to another instruction you want executed. For instance, should you decide that temporarily, while you're performing a transition that you want mouse clicks to be absorbed and ignored, you can do this:

```
set the mouseDownScript to "dontPassEvent"
```

This means that a mouse click will execute the dontPassEvent command, which prevents that mouse click from going further. Or, you could set it up to call a particular handler for you:

```
set the mouseDownScript to "leaveItAlone"
```

Of course, you have to define the handler:

```
on leaveItAlone
  beep
  alert "Leave that mouse button alone!"
  dontPassEvent
end
```

You need to put the handler in a movie script so that it can be found at the time when it is needed to be called.

You noticed the reference to dontPassEvent. When you set the mouseDownScript to some instruction, you're giving it first crack at the event.

However, the `mouseDownScript` behaves very differently from the regular event handlers we discussed earlier, like on `mouseDown`.

I described how, when an event occurs, Director tries to find a regular event handler (like on `mouseDown`) to give the event to. Director will work its way through the hierarchy until it manages to deliver the event. At that point the event goes no further.

It's possible that you might have a situation where you want the event to get picked up by more than one handler. For instance, if you had a screen with a particular sprite on it, normally clicking anywhere on the screen would make the program go on to the *next* screen. If, however, you happen to click on that sprite, you might want something to happen first and *then* go to the next screen.

So it might be that the movie or the frame has a mouse handler to take care of the click and move on to the next screen. It might look like this:

[Script in frame script channel]

```
on mouseDown
   go to the frame + 1
end mouseDown
```

If a `mouseDown` event ever works its way to this script, it would be picked up by this `mouseDown` handler. However, I mentioned that if someone clicked on the sprite that I wanted something to happen and *then* have it go to the next screen. This is where the `pass` command comes in handy. I could set up the sprite with a script like this:

[Script attached to the sprite]

```
on mouseDown
   puppetSound "giggle"
   pass
end mouseDown
```

If the sprite was clicked on, it would play a giggling sound. As we described before, because the event was delivered here, Director would make no attempt to deliver the event beyond this point. However, we need to go to the next screen, which means that although we wanted this sprite script to process the event, we want the other script to process it *also*.

We resolve the situation with the Pass command, which tells Director that although we handled the event here, we want Director to pass it on to the next available handler in the hierarchy. Director will do so, following the rules described previously, until it again manages to deliver the event (unless that handler, too, has a Pass command).

Now the mouseDownScript gets to avoid the hierarchy because it's special. When an event occurs, the mouseDownScript, if defined, will execute first, but it *will not block delivery to the rest of the hierarchy.* This means that if a mouseDownEvent occurs, it will first execute the instruction defined in the mouseDownScript and then it will still be delivered through the hierarchy as described.

You can stop this, though, by telling it *not* to pass the event. That's done by the dontPassEvent instruction.

A Debugging Plug-In

You might want to use the mouseDownScript for debugging purposes. For instance, you could use this trick to provide feedback on mouse clicks.

```
on showMouseDownInfo
  put "Mouse down received!"
  put "The clickLoc: "& the clickLoc
  put "The mouseCast: "& the mouseCast
end showMouseDownInfo
```

You can still have your regular mouseDown handlers in your scripts, but if you issue the following instruction:

```
set the mouseDownScript to "showMouseDownInfo"
```

Director will first execute your little handler before going on and delivering the event to the hierarchy. The benefit of this is that you can insert code to advise you of what's going on without disrupting the operation of anything else in your movie.

If you actually want to *override* the behavior elsewhere, and capture the event and not let it percolate through the system then you have to specify dontPassEvent:

```
on showMouseDownInfo
  put "Mouse down received!"
  put "The clickLoc: "& the clickLoc
  put "The mouseCast: "& the mouseCast
  dontPassEvent
end showMouseDownInfo
```

Remember, this is only for when you use the primary event handlers that you define by the `mouseDownScript`, the `mouseUpScript`, the `keyDownScript`, and so on. These normally allow events to get past them into the hierarchy (they're good for peeking at the events). `DontPassEvent` stops that behavior. If you're not using one of these, then the event just gets delivered into the hierarchy like normal.

Scripts

There are four kinds of scripts that you can encounter. All are cast members that have text and can be edited. The way they differ is in their *scope*. That is, the portions of the movie over which they have influence and can be called from.

Three of the four are types that you will come across in most general work that you do with scripts. In descending order of influence they are the movie script, the cast member script, and the score script. Actually, the influence of the score script varies depending on how you use it.

The fourth type is called a parent script, and is used specifically for creating and working with objects, which I'll cover in a later chapter. At the moment, just focus on the first three script types.

Score Scripts

Previously, I made reference to frame scripts and sprite scripts. These both are actually different names for a score script. A score script is so called because it's applied only to items in the score. The only items in the score that can accept a script are a sprite in a channel, or the frame itself.

When a score script is applied to a sprite, we refer to it as a sprite script, because that's how we're using it. When it is applied to a frame, we refer to it as a frame script because that's how we're using it. Simple enough?

When you click on a script cast member and look at its info dialog box, there's a drop-down box marked Type (see fig. 3.2). This can be set to Movie or Score or Parent.

Figure 3.2

The script type can be set from the Script Cast Member Properties dialog box.

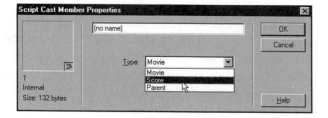

As a score script, the handlers in it are only evaluated if they're attached to something, like a sprite. This is because sprites can each have their own scripts, meaning that there could be hundreds of on mouseDown handlers scattered throughout the cast.

When we work our way down through the hierarchy, and need to try to deliver an event to the movie, we need to know which scripts are intended for the whole movie, and not individual sprites or frames. By distinguishing between a movie script and a non-movie script (meaning, a score script) it becomes possible for Director to implement the hierarchy without causing havoc because it won't be confused trying to determine which script is intended for what.

Because a score script is only evaluated if it's attached to something (and that something is being evaluated), it also makes it an easy way to temporarily prevent a movie script's handlers from being used—sort of a way to put them in storage. Just set the type to score script. If you don't attach it to anything, it won't ever be evaluated!

Pitfall

By the way, that's one reason why some people's on startMovie handlers never get executed—Director looks to see if the movie has an on startMovie handler defined for the movie. If the thing is defined, but it's sitting in a score script, Director won't even glance at it. It needs to be in a movie script.

Movie Scripts

Whereas a script attached to a sprite is used to handle specific sprite events (like a mouseUp), handlers that appear in a movie script are available to other handlers that want to call them. For example, you might want to have a common service that handlers in your sprite or frame scripts could call. You'd put it in a movie script so they all would be able to access it.

A movie script is also a place to put handlers that either handle some event for the whole movie, or that serve as a fallback position (a default) in case you don't specifically handle the event at the sprite or cast or frame level. For instance, you could put a generic on mouseDown handler in a movie script that could take care of times that the mouse has been clicked even if you don't have a sprite that it was clicked on. In theory, you can also do this in a frame script, but if the desired behavior would be the same no matter which frame you're in, then why bother putting the handler in all the frame scripts? Just put it in a movie script and use the frame scripts to override the handler as needed.

Multiple Movie Scripts

Let me clarify something about the scripts: you can have as many as you want. Use the cast window to your advantage and make all the scripts you need, broken up into manageable portions.

You can create a thousand sprite scripts, so each sprite has its own script. Or, you can create just one sprite script, and have them all share that one script. The same goes for frame scripts. The same goes for cast scripts.

Remember, both the "sprite script" and the "frame script" are secretly *score scripts*.

You can also create a million (well, okay, maybe a thousand) movie scripts. Unlike cast or score scripts, which need to be assigned to an item like a cast, a sprite, or a frame in order to be valid, a movie script is *always* valid. You can also have as many of them as you would like.

The way things work when you call a handler is that Director will try to see if the requested handler is in the current script. For example, you have a script with four handlers in it, Director tries to see if the requested handler is one of those. If Director can't find it there, it'll try to see if the handler is in one of the movie scripts. From this you can divine two things:

✢ Director will look in all your movie scripts for the handler.

✢ You can only effectively have one handler of a given name at a time in your movie scripts.

Because Director will look in all your movie scripts for the handler, it makes sense to take advantage of the capability to have more than one movie script. I segregate my scripts by feature. For instance, I have one movie script to handle startup and shutdown issues, one script to handle audio, one script with all my text functions, one script with all my video functions, and so on.

Because score scripts are not global in scope (unlike movie scripts) you *are* allowed to have the same-named handler in more than one score script.

If you create a movie script and put in it two handlers of the same name, Director will catch the attempt and tell you that the name's already taken. That's because Director will have trouble building the name table of the handlers for that script, so it needs the problem resolved before it can successfully compile the script. As a result, you won't be able to go ahead until you resolve the name conflict.

On the other hand, you can create *other* movie scripts that happen to have a handler of the same name as one in a preceding movie script. These scripts will compile successfully, and their handlers' names will be added to Director's Big Name Table of the Universe. (Director maintains an internal name table of all the handlers that are available globally.)

When you call a function that Director doesn't recognize, Director looks to see if the function is in the local name table of handlers (those in the current script). If not, it looks in the global name table. If the function is *there*, Director will take the first instance it finds of that name. Subsequent entries will be ignored. If Director can't find any matching entries, it will raise an error about an undefined handler.

This means that if you have more than one handler of the same name scattered throughout your movie scripts, only the first one in the cast will count, and only the first cast that has one will win. You can put in a million handlers of the same name, but you'll never execute anything other than the first one that appeared in the first cast that had it.

Predefined Handlers

There are certain handlers that Director will attempt to execute at certain times if they're present. If you look in your Lingo Dictionary, you can find a list of these under the keyword "on" but, as an example, a few are:

on exitFrame	Invoked at the completion of a frame
on startMovie	Invoked at the start of the movie
on stopMovie	Invoked when the movie stops
on mouseDown	Invoked when the mouse is clicked
on keyDown	Invoked when a key is pressed

...and so on (no pun intended).

Director will attempt to call these if it can find them in the name table of available handlers. To be available, a handler must be in a movie script, or else it won't make it into the table (and as a result, won't be found by Director).

Depending on how you create your script, you can end up with a movie script or a score script. As a general rule, if you create it from the score (using the box in the upper left corner) you get a score script. If you create it from the Movie Cast window, you get a movie script. Reasonable enough? You'd think so, but a surprising number of people put their startMovie handlers in score scripts and then can't understand why they don't execute.

The startMovie handlers don't execute, obviously, because they're not sitting in a movie script, so they're not in the name table. Therefore, Director isn't even aware they exist when it goes looking for a handler by that name.

Cast Member Scripts

Cast member scripts are scripts attached directly to a cast member, like a bitmap cast member. Whereas the other kinds of scripts take up a slot in the cast, cast member scripts do not.

A cast member script applies to all sprites you create based on that member. For instance, if you create a bitmap button with a script attached to it and put it on the stage, any sprite that you make with that member would have access to the script. This is a lot easier than duplicating the same sprite script over and over.

> If you need to override the script for some particular sprite, just give that sprite a sprite script (because the sprite script takes precedence).

The only real drawback to the cast member scripts is it's easy to forget they're there because they don't appear in the cast window like the other scripts do. I once spent more hours than I care to admit trying to debug someone's movie and not being able to figure out what was going on. Finally, I realized they were using cast member scripts, which is why I couldn't see them.

> There are, however, a couple of tricks you can use to see the scripts, or at least be more aware of them.
>
> First, make sure you have the little "cast script icon" enabled for the cast window. This lets you know at a glance that the cast member has a script associated with it. I find this of questionable value, though, because there are so many of the little icons that I forget which is which. Still, it's a start.
>
> Then, open up some nearby script and use the arrow buttons (see fig. 3.3). The arrow buttons let you move back and forth through the cast members with scripts, including both scripts that you wrote and those with embedded cast scripts. The only catch is that you have to pay attention to which cast member you're on (by looking at the title bar), so you don't get lost.

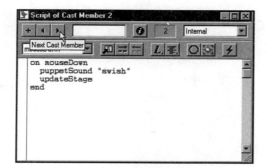

Figure 3.3
Using the arrow buttons in the Script of Cast Member 2 dialog box.

Variables

Goals

What variables are

Differences between local and global variables

The problem is that my variables keep changing!
Name withheld to protect the innocent

Computers store information in memory locations. Heck, computers store *everything* in memory locations. The compiler, which translates what you type in a file into code that the computer can execute, has two jobs:

* To create code that the computer can execute (if it can't do this, it's pretty useless)

* To have the program run at a halfway decent speed (if it takes it five minutes to add four numbers together, it's a pretty miserable implementation of a compiler)

Compilers eke extra speed out of programs by cutting corners, albeit safely. Any available shortcuts should be taken, as long as they don't adversely affect the program's behavior. You call a compiler that takes shortcuts to improve a program's speed an *optimizing compiler*.

One way to optimize is to take what you know about your code, and the variables within it, and leverage that information to speed things up. That's why compilers started to distinguish between constants and variables. Both occupy your average everyday memory location. When you use a *constant*, you're declaring to the compiler that in that specific location, the information will not change, ever. (That's where the name comes from!)

In other languages, such as C, constants might be declared to the compiler like so:

```
const int maxTries =99;
```

Because the variable `maxTries` is declared as a constant, the compiler can use this information to take some shortcuts (optimize) when creating the final compiled code that will run on the machine. For instance, it can always put the actual value 99 in the compiled code, because it knows the value will never change (with a variable, which *is* allowed to change, the compiler would have to insert code to look up the current value each time).

When you use a variable, you're also reserving a certain amount of memory space, but you're declaring that the contents of the space can vary. This means that you can set the value of that memory space and then set it to something else later on in the program (one line later, or many lines later). With variables, the compiler knows that just because it looked at that space a few moments ago, it's possible that you might have changed the contents since then. In other words, the contents are *variable*.

For instance, we might keep the score of a game in a variable:

```
set blueScore =0
set redScore =0
```

To start, they might be zero, but as soon as someone earns a point, that person's point score would be changed. For instance:

```
set blueScore =blueScore + 1
```

Because variables, in almost all programming languages, are assigned the result of whatever's on the right of the equals sign, this takes the old value of blueScore (looked up to be 0), adds 1 to it (making a total of 1), and assigns what's on the left (blueScore) the value of the results on the right, in effect, making blueScore equal to one more than its old value. Whenever blueScore is referenced in the program, its current value needs to be looked up in case it has changed (like it did here).

Variable doesn't mean that the compiler changes them on *you*, but that you can change them on the *compiler*.

Whereas some languages do support constants, Lingo doesn't. Lingo assumes that *everything* is a variable. This is both for reasons of convenience (nothing to declare) and simplicity (even in languages with both variables and constants, most people use variables anyway).

Lingo can afford to take this shortcut because variables can serve as constants (just don't change their value), but the reverse isn't true. The only place you lose out is that Lingo doesn't have an opportunity to optimize as a result of *knowing* that you don't intend to change the value, but it seems that the vote was made in favor of simplicity.

How Variables Are Represented Internally

You get to name your variables as an easy way to refer to your memory locations. A variable named subTotal, for instance, might be assigned to a particular memory location off in the Bahamas. As a convenience to you, the Lingo compiler enables you to assign that location a name rather than refer to it by some numeric value.

Each variable represents a certain amount of memory space. Exactly *how much* space depends on the kind of information you want to store. If you want to store numbers, they take only a few bytes, because by some creative methods of subdividing bytes into many 1s and 0s (*bits*), you can arrange for just four bytes to represent a number as large as 4,294,967,295. That's *billion*, not million, in case you weren't counting commas.

So, most numbers represented in Lingo take up only four bytes each, regardless of their size (unless you expect your numbers to exceed four billion). A variable that represents a number, therefore, takes four bytes. Remember, the variable is just a name you picked out to reference that memory location (the computer automatically chooses that location for you).

A string (anything in quotes, like `"these words here"`), on the other hand, takes up one byte per letter, because you can insert any one of 256 possible characters, including the 26 English-language letters, a variety of special letters from other languages, as well as symbols and punctuation, and some other fun things. Each byte, therefore, could assume the value of any one of the 256 things, limiting you to just one byte per character if you wanted to allow such a wide variety of expression.

It's because of this wonderful capability to represent a variety of characters that you can create such colorful phrases as "Why isn't this !@(*&^#$ script working???"

But I digress. The point I was getting at is that strings take up much more memory than numeric variables. Lingo can allocate as much memory as it needs to accommodate your nefarious requirements, up to some ridiculous limit, like 32,000+ characters. But don't laugh—some people really do run into such a limit in honest projects and for them it's a real barrier. Of course, such a limitation is one characteristic or requirement that you need to keep in mind when you design programs.

Variables also can represent almost any other entity in Lingo, as well. For example, variables can represent objects, lists, and windows. In the next section, I talk about how to create variables.

Inside the Secret Variable Laboratory

Language designers have great latitude in determining what the user must do to have a variable available for use. At one extreme is Assembly language, which is as close as you can get to true computer language and still call it human-readable. In Assembly, you can use internal computer registers, must declare your variables in advance, and can pick your own locations. This requires a tremendous amount of familiarity with computer internals, degrees from college, references from employers, and so on.

At the other extreme is Lingo, about as far as you can get from Assembly and still be truly programming.

In Lingo, you create variables simply by using them. Consider the following code:

Nothing there, right? Right. No variables, no nothing. Now, suppose you're building a game and you want to keep track of the scores:

```
set us = 0
set them = 0
```

Presto! Two variables: us and them. In Lingo, if you need to make a variable, just use one. As soon as you use the variable, it exists. Lingo creates it for you instantly.

When Lingo comes across a line like set us = 0, it first checks to see if it has a variable by that name. If one exists, Lingo makes the assignment and that's that.

If the variable doesn't exist, as in this case, Lingo needs to create one. The first thing it needs to do is determine how much memory is needed for this variable. Fortunately for you, you don't have to worry about this—it's

Lingo's job. You should know, however, that different types of data take different amounts of memory, and Lingo changes the allocations to match the requirements. So, internally, Lingo recognizes that you're setting the variable to 0, a numeric value, and reserves enough space for a number.

But you don't care. You just get to go `set us = 0` and Lingo does the rest for you.

What's even neater, though, is that you don't even have to keep the same type of information in the variable. If you want to reassign the variable to a string mid-program, you can. For instance, the following would be perfectly valid in Lingo:

```
set us =0
set them =0
... sometime later ...
set us ="Winner!"
```

This sets starting values for each (numeric), but later sets one of the variables (us) to a string (`"Winner!"`). Each time you make an assignment, Lingo reevaluates the variable and works to accommodate it.

In general, though, one doesn't go around resetting variables from one type of information to another, but as you get going on some special project you might encounter a scenario in which taking such an approach would make sense. At least you know it can be done.

Lingo Breakdown

Although I know you've read the manuals (right?), I'll just remind you that variable names begin with a letter, and can be any manageable, continuous string of letters and numbers and underscores. For instance, `thisCouldBeAVariableName`, and `so_could_this`, but not `this` and not `2WongFoo`. If you need a space, use an underscore, but don't begin with a number and don't use other punctuation. A common mistake is to use hyphens or apostrophes. Hyphens act as a subtraction sign in Lingo, so they're particularly prone to generating unlikely results. For instance, Lingo actually evaluates `Biddle-Barrows`, which you might think of as a hyphenated last name, as the variable `Biddle` minus the variable `Barrows`.

Local and Global Variables

Remember my discussion on movie scripts in Chapter 3? I explained how a movie script differs from other scripts because of its *scope*. A movie script is movie-wide. Handlers in a movie script are accessible to any other script in the movie, regardless of whether the other script is a movie script (it could be a score script or a cast member script).

Likewise, variables can vary in scope. Most variables are valid only in the handler in which you use them. Global variables, on the other hand, can be referenced from any handler, and in fact, from other movies as well.

So that you can understand this concept, take a look at how variables work within handlers.

Local Variables

Take the bare structure of a handler:

```
on myHandler
end myHandler
```

You can have one of your other handlers call this one (not that it would do much). It jumps to the handler and then returns where it came from.

Now, I'll add a variable to this handler:

```
on myHandler
  set numTimes =10
end myHandler
```

Something now happens when you run the handler. Lingo transfers over to the handler and executes the first line, (`set numTimes = 10`). Lingo *always* assumes a variable to exist *only within the handler* unless you tell it otherwise. The first time that Lingo encounters a variable by a certain name after beginning to execute a handler, it allocates space for it, creates it, and assigns it a specified value (in this case, 10).

At the end of the handler, we return to wherever we came from, and Lingo automatically destroys any variables created during the course of the handler. This means that this incarnation of the variable `numTimes` is lost forever in the mists of time.

This particular example was a little bit silly in that it created a variable and then immediately exited, thus destroying it. Still, it demonstrates something of the mechanics involved.

This example can serve to demonstrate something else, too—a variable that's *local*, meaning a variable whose scope is confined to its immediate handler. It didn't exist before that handler, won't exist after it, and can't be referenced in any other handler.

Further, the next time the handler executes, Lingo does the same process all over again. It creates and then destroys the variable, exactly as it did the first time. The variable and its value are destroyed, thus lost, every time at the end of the handler—the variable has no *persistence*. If it *did* have persistence, its last value would still be available the next time around.

For instance, in other languages like C and Pascal, you can make a variable local to a handler that "remembers" the value it had the last time that handler was called. Lingo doesn't have that feature specifically, although you can simulate it. One way to get around the persistence problem is by using global variables.

Global Variables

Like local variables, Lingo creates global variables the first time you use them. Unlike local variables, however, Lingo doesn't destroy them. A global variable persists until your program ends. Also unlike local variables, you must *declare* them, or use a special Lingo statement that says you intend to have it available *globally*; that is, so that it can be referenced anywhere.

You do that by using the `global` declaration before you reference the variable for the first time that it appears in that handler. For instance, you could do the following:

```
on startMovie
  global numPigs

  set numPigs = 10
end startMovie
```

In a startMovie handler here, I just set a variable called numPigs to 10. I chose to do it in a startMovie handler because startMovie is called only once during the life of a movie. This way, I can arrange a definite starting value.

Notice what I did to declare it global. If I didn't include that line, the compiler would assume that numPigs is just another local variable like the one I described earlier, and consequently, would destroy it at the end of the startMovie handler—making it pretty much useless.

As with locals, if Lingo encounters a global variable name for the first time (one that's not in the internal global name table), it makes an entry, allocates some space, and assigns the value. The only difference is that Lingo reserves the memory in an area for global data only, to keep it from being destroyed.

A global declaration is valid for the duration of a handler. If you declare it once at the top of a handler, the variable's scope is for the entire handler. Look at the following bit of code:

```
on startMovie
  global numPigs

  set numPigs =random(12)
  put numPigs
end startMovie
```

I declared it only once, but all references to numPigs from that point on refer to the global variable numPigs, at least until the handler ends.

Lingo Break down

As a general practice, you should list all your global declarations at the top of a handler, but all you technically must do is declare them before you use the variable. In fact, you could do the following:

```
on myHandler
  set numPigs =4
  global numPigs
  put numPigs
end myHandler
```

What do you think would happen here? Probably not what you think. The output, in fact, would be <void>, because we came across the name numPigs and, being a new reference, created a

continues

continued

local variable for it. *Then*, we see a global declaration for it, which means that any future reference refers to the global variable `numPigs`. The very next line, `put numPigs`, attempts to put the value of the global variable. The global one has no value yet, however, so we end up putting out <void>.

I can't think of any reason you'd want to do this intentionally; I'm just providing an example of possible behavior. My point is that you could end up with undesirable effects if you don't maintain a habit of declaring your globals at the top of each and every handler or script in which you use them.

If you have more than one global variable, you can declare each on their own line, or bunch them up and make them share a line; for example, both of the following approaches are valid:

```
on startMovie
  global numPigs
  global numFrogs
  global numSnakes
  ... whatever else...
end
```

and

```
on startMovie
  global numPigs, numFrogs, numSnakes
  ... whatever else...
end
```

If you have a very common global variable that you use often, you can declare it at the top of a script, *before you declare any handlers*, giving it a scope of the entire script, and thereby eliminating the need to declare it in each and every handler in which you use it (within that script). If you have other scripts that contain handlers that reference those variables, you need to declare them at the top of *those* scripts as well.

Now, declaring one variable might not seem like a big deal, but if you get to where you have twenty or thirty global variables that you reference throughout your script, putting them out of the way at the top starts to look pretty attractive. Technically, it's an undocumented technique, but it's so darn common—Macromedia even uses it in its demo programs—that I'm hard-pressed to find a good reason not to use it. I use it everywhere, and it hasn't caused me any problems (yet).

The Need for Multiple Global Declarations

In practice, it might quickly become evident that declaring globals in each and every handler (or script) in which you use them is a pain. You might soon be asking, *why?* Why can't you just declare them once and be done with it?

The main reason is because Lingo doesn't have any defined starting point. Although you *can* define a startMovie handler, you don't *have to*. Heck, you don't have to have any handlers at all in Director, although your functionality could prove somewhat limited if you don't.

Because a defined starting point doesn't exist, there's no real place to declare globals where you know they'll be executed.

You are thinking that it would be nice for Lingo to support an on declareGlobals handler, much like it supports on startMovie. Then you could use that handler to contain declared globals for the entire movie. Unfortunately, that sort of arrangement would hinder compiling scripts. With no reference to globals anywhere in a script (the references are all in another script somewhere else), Lingo can't properly compile the script because it doesn't know if any of the referenced variables are supposed to come out of the global pool.

The way to get around this problem quite neatly and allow scripts to compile would be to declare the globals you intend to use within each script. In fact, that's exactly the technique I currently use when I put the global declarations at the top. See, you've got the feature already!

Anything Worth Doing Is Worth *Over*doing

That was my philosophy through college, but alas, it isn't appropriate for the "real world." Likewise, it's not appropriate for global variables.

You don't have to go nuts trying to *avoid* using global variables, but don't go nuts *using* them either. The reason to be careful is that they use up some of your precious global data space, and if you overdo it, pretty soon you'll find that you can't do anything.

Some schools of thought consider globals to be an impure way to program, that you should never, ever use globals, and that you should pass everything in parameters, and so on and so forth. To minimize the use of globals to improve performance (or at least, not hamper it), or to conserve memory, is valid. To not do it ever because it's "impure" strikes me as overkill.

But be prudent. If you're writing a handler that you expect a variety of programs to call but that really shouldn't depend on the design of any of those programs, then don't make it depend on globals to communicate with the handler.

On the other hand, if your handler won't ever get used in anything but that one program you're writing, then by all means, do whatever you have to do. Don't jump through hoops of calling ten million handlers in succession and passing parameters just to avoid using a global—that would be mind-numbingly silly. Do what you need to do to get the job done. Over time, if you find that you write in a confusing style, you'll probably end up simplifying your code out of necessity. Or if not, you'll probably spend forever trying to debug your old code.

5

Handlers and Parameters

Program Flow

Using Director gives you a taste of *event-driven programming*. In the old days (before Windows), you'd write a program and it would start at the beginning and end at the end. And in the middle, it would go where you told it to go. You could take a debugger and go from line to line, and always know where you were going next.

I kind of liked that; it was all laid out, all very straightforward, with no surprises.

When your program had to run in a pseudo-multitasking windowed environment like Windows, however, you had to get into event-driven programming. And yes, Mac people, I know you were doing event-driven programming long before Windows was even a bad dream in Mr. G's head, but the reality is that the PC platform is the commercially dominant platform, and that most PC programmers didn't have to even think about event-driven programming until Windows 3.1 rolled around.

Now it seems you can't avoid it.

If you're working in Director, you're doing event-driven work. Director starts when you press play and ends when you quit the movie. If you have a `startMovie` handler, it gets called at the start of the movie (an event) and when the mouse gets clicked, you get a `mouseDown` event (should you choose to respond to it), and then you have events for entering a frame, exiting a frame, activating windows, handling occurrences of idles, and so on.

Events stem from actions in the environment and you can choose whether to handle them or not. After you finish handling an event, control returns to Director, and you might or might not be back in Lingo for a while, depending on the events and your program's setup. This aspect of event-driven programming distinguishes it from linear programming. What can make debugging hard is that you can't always predict the events that might happen. In Director, though, only a limited number of events can happen, so covering or otherwise accounting for all of them isn't too hard.

Handlers

If you choose to handle an event, you do so by writing a *handler* for it. Although the Lingo documentation doesn't really make a distinction, you really have two basic types of handlers in Lingo: *event handlers*, which already have specific names for handling Director events, and all the rest (the ones for which you choose a name and invoke only by calling).

Event Handlers

I discussed event handlers back in Chapter 3, "Scripts and Events." Event handlers are documented as being invoked (if present) in response to specific Director events. For instance, the on `exitFrame` handler responds to the *exitFrame* event. And, in fact, these event handlers are your only entry points into Lingo. Other than the message window, you can't have any Lingo instructions executed unless you come in through one of these entry points. (Actually, one more exception would be a handler of your choosing that gets invoked from an xobject or xtra.)

That's not to say that these are the only handlers that get executed, just that you have to *start* with one of these handlers. After an event occurs for which you have a handler defined, things then fall into Lingo's province, and Lingo doesn't relinquish control to Director until you exit the handler (well, that's actually a generalization, but one that's true for the most part).

Within a system event handler, you can do all the work you want and then be done with it, but some of those handlers can get pretty extensive. This is particularly true if you have similar Lingo instructions that you have to repeat over and over again in different event handlers. At this point, you need to think about breaking things down—and that's where your personal handlers come in.

Personal Handlers

A personal handler is one that you create, not to respond to an event, but simply to keep things more organized or efficient. I call them *personal handlers* for lack of a better name, because they're your own personal handlers, not the system's.

You can get to a personal handler, however, only from another personal handler or, if you go back far enough, from one of the event handlers responding to an Director event.

The personal handlers in score scripts are available only to the other handlers in the same script, whereas the personal handlers in movie scripts are available to *any* handler in *any* script.

Personal handlers and event handlers basically are the same, aside from how they're named and what calls them.

Handlerus Genericus: Your Basic Handler

The *handler* simply is Lingo's implementation of a very old programming concept: the subroutine. The subroutine is so called because it's beneath, or utilized from, the *main* routine.

The *main* routine is what programmers used before this event-driven programming stuff came along. The program starts, runs the first line of the main routine, and continues executing each line until it gets to the last line, whereupon it ends.

Somewhere deep down in Windows, and the Mac O/S as well, is a main routine. Buried deep in the swamp of the operating system is a section that gets called when power is applied to the computer, and ends when the power is shut off. On the Mac and in Windows 95, the operating system's main routine has a definable end, because each has controlled shutdowns. Before Windows 95, though, on the PC side, things just ended when you turned off the power—Windows had no "official" way to shut down the machine. The same applies to the early Apples and most other microcomputers.

A division of labor usually is the point behind a subroutine. A boss of a company might have 5 departments, each with a particular function. Each department might require work of subdepartments. For instance, the Maintenance department might divide its work into several subdepartments, one of which being *repairs*. However, due to the way the company is organized, any other department in the company can call the maintenance department and schedule a repair.

If all the people in the company were in one huge room and went through one person to handle everyone's scheduling, you'd have a logistical nightmare. Only by dividing things up do you make them easier to manage.

It's the same theory with subroutines. The main routine, to make things easier, has separate subroutines that it calls to perform a function and then return so that the main routine can go on and do its next important thing. Breaking it down into separate functions means that you can work on and see an individual function in its entirety, without being distracted from anything else. When you look at the main routine you can see it in broad strokes without being weighted down by the details.

For instance, a main routine for a fictional computer operating system might look like this:

```
start_up_all_devices
allocate_some_memory
start_up_this_subsystem
```

```
start_up_that_subsystem
put_logo_up_on_screen
do_something_else
signal_user_ready_to_go
repeat
    get_command
    execute_command
until command = "STOP"
shut_down_this_subsystem
shut_down_that_subsystem
shut_down_all_devices
power_off
```

The division of labor here enables you to easily see how everything flows. Power goes on, things start up, logos go up, everything gets ready, and then we loop around taking commands until we get the command to stop, at which point we shut down everything and turn off the power.

Minus a division of labor, this program would be zillions of lines long. Not only would each subroutine be incorporated in full, but every subroutine of those subroutines would be incorporated in full, too. The program would run the same, except it would be excessively huge.

Imagine what goes into simply having a character appear on-screen. Even at the most basic level, it involves setting up video card registers and latches, loading values into ports, watching for vertical traces, and all sorts of things—it's sort of complicated.

Because getting a character up on the screen is a fairly specialized process, it would be nice to get it down to a science and then just have that routine in a place where everyone can use it. Otherwise, you would be obligated to write the whole routine out each and every time you want to perform that function, which is how a program without subroutines can get to be so vast. So, if you gave the process a name and rigged it up as a subroutine, anyone could call that routine and ask that it put a character up for them. And that, indeed, is the benefit of subroutines—write once, use often.

The same theory applies to handlers. You can use them to separate out specific tasks performed only once—for organizational purposes—or you can take some function performed multiple times and name it so that everyone doesn't have to write the same code over and over.

Think about a simple task like playing audio. Suppose you want to play a sound effect in several places in your program. I cover audio more in Chapter 25, but for now let's stick to these instructions necessary for making a sound:

```
puppetSound 0
puppetSound "gong"
updateStage
repeat while soundBusy(1)
end repeat
```

Not too much, admittedly, but still a little annoying to deal with each and every time you have to make a sound. A better idea would be to encapsulate this in a handler so that anyone could call it.

```
on playGong
  puppetSound 0
  puppetSound "gong"
  updateStage
  repeat while soundBusy(1)
  end repeat
end playGong
```

Now, anytime you need to play a gong sound, you can just have `playGong()` rather than list all the instructions.

Notice that I had parentheses follow the name. Actually, you could just have the statement `playGong` without the parentheses, but I used them for a reason (which I'll get into a little further on in this chapter).

Parameters

So we have now taken our gong sound and stuck it in a handler. Very nice! And if we wanted to make a *swoosh* sound, we could make a handler for that too. Also very nice! Also very redundant.

If you can use a handler for things that are only slightly different, rather than copy the handler, make that change, and call it something new, you're better off having your handler do both. A good rule is this: Whenever possible, have a handler that does a *type* of thing rather than a *specific* thing.

Keeping that in mind, observe how the following handler does just that:

```
on playSound
  puppetSound 0
  puppetSound ??
  updateStage
  repeat while soundBusy(1)
  end repeat
end playSound
```

The `playSound` function is identical to the `playGong` one, except that it doesn't specify what to pass as an argument to the `puppetSound` function. The `playGong` function uses the string "gong," but that's limiting. How can we resolve this problem?

You can resolve it by determining the name of the sound to play at the time that you call the function, and just keeping the function generic (that is, not tied to any specific sound).

One way to do this (it's not recommended, however) would be to use a global variable. If you used this technique, the handler would look something like this:

```
on playSound
  global soundToPlay
  puppetSound 0
  puppetSound soundToPlay
  updateStage
  repeat while soundBusy(1)
  end repeat
end playSound
```

You can see how I reference the global variable, `soundToPlay`. Whatever `soundToPlay` is will play. To make it play the gong sound, you could do it like this:

```
global soundToPlay
set soundToPlay = "gong"
playSound
```

Unfortunately, that's a little cumbersome, and creates a global variable for no good reason. Also, you run the risk of forgetting to declare it global before using it, which means that you would set a local variable to "gong." Because that local variable wouldn't exist in playSound, playSound would play nothing, because it wouldn't know what to play.

All in all, it's not very satisfying.

Just being able somehow to tell the playSound routine what sound you wanted to play would be much nicer. You know, something like this:

```
playSound "gong"
```

Then it's all taken care of for you. Why, that sounds like the solution for us! And, in fact, setting it up this way is the proper way to do things. It's the cleanest and most professional method.

Remember my discussion on local variables in Chapter 4, and how to create them? Well, you're going to use local variables to implement this solution.

You can do this trick, see. If you put the local variable on the same line after the handler name, it becomes a parameter; like so:

```
on playSound whichSound
  puppetSound 0
  puppetSound whichSound
  updateStage
  repeat while soundBusy(1)
  end repeat
end playSound
```

In this handler, whichSound is a local variable. Remember, local variables are created when they're first referenced in a handler, assigned a starting value, and destroyed when the handler exits.

Because I put the whichSound variable on the same line after the handler name, it receives special treatment. Like all other local variables, it too is created here for the first time and destroyed when it exits. It differs, though, in how it's assigned its starting value. It gets its starting value from the arguments passed in when you call the function. Consider:

```
playSound "gong"
```

Here, you have the name of a handler, playSound, with one argument, or parameter, passed in. The argument in this case is a string, "gong".

On the other side (inside the handler), the handler will create whichSound and assign it the value of the first (and in this case, only) parameter passed in:

```
on playSound whichSound
  puppetSound 0
  puppetSound whichSound
  ...
```

So, in other words, it's just like a local variable (heck, it *is* a local variable), except that you get to set its starting value when you pass your parameter in. What you end up with is a generic function that can play any of your audio cast members if you tell it their name.

Multiple Parameters

You're not limited to passing in just one parameter. You can pass in as many as you can manage, usually something like seven, tops, and preferably no more than two or three. Technically, you could use however many you want, like you could use 81 if you wanted, but I'd say that if you get up over 9 or 10, you've got a serious design problem and you might want to rethink your approach.

If you're familiar with the audio calls in Lingo, you might have recognized that after my handler started playing the sound it would then wait until the sound finished before returning. Suppose you want to make that feature optional, so you can turn it on or off at will. You would write the handler like this:

```
on playSound whichSound, waitUntilFinished
  puppetSound 0
  puppetSound whichSound
  updateStage
  if waitUntilFinished = TRUE then
    repeat while soundBusy(1)
    end repeat
  end if
end playSound
```

I accepted a second parameter into another local variable, called `waitUntilFinished`. So, if the user calls the following function, it sets the `whichSound` parameter to "gong" and the `waitUntilFinished` parameter to `TRUE`:

```
playSound "gong", TRUE
```

This is the primary danger point where half the audience gets confused (not the half who is reading this book, mind you... the other half): *How does the computer know to set* `whichSound` *to "gong" and* `waitUntilFinished` *to* `TRUE`*?* Or, how do whichSound and waitUntilFinished get assigned correctly, not mixed up?

The computer doesn't know. *You* do. The secret is that parameters are *position dependent.* The order in which you send them down is the order in which they are received.

In this particular example, I sent them down like this:

```
playSound "gong", TRUE
```

and picked them up like this:

```
on playSound whichSound, waitUntilFinished
```

See the one-to-one correspondence? *You* are the one who coordinated everything to get them lined up. I could easily have screwed up the call and made it like this:

```
playSound TRUE, "gong"
```

in which case, it would have been picked up just the same:

```
on playSound whichSound, waitUntilFinished
```

except, the end result would be that `whichSound` would be `TRUE`, and `waitUntilFinished` would be "gong," thus rendering the whole thing ridiculous.

So, it's important to remember that position dependence is the key. The handler doesn't care what's on the other side, whether it's a variable, an actual number, or whatever.

Neither should the statement calling the handler have to know the names of the parameters in the handler. It *does* need to know what to expect in what location; that is, that it can expect the first parameter to be a string of some kind that represents the name of a cast member sound to play, and the second parameter to be TRUE or FALSE to indicate whether to wait for the sound to finish.

How you derive those arguments on the calling end is up to you.

You could keep the name of the sound in a list or in another variable. It doesn't matter to the handler. The arguments you pass must ultimately be translated to their true meaning. If you did use variables, they could even be of the same name as those local variables in the handler, or they could be totally different. It wouldn't matter.

Returning Values

Parameters, alas, are just one-way. You can't set a parameter to a value from within the called handler and have it automatically changed on the side that called it.

There are, however, Lingo functions that return a value, like Lingo's ABS() function. ABS is a function that returns the absolute value of the number you pass into it. You can do something like this:

```
set positiveNum =ABS(-32)
```

and postiveNum comes out to be 32. How so? Yes, it does take one parameter, a number, but how does it send back a resultant answer?

The answer is that it uses the return statement. Here's how the absolute value function might have been written:

```
on abs numberToConvert
  if numberToConvert < 0 then
    set answer = 0 - numberToConvert
  else
    set answer = numberToConvert
  end if
  return answer
end abs
```

You can see how the function sends back the answer with the `return` statement, but how does the caller of the function retrieve that value? By either assigning it to a variable or sending it down as a parameter to another handler.

The prior example showed the assignment method:

```
set positiveNum =ABS(-32)
```

The left side of the equal sign is evaluated, and the result is passed back and assigned to the variable `positiveNum`.

If you passed it to a handler, it might look like this:

```
put ABS(-32)
```

Yes, that's right: the put statement is a handler, too. It's internal to Lingo, but still behaves as a handler. In this example, the result from `ABS(-32)` is determined and in turn given to put, which in turn displays it in the message window.

Now, you don't *have* to assign it to anything. You could simply have the statement as is, all by itself:

```
ABS(-32)
```

Unfortunately, that would be a waste of everyone's time, at least for this particular statement. You see, this function merely calculates an answer and returns it to you—it does nothing else. So, if you choose to ignore the answer by not picking it up anywhere or doing anything with it, just calling the function is a waste.

On the other hand, many functions perform a valuable task and return status information as a return value. In those functions, the status information is valuable but not the function's focus, and choosing to retrieve it is optional.

The `preloadCast` function is a good example of this. It attempts to preload all the cast members into memory, so you could give the instruction all by itself:

```
preloadCast
```

If you do that, `preloadCast` tries to do what it can. Unfortunately, you don't know if it succeeded. The documentation states that `preloadCast` returns the number of the last cast loaded. So, you might want to find out what that is. You can retrieve it by having some variable pick up the return value:

```
set lastOneLoaded =preloadCast()
```

But in this case, preloadCast actually performs a valuable function regardless of whether you bother to get the return value. You also can just leave it alone and it still works just fine.

Using `return` as an Alternate Exit Point

When you execute the `return` statement, you're leaving the handler with the return value, if any, in hand. `return` doesn't *have* to have a value; you could just decide to jump out of the handler. But no matter whether you include a value when you return or not, when you reach that line you cause the handler to exit. Like in this:

```
on divide firstNum, secondNum
  if secondNum = 0 then
    return(0)
  end if
  return(firstNum / secondNum)
end
```

This example actually demonstrates several points. First, a `return` doesn't have to be at the end of the handler, but wherever it is, it marks the exit point of the handler. You don't execute a `return` statement and keep on going.

Consequently, the only time you see `return` statements other than at the end of handlers is at the end of `if` statements. If the `return` statement is located anywhere else, it prevents the remainder of the code from executing.

For instance, consider this well-intentioned, but ill-conceived, method for returning two results from the handler:

```
on getEnds whichString
    set firstWord = word 1 of whichString
    set lastWord = the last word in whichString
    return firstWord
    return lastWord
end getEnds
```

It never makes it to the `return lastWord` line. That's considered *unreachable code*. Your program never gets there, because it gets kicked out when it hits the first `return` statement.

You also might infer that you can't return two variables at once. And that's true. You can't. It's easy to understand why. Remember how you can pick up the result on the other end by assigning it to a variable?

```
set positiveNum =ABS(-32)
```

That's the only way to receive a return value, but undoubtedly there's going to be some situation *sometime* when you'll need to return more than one.

In such a situation, then, what would you do? You'd have to put both the items in a list and then return the *list*. A list is an entity that counts as one item, so it'd be a way to pull off this trick. I discuss lists more at length in Chapter 11.

Break down

Going back to the previous divide example, I just wanted to point out one more thing about this:

```
on divide firstNum, secondNum
if secondNum = 0 then
return(0)
end if
return(firstNum / secondNum)
end
```

You will notice that with the final line, I do the division within parentheses rather than ahead of time. What happens is that the expression within the parentheses (in this case, `firstNum / secondNum`) is evaluated, and the *result of that* is sent back rather than the whole expression.

The Parameter Wrap

In many of the prior examples, I wrapped my function calls in parentheses. In Lingo, for the most part, parentheses are optional. The exception is when you're evaluating complex expressions, but as far as general handlers and parameters go, they're just optional.

I prefer to use parentheses, though. First, most of the other languages I work in *do* require them, and it's just easier for me to be consistent, and second, and perhaps more importantly, they remove any ambiguity about what I'm doing. If I see a reference to something like this:

```
set answer = total
```

I don't know whether `total` is a variable or a handler that returns a value. If I put parentheses around the parameters, even if there are none, it makes it very clear and unambiguous—just who's who and what's what:

```
set answer = total()
```

In this case, I know just by looking that `total` is a function. Also, the compiler doesn't have to make a distinction or a decision; I've gone and told it.

This little layer of explicitness helps contribute to the clarity of my program. It's little things like this that make debugging easier, and that help prevent mistakes from happening in the first place.

6

Expressions

Grant me some wild expressions,
Heavens, or I shall burst.
> George Farquhar
> (1678-1707)

But not too wild! In Lingo, an expression is something that reduces to a value. It might be a value to begin with, like 2, or it could be a complex formula that needs to be reduced down to its answer, or it might be a combination of function calls and other things, all of which need to be evaluated to come up with a final answer.

For instance, the following subexpression reduces to some number:

```
subTotal + 200 + numPictures + ¬
getNumPicturesInLibrary()
```

Each of the components is evaluated in turn.

subTotal is a variable, as is numPictures. Each has values that can be plugged in. Obviously, 200 is a value. getNumPicturesInLibrary() is a handler that returns a value. To evaluate this subexpression, this component must be evaluated, and to evaluate this component, the handler must be executed.

So the handler is executed, and does whatever it has to do, and *returns* a value. That value then gets plugged in with the rest and the result is something like, let's say, 614.

The concept of comparison expressions, such as the following two examples, is pretty straightforward:

```
if (a=b)
```

or

```
if (tries < (clues + handicap))
```

I'm not going to spend any time on them. The confusion basically tends to set in with combining multiple expressions.

Combining Expressions

Combining expressions is a shortcut around having a million if statements. Suppose I'm doing a game, for instance, and I want to see if the user is done or if all the cards have been used. I need to do an if statement, such as the following:

```
if (cardsUsed = 52) then
   ... do something
else if (done) then
   ... do the same thing
end if
```

What I really want to do is combine them like this:

```
if ((cardsUsed = 52) or (done)) then
   ... do something ...
end if
```

The first thing you might notice is that I wrap parentheses around each expression to make my intention unambiguous. The next thing you might notice is that little word "or" that worked its way in there.

The and & or Operators

Operators like and and or work by evaluating their left and right sides and returning a result.

In the prior example, where I had the following, the OR operator had the left side reduced as far as it could go, and the right side reduced as far as it could go:

```
if ((cardsUsed = 52) or (done)) then
```

The left side, (cardsUsed = 52), for instance, will evaluate to TRUE (if 52 cards were used) or FALSE (if not). Either way, I need to distill the subexpression down to a number or a final value somehow.

Continuing this same example, done also can be TRUE or FALSE. After I distill both the left and right sides of the OR statement down to a final value of some kind, I can try to evaluate the OR statement itself.

As logic dictates, one side or the other needs to be true before the OR statement can evaluate to TRUE. If *neither* of them qualify as true, the final expression evaluates to FALSE.

AND works the same way, except, of course, both the left side *and* the right side need to be true before the expression can evaluate to TRUE.

What's TRUE?

Here's the truth: TRUE is true, but true is not necessarily TRUE. Got it?

If so, you're ready for your metaphysics degree.

Actually, that statement *is* true. Lingo makes a distinction between what qualifies as a true statement and TRUE. You will notice that whenever I refer to one of these in particular I capitalize it. That's because Lingo has a constant called TRUE, which has a value of 1.

FALSE also is a constant, with a value of 0, and any expression that evaluates to 0 is considered false. In accord with that same line of thought, then, if it's not false, it must be true. And so it is. Anything that evaluates to something *other* than zero, and therefore has a value, is considered to be true.

This can come in handy when evaluating expressions. For instance, if you had a variable called cardsRemaining and it had a value of 24, for 24 cards remaining, you can use it in an expression like the following:

```
if cardsRemaining then
    ... do something ...
```

The expression cardsRemaining didn't need much evaluation, because it's just one variable—but it did have a nonzero value. As a result, the if statement is TRUE and the contents of the if statement are executed.

In fact, you would be in trouble if you tried a comparison such as the following:

```
if (cardsRemaining = TRUE) then
  ... do something ...
```

This might normally be okay if you used cardsRemaining as a flag that was either TRUE or FALSE, but in this case it's serving as a count of cards (remember how it had a value of 24?). Therefore, the idea is to determine whether the cardsRemaining (24) is equal to TRUE (1), which would cause the whole expression to fail, or at least that would be the case until you got down to one card left, at which point you'd be comparing 1 and 1.

So, an expression could be true without being TRUE. For instance, this is true:

```
if cardsRemaining then
  ... do something ...
```

(At least until only zero cards remain.)

The reason Lingo has a constant TRUE with a value of 1 is so you can do convenient things like:

```
set gameOver = FALSE
```

```
if not cardsRemaining then
  set gameOver = TRUE
end if
```

Without them, you'd have to do it like this:

```
set gameOver = 0

if not cardsRemaining then
  set gameOver = 1
end if
```

It evaluates to the same thing—it's just that the first one is easier to read and understand.

What's NOT?

Perhaps you noticed me sneak in a little example of NOT, when I did this:

```
if not cardsRemaining then
```

The way NOT works is that the expression to NOT's *right* is evaluated. Then, whatever it comes out to be, NOT *expression* is the opposite.

It's very handy for stuff like what I just did there. On the other hand, it just confuses some people too much. If it hurts your head, just leave it alone for now.

Segregating Expressions for Clarity

I took you through that discussion of evaluation because it's really key to understanding how combined expressions work.

For instance, somewhere online recently I saw a question from someone who was trying to recognize either the ENTER key *or* the RETURN key when a key was pressed. He was doing it like this, and it wasn't working:

```
if the key = ENTER or RETURN then
```

Can you see what's wrong?

If you think about how expressions are evaluated, where each side of the AND or the OR has to evaluate first, it should be clear.

In this case, (the key = ENTER) might or might not be true; this part of the expression doesn't have anything wrong with it. But the other side of the OR operator simply has RETURN. What is RETURN? It's character # 13. So, technically it's non-zero. How do you think that expression evaluates? Because the right side of the OR is *always* non-zero the way he had it written, it's always going to end up being true.

He *should* have had separate expressions on each side of the if statement:

```
if (the key = RETURN) or (the key = ENTER) then
```

This way each side of the OR statement can be evaluated down, and the final expression can evaluate the way he wants it to.

I used this example because it is absolutely the most common mistake that I see people make with expressions.

Because Americans grow up using the English language, we tend to make statements like, "If they have today's *Herald* or the *Courier*, then bring me a paper please." Unfortunately, the way we speak English doesn't translate well to computer if statements. For a computer, you'd have to phrase it as the following so that each side could be independently evaluated and the whole expression could reach a conclusion:

```
if (they have today's Herald) or (they have today's Courier)
```

Finally, I just want to mention that you certainly can mix and match these things as long as you keep things straight. You use parentheses to keep them straight.

For instance, you could do this:

```
if (cardsLeft and not done) or ((quit = FALSE) and stillTime)
```

The trick is to work from the inside of the parentheses out, and reduce everything to its own little subexpression. By breaking an expression into its smallest parts, you can get a real doozy of an expression going. But if you don't use parentheses to remove ambiguity, you're just asking for trouble.

Loops

I've seen some people go to extraordinary, and often awkward, lengths to write code that would be so much better served if they used a loop or a list. Often they're aware that loops exist, but are unfamiliar with them, or may feel intimidated by them.

It's understandable to be unfamiliar with them, but there's certainly no reason to be intimidated by them. In fact, I suspect most people do know how to use them, but typically fail to consider them as a solution for a particular problem that's vexing them. So let's review, first, what they are, what kinds are available, and how to use them to solve some common Lingo situations.

Understanding Loops: A Boy and His Loop

Many, many years ago, in a land far, far away, lived a young lad. Although he was eager to please, his short-term memory was shot to pieces owing to the excesses of youth. Consequently, if members of his family wanted him to do a favor for them, they had to write it down.

Usually, his memory problem wasn't a big deal. Most of the instructions fell along the these lines:

1. Go to the baker

2. Get bread

3. Pay for bread with money

4. Bring bread home

One day, unfortunately, his father, a shopkeeper, suffered an unexpected but fatal sickness and passed away. The task of running the store fell to the son (in those days, in that land, a woman was forbidden to run such an establishment), so his mother had to write everything down for him so he could keep the store going.

His mother wrote down the instructions for him:

1. Greet customer

2. Ask customer what item they want to buy

3. Locate item

4. Tell customer price

5. Receive money

6. Thank customer

Although his mother admirably enumerated the steps for handling a single-item purchase, she failed to consider that some customers would have more than one item to buy. Indeed, some customers didn't even know ahead of time how many items they would end up getting.

His mother could handle such a situation with ease, but had forgotten that her son would be lost and unable to improvise in such a situation. Indeed, without every single instruction laid out for him, he would be incapable of handling anything beyond the first and only purchase by the customer.

Racking her brains, she considered making an instruction list for each possible occurrence. She tried to remember the most items they'd ever sold at one time. The most she could recall was twenty items. Her first effort, therefore, looked like this:

1. Greet customer

2. Ask customer how many items they want to buy

3. If the customer wants twenty items, find the instructions for twenty items

4. If the customer wants nineteen items, find the instructions for nineteen items

5. If the customer wants eighteen items, find the instructions for eighteen items

6. ...and so on

Each of the individual instructions were accordingly lengthy. The instructions for twenty items had twenty repetitions of asking which item, locating it, telling price, and receiving money. The nineteen-item instructions were similar, but she only wrote the series down nineteen times.

This worked well for the first customer that came into the shop, but immediately hit a snag with the second customer. This is how that conversation went:

Boy: "Good day, sir, welcome to our shop. How many items did you wish to buy today?"

Customer: "Ummm, I don't know yet. We'll start off with a couple items and work from there."

Needless to say, this stymied the boy immediately and he forced the customer to do each transaction one item at a time, from greeting to payment to thanks, to accommodate the sale. His mother, watching, realized the awkwardness and now-obvious limitations of her instructions.

That evening, his mother had a flash of inspiration and prepared this for him:

1. Greet customer

2. Start new bill for customer

3. Ask customer which item to help find; if they name an item, then do steps 3a through 3d, otherwise go to step 4.

    3a. Locate the item

    3b. Tell customer price

    3c. Add price to bill

    3d. Go back to step 3 again

4. Tell customer total of bill

5. Receive money

6. Thank customer

What she particularly liked about it was how it would work for any number of transactions, even those higher than twenty. It would also work for none.

The son liked it because it took care of any situation. It also eliminated the many lists he previously had to use (the one for twenty items, the one for nineteen items, the one for eighteen items, and so on).

It became so useful, that their business stopped losing customers and actually grew, and soon they could hire salespersons and clerks, and this technique was taught to each clerk, who taught it to the next clerk, who taught it to their children, and so on and so forth, until it became the Lingo `repeat...while` loop that we know today.

Although most of this story has been buried in the shifting sands of history (perhaps appearing here in print for the first time ever!), its most valuable points continue to stand the test of time:

❄ If you have more than one or two similar operations in a row, you ought to be able to create a loop for it.

❄ If you find yourself creating extravagant instructions to handle cases for twenty of this, nineteen of that, and eighteen of the other, something's wrong. Chances are, you can adapt your instructions to use a loop.

❄ You have a test at the beginning of a loop. If the test fails, none of the steps in the loop are executed. In the example from our tale, if the customer doesn't name an item when the boy performs step 3 (asking the customer which item to help them find), the boy doesn't perform the loop (3a through 3d).

❄ When the test fails, the next item to be executed is the one that *follows* the loop. In the example from our tale, when the customer fails to name an item (the test at step 3 fails) and the boy doesn't perform the loop (substeps 3a through 3d), the boy skips on to step 4.

In Lingo, a loop has a test condition at the top, and perhaps a few other things (which we'll get to in a minute). This is the line that has the `repeat` keyword on it. Examples are `repeat with ...` and `repeat while...` There are some variations to these. The end of the loop is marked by a line that says `end repeat`. Everything in between acts as the body of the loop. Figure 7.1 illustrates the Lingo loop.

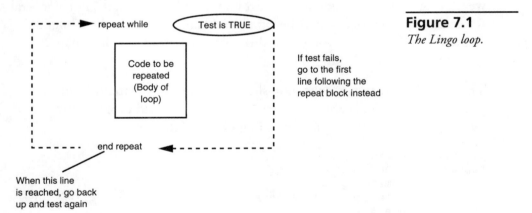

Figure 7.1
The Lingo loop.

Let's take a look at the different kinds of loops you can create...

repeat while...

This type of loop continuously executes the body of the loop until the expression at the top of the loop proves FALSE (that is, evaluates to zero).

The expression can be anything you want, as long as it eventually evaluates to a TRUE (nonzero) or false (zero) state. For example, these are all valid loops:

```
repeat while (the mouseV < 20)
   ... do some instructions ...
end repeat

repeat while not done
   ... do some instructions ...
end repeat

repeat while soundBusy(1)
end repeat
```

The first of these three loops (does something) when the mouseV is less than 20. The mouseV happens to be a Lingo property that indicates the mouse's vertical position. The loop executes its contents as long as the mouse stays at the top of the screen within the first 20 pixels.

Note that because the loop doesn't even start unless the expression is TRUE for the initial test, if the mouseV isn't 20 or less at the time that the loop begins, we skip right over that loop to the next line. In other words, it's not a general statement "If the mouseV ever becomes less than 20 then do these lines...." Rather, it says "If, when you get to this point, the mouseV is less than 20, then do these instructions."

The repeat while not done loop shows a continuous loop until such a point that the variable *done* becomes TRUE. This is an old programming technique, usually utilized in something like the following:

```
set done = FALSE
repeat while not done
    ... do something ...
    if something special happens then
      set done = TRUE
    end if
end repeat
```

The idea is to loop continuously until some particular event happens, at which point we consider the job to be finished. We set the variable to FALSE at the start, just to make sure the loop does begin, then we loop around until our magic happening occurs. At this point, we set done to TRUE, which causes the test to fail, thus tossing us out of the loop (execution continues on the line that follows the end repeat statement).

This technique once was the mainstay of the old pick-an-item menu selection interfaces, where you'd have anywhere between two and twenty (or more) menu items. If you chose the item Quit, however, some variable, such as *done*, would be set to TRUE and the loop would terminate.

Because of Director's event-driven nature, we don't use this technique on such a grand scale, but you could use it on a smaller scale. Perhaps our program has to scan through all the words in a text member until it finds one or runs out of words. We'd use something very similar to pull this off, with *done* set to TRUE at the point at which we're ready to end the loop (that is, when we find the word we want or otherwise run out of words).

The third loop was this one:

```
repeat while soundBusy(1)
end repeat
```

This loops continuously as long as the soundBusy() handler returns TRUE. As you can see, the loop is empty of instructions, which is perfectly okay—the purpose here is to kill time until a certain condition is FALSE.

In this example, if soundBusy() is FALSE when we do our initial test, we never even make it into the loop. This loop typically is used immediately following an instruction to start the sound playing. For instance, the following would start the sound "anthem" playing, and then loop around while it's busy:

```
puppetSound "anthem"
updateStage
repeat while soundBusy(1)
end repeat
```

Because the puppetSound and updateStage instructions should get the sound playing, by the time we hit the repeat loop we know that soundBusy()

should be TRUE. We then loop around, testing soundBusy() each time until it returns FALSE. In other words, as long as the sound plays, soundBusy() is TRUE. As long as soundBusy() is TRUE, the loop continues one more time. The net effect is that we stay in the loop until soundBusy() is FALSE or, effectively, until the sound stops playing. It's a way to wait for something to happen (or stop happening).

repeat with...

The next variation is the counting loop. A counting loop also continues until reaching a condition, but changes a variable automatically for you, counting up or down.

It looks like this:

```
repeat with x = 1 to 200
  put x
end repeat
```

or this:

```
repeat with thisSprite =1 to 48
  set the visible of sprite thisSprite to FALSE
end repeat
```

or this:

```
repeat with bottlesOfBeer = 99 down to 0
  put bottlesOfBeer & "bottles of beer on the wall"
end repeat
```

The last one differs only slightly because it counts down, using down to rather than repeat with x = y to z.

The condition in these loops is whether the to point has been reached. The way they work is as follows (see fig. 7.2):

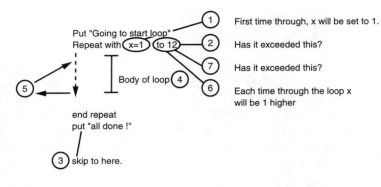

Figure 7.2
The way a Lingo loop works.

1. The variable you specify is assigned the starting value.

2. A test is made to see if it has exceeded the to limit.

3. If it has, we skip out of the loop to the first line after.

4. Otherwise, the body of the loop is executed. The variable holds its value during that time. You can, in theory, modify it, but doing so is not recommended.

5. When we reach the end repeat statement, we jump back to the first line of the loop.

6. The variable is then incremented (or decremented, if using down to) by one.

7. Go to step 2.

The syntax of the statement looks like this:

```
repeat with variable = firstValue to secondValue
```

The *variable* is any variable you want to specify. It could be *thisChar* or *x* or *cardsRemaining* or *myVar*—whatever you need, as long as it's a variable. It couldn't be, say, a handler or a literal value (like 2).

FirstValue and *secondValue*, however, can be anything as long as they eventually evaluate to some numerical value. In other words, they could be a handler, or even another variable. For instance:

```
repeat with x = 1 to count(myList)
```

or

```
repeat with whichCard =firstCard to lastCard
```

The first example calls the built-in function count() to determine the number of items on the list. This becomes our stopping point. The second example runs from firstCard's value to lastCard's value. Again, remember, if firstCard exceeds lastCard, the loop never executes.

Lingo evaluates the items in the test every time it hits them. In the following example, every time it increments *x* and runs the test to see if the loop has expired, it has to call count(myList), evaluate it for the answer, and do the test:

```
repeat with x = 1 to count(myList)
```

Once you understand this, you're ready to do a little optimizing. If you have a time-critical loop that you need to execute quickly and you find yourself doing unnecessary tests, you can rearrange things to eliminate those unnecessary tests to speed things up.

The previous loop, for instance, constantly calls to get a count of the list myList. If you know that the size of the list isn't going to change, however, continuing to ask for a count is pretty silly. A better way would be to call the handler once up-front, store the amount, and then just check against the amount in the test. Like so:

```
set myListSize =count(myList)

repeat with x = 1 to myListSize

    ...

end repeat
```

Here, we've moved the handler call out of the evaluation test area. We know (because we wrote the program) that that particular list's size doesn't change. We then can take advantage of that fact by recording the result of the handler call *once*, storing the result, and using the *result* in the loop.

This probably is a good place to mention that you can optimize your loops by moving other repetitive, unchanging, stuff out of the loop as well.

For instance, this loop changes the cast of a sprite 100 times:

```
repeat with x=1 to 100
    set the membernum of sprite x to member "Sad Face"
    updateStage
    set the membernum of sprite x to member "Happy Face"
    updateStage
end repeat
```

Although this really isn't the place to discuss cast lookups, you should know that when you refer to a cast member by name, it has to go through the cast looking for one that has that name. String lookups, which this is, take some time. Eventually, it determines the number of the cast and then uses that. In a loop, this gets a little ridiculous because we keep looking up the same member over and over.

To optimize it, since the position of the cast isn't changing, we could just do this:

```
set sadFaceMember =the number of member "Sad Face"
set happyFaceMember =the number of member "Happy Face"
repeat with x = 1 to 100
    set the membernum of sprite x to sadFaceMember
    updateStage
    set the membernum of sprite x to happyFaceMember
    updateStage
end repeat
```

Now we're just assigning it to the value held in the variables `sadFaceMember` and `happyFaceMember`. This takes nowhere near the amount of time previously spent, because instead of doing a total of 200 lookups (one for each, 100 times), we now do just two.

repeat with... in...

The final variation is the `repeat with... in...` loop. Whereas the other loops styles commonly have equivalents in other languages, you don't typically find the `repeat with... in...` loop in languages other than Lingo.

`repeat with... in...` is used exclusively with lists. Although we haven't covered lists yet in this book (see Chapter 11), you might be somewhat familiar with them if you've been reading the manuals.

This particular variation of the loop is more of a convenience than anything else, although I've heard that it's also a little bit faster. I've also heard the opposite, so I really think of it as more of a convenience.

Whereas with a traditional loop you might do something like this:

```
repeat with x=1 to count(myList)
  set thisItem =getAt(myList, x)
  .. do something with thisItem ..
end repeat
```

You can use this loop variation to have it automatically extract the value for you, like so:

```
repeat with thisItem in myList
  .. do something with thisItem ..
end repeat
```

Basically, it skips a step and avoids the intermediate variable (*x*, in this case). There are alternatives, as shown in the first example, so using this particular loop type is optional.

Variations

So far, we've just seen the more traditional implementations of loops. There are some traditional variations of them, which we can take a look at here.

Counting by Twos and Other Strange Fetishes

The repeat with loops increment or decrement a variable, starting at some number, by one, until it surpasses an end limit. But what are you going to do if you need to count by twos? Or by tens? Perhaps you need to move a sprite 20 pixels at a time. Or maybe you need to count by halves, or even by some formula.

You can make your own variation of the repeat with loop by using the repeat while loop. For instance, say you want to count by twos. You could do it this way:

```
1)   set x=1
2)   repeat while x < 20
3)     .. do your stuff
4)     set x = x + 2
5)   end repeat
```

What this does is set the initial value (line 1), declare the limit (line 2), and then do the stuff (line 3 and more), then increase the counting variable (line 4), and continue the loop, which applies the test again on line 2.

The set x = x + 2 statement takes the old value of x, adds 2 to it, and then reassigns it to x (thus increasing x by 2). You could just as easily have some extravagant formula here.

Pitfall

The only caveats are that you *remember to assign your starting value* (you'd be surprised how many people forget to do this) and make sure that you end when you're supposed to. Write down on paper, if you need to, what the variables will be. In this example, notice that I have it go as long as it stays less than 20. I didn't say while it didn't equal 20, just while it was less than 20. The reason is, if I keep adding 2 in this case, but it starts with 1, I keep producing odd numbers. It *always* ends up not equal to 20. So unless you know exactly where it will end, consider using a relative comparison, like a less-than comparison. Otherwise you end up in an infinite loop.

Infinite Loops

An *infinite loop* is, as the name implies, infinite, as opposed to a finite loop, which has a definite end. Finite loops can end when x reaches 100, or `myVar` `> 42`, or when `done` `=` `TRUE`, depending on how the program is set up. An infinite loop, however, usually is defined by the following characteristics:

* The loop continues without ending; there's no way to fail the test that would break the loop.

* It's unintentional.

You know you have a potential infinite loop when your program gets to a particular spot in your program (a loop) and you never see or hear from it again.

By definition, it couldn't be a `repeat with` loop, because those have defined endings. Only the `repeat while` loops have the potential for trouble, because they repeat forever as long as the condition is true. If the condition is never false, only killing the process or turning off the power can end it.

It's very important to make sure your loop gets an opportunity to stop somewhere along the line. If you don't take the time to verify this, a few hours debugging, a bunch of rebooting, and time spent retyping scripts you lost because you didn't save your program before you ran it should convince you to check in the future. I've had my share of this happen to me. I'm just doing my good deed and telling you now.

Nested Loops

The only remaining concept we need to cover is *nested loops*. Much like the fabled Ukrainian Easter Eggs, nested loops are loops within loops.

Here's an example of a nested loop:

```
repeat with x = 1 to 100
  repeat with y = 1 to 100
    put x && y
  end repeat
end repeat
```

What this would do, if you ran it, is set x to y, then loop y from 1 to 100. Then x would become 2, and y would again loop from 1 to 100. This would repeat 98 more times, until x had gone through the list 100 times and y had gone through the list 100×100 times.

Why would you use one? In programming languages that offer arrays (Lingo doesn't), nested loops are used all the time to access two-dimensional arrays. In Lingo, you have less need to use nested loops, however there are still lots of instances to use them. For instance, if you simulate a two dimensional array, like we do in Chapter 21, or use lists within lists, or are doing animations, nested loops can be quite valuable.

You do use them under certain circumstances, but identifying them all here wouldn't be all that convenient (or necessary). Just know that you can nest loops, and that the outer ones move more slowly than the inner ones.

Loop-de-Loops

Loop-de-loops are a variation of the normal roller-coaster ride. They allow you to experience vertigo, thrills, nausea, and the feeling of impending disaster. They have no exact equivalent in Lingo, and aren't available through the language, but I thought I'd mention them here, because they sort of parallel the software development process.

Debugging

Man is a tool-using animal... Without tools he is nothing, with tools he is all.
Thomas Carlyle (1795–1881)

If you're learning Lingo, you might think you're going to spend your Lingo time "programming." However, you need to expect to spend between 10 and 90 percent of your time debugging. If you're a beginner to programming concepts, you can expect to be nearer to 90 percent. If you've worked in many languages and are a halfway-decent programmer, you might be able to keep it down to 10 to 30 percent. But no matter where you sit on the curve, you're going to do a certain amount of debugging. And if so, you need to learn what your tools are.

Message Window

The message window is your first tool. You really have two ways you can use it. First, you can experiment by typing Lingo commands in it and watching them perform (or *execute*) right away. Second, you can use it as an output device to display messages as your program runs (authoring mode only, not in projectors). The messages in the latter method can be ones that you generate (via the put command) or that Lingo generates for you (via the trace feature).

Features of the Message Window

The new message window in Director 5.0 is somewhat different than in older models (see fig. 8.1).

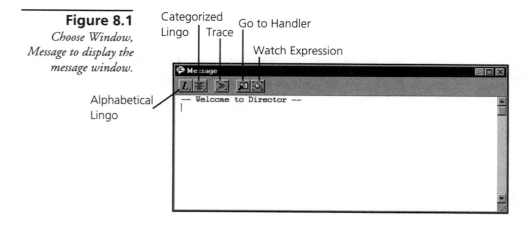

Figure 8.1
Choose Window, Message to display the message window.

The two Lingo buttons give you quick access to the Lingo syntax. The Alphabetical Lingo command lookup enables you to look up commands by name. The Categorized Lingo command lookup is particularly helpful, because it attempts to lump all related Lingo commands together. For instance, to see a list of all commands related to Score generation (covered in Chapter 14), you could use the Categorized Lingo button to pull it up (see fig. 8.2).

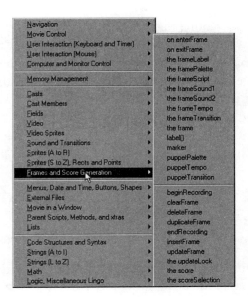

Figure 8.2

By clicking on the Categorized Lingo button and choosing Frames and Score Generation, you can see a list of all the Lingo commands related to score generation.

The only drawback to these two Lingo buttons (in my estimation) is that they simply insert the command into the window rather than furnish help for that item. The idea is that you don't have to memorize the syntax, that you can simply select and insert the command. Of course, most of these commands take parameters, and you would need to know which is the parameter. Director tries to help you by highlighting the part that you need to replace (so you can just type the part yourself), as shown in figure 8.3.

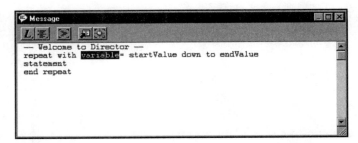

Figure 8.3

Director highlights at least one part that you need to replace.

The big problem here is that you often need to replace more than one thing, such as in this example. variable is highlighted, and needs to be replaced, but so does startValue, endValue, and statement. Personally, I'd just prefer access to the help system because it would at least explain what the various commands are.

The other buttons, however, are quite helpful. If you highlight a word in the message window, and that word is actually the name of a handler, the Go to Handler button will take you to the script where that handler is defined. If the word is a variable or an expression of some kind, you can use the Watch Expression button to add it to the debugger watch window. The watch window keeps certain variables displayed at all times with their current values so that you can *watch* what the values are, and notice if they change. It's part of the Lingo Debugger, which we'll cover shortly.

Using the Message Window for Experimentation

You can type Lingo commands directly into the message window and have them execute right then and there, which makes it great for experimentation.

You can experiment with puppeting sprites, moving sprites, updating the stage, playing sounds, calling handlers, and opening MIAWs, all from the message window.

For instance, when I cover lists in Chapter 11, you can experiment with them by directly typing the commands. I'm getting a little ahead with this example, but try typing the following:

```
set myList =["sword","shield","axe","water","lamp"]
```

Then type this:

```
put count(myList)
```

You then see this:

```
-- 5
```

The double dashes (--) indicate a comment in Lingo, and they precede most output in the message window so it's not accidentally executed.

The 5 results from the command put count(myList), which displays the count of the list (which is five items). I know I haven't really covered lists yet, but when I do, you can use the message window to experiment with them.

Restrictions and Other Considerations

There are some limits to what you can do in the message window; for instance, you *cannot* try multiline Lingo commands, like repeat loops. You can use only single-line commands. If you must test a multiline command, put it in a handler in a movie script, and then just call that handler from the message window.

Any variables you access from within the message window are considered to be global variables. You can stop the program and then use the put statement or the ShowGlobals command to examine the values of any of the globals in the message window.

Using the Message Window for Status Messages

The put command is your friend. I don't mean the one that has put x into y, but rather just plain old put info, all by itself.

All by itself, the put command prints the info out to the message window. You can use this command to determine which part of your program is executing, as well as the status of certain things, without really interrupting your program in the process.

For example, you could use the put command like this:

```
put "The memberNum of sprite 12 is " & the memberNum of sprite 12
```

or this:

```
put "MouseUp!"
```

The first example would print out the value of something you need to know about. I say "you need to know about" because for some reason you've probably had a question about the memberNum of that particular sprite. One way to find out is to have one of the handlers print out that value. That way, you can confirm that it's what you expect.

The second example would just print "MouseUp!" You probably would put this one in your on mouseUp handler. You might do it, for example, if you weren't convinced that your `mouseUp` handler was getting invoked. Perhaps the handler was supposed to do something when the mouse was clicked, but you couldn't figure out why it wasn't working. Your first line of inquiry should be to figure out whether the handler is even being reached at all. The easiest way to do that is to have it print out a little message when it gets there.

You also can print out messages when you're done with a handler, or when an `if` statement executes (to do so, just stick it inside the `if`).

They're also particularly good for showing the status of certain things that are hard to track any other way, such as the mouse position. You could track the mouse position with a handler like this:

```
on idle
  put "The mouse is at " & the mouseH & ", " & the mouseV
end idle
```

This handler would continually put the mouse location to the message window whenever the program has a free moment.

Likewise, you can use a handler to obtain the coordinates of a click action:

```
on mouseDown
  put "Mouse down at position "&the clickLoc
  ... do other stuff ...
end mouseDown
```

I can think of two possible reasons you might want to use such a handler right away. One, you might have rigged things up so that a click in a particular location makes something happen, but it's not working, so you need to see where Director thinks the click has occurred.

And two, you might need to know the coordinates of a certain object or location on-screen. You would make a handler like the ones I just showed you, put it in a Movie script (but you knew that), and then click away. As you move the mouse or click on things, the coordinates appear in the message window, as shown in figure 8.4.

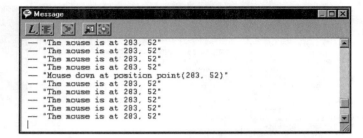

You should be aware, though, that heavy output to the message window slows things down. It's okay to use it while debugging, but you should have very little output activity while finalizing your product. The reason is that string operations and video output are two of the slowest things you can do on a computer, and message window output consists of them both.

Also, the messages themselves take up space. If you litter your code with long put messages, you can chew up data space that you might better put to use for something else or not use at all. Sticking messages in at key points, like when you enter a particular handler or a movie or something, and certainly when you *must* know a particular value (like you're not sure where the mouse thinks it's clicking in relation to a sprite), is fine, but be sure to remove the messages after you're done so you don't unduly burden your program.

A projector, of course, has no message window, so this technique is just limited to authoring mode.

For Tracing

The trace button (formerly a checkbox in Director 4.0) is helpful for enabling Director's trace function. The trace function displays each line and handler as it's entered, and the contents of variables as they change. In Director 4.0, it occasionally proved invaluable for finding out just where a program was going or getting stuck, but it was easy to succumb to information overload. It's not quite as invaluable in 5.0, thanks to the debugger, but it's still useful sometimes.

For instance, figure 8.5 shows a moment spent in the execution of one of Director's demo programs.

Figure 8.5

*Tracing the execution
of one of Director's
demo programs for a
moment.*

```
Message                                              _ □ ☒
 L ⊞  ⬛ 🗔⊞
 --- Welcome to Director ---
 == Movie: E:\MACROMED\DIRECTOR\SAMPLMOV\LINGOEXP\Navigatr.dir
 Frame: 1 Script: 9 Handler: startMovie
 ---> if  the colorDepth > 8 then
 ---> set IndexHighLite = FALSE
 == IndexHighLite = 0
 ---> set  hiLiteLine = 1
 == hiLiteLine = 1
 ---> set the stageColor = 240
 ---> set codeExampleList = []
 == codeExampleList = []
 ---> set manualHeaderList = []
 == manualHeaderList = []
 ---> set INDEXTEXT = 30
 == INDEXTEXT = 30
 ---> set MAXINDEX = 102
 == MAXINDEX = 102
 ---> set BASEmmCAST = 88
 == BASEmmCAST = 88
 ---> set CONTROLPNEL = 23
```

The lines marked with a ` --> ` are the lines within the above-named handler
that's being executed at that moment. The lines with == show the new value
of a variable you just changed. For instance:

```
--> set hiLiteLine = 1
== hiLiteLine = 1
```

Director executes the line set hiLiteLine = 1, and then you're told the new
value of hiLiteLine. It should match whatever you set it to. This particular
feature is more valuable when setting one variable to another, rather than to a
plain old number or string, because the final value would not be obvious
simply by looking at the code itself.

My main complaint is that it doesn't show the line number of the line it's
executing, so it's hard to know whether you're in a loop, or, if you've jumped
from an if statement, where you've jumped to. Of course, no line numbers
are visible in the script window either, so line numbers would be of limited
use even if they did appear.

The main drawback to the trace button is that there can be a ton of information that gets sent your way. Using the trace messages in the message window
drags everything down because it takes time to print the messages out.

It's easy to forget to uncheck the trace button. If you find your program suddenly running incredibly slowly in Director, check to see whether your message window is full of trace messages. If so, you probably forgot to turn off the trace feature. Click the button back out to turn it off.

A way to improve your content is to set the Lingo property the trace. If you set it to TRUE, tracing occurs; if you set it to FALSE, no tracing occurs. You can use this in your code to see what's happening in a handler.

You can use the trace for real-time monitoring of events (well, more or less real-time, taking into account the considerable delay for printing out the messages), but using it for much of anything else is a pain. It used to be the only game in town, but now we have a much more powerful alternative: the debugger.

Debugger

I can't even begin to describe the joy of having a debugger available now in Director. If you've never worked with one, you probably don't realize what you're missing, but if you've ever used one, you feel its absence acutely.

I know this is a book on Lingo, but if you don't know how to use the debugger, you can really hamper your productivity in Lingo. Using the debugger enables you to do the following:

* Step line by line through your program from the beginning

* Stop your program at a particular point so that you can then step through it line by line, and then resume running it full-speed when you're ready

The main windows of the debugger are the *execution history window* (also known as the Handler History pane), the *variable* pane, and the *script* pane. The buttons are the *step over, step into*, and *run*, as well as buttons for setting a breakpoint, ignoring breakpoints, adding an expression to the watcher window, displaying the watcher window, and going to a particular handler (see fig. 8.6).

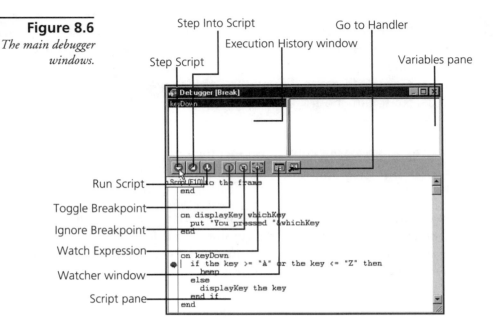

Figure 8.6
The main debugger windows.

Step Into Script

Step Script

Execution History window

Go to Handler

Variables pane

Run Script

Toggle Breakpoint

Ignore Breakpoint

Watch Expression

Watcher window

Script pane

```
on displayKey whichKey
    put "You pressed "&whichKey
end

on keyDown
    if the key >= "A" or the key <= "Z" then
        beep
    else
        displayKey the key
    end if
end
```

Stepping

You can use the debugger in Director to step line by line through your programming from the beginning. The step buttons let you *step over* a line (meaning that it executes without showing you the details) or *trace into* a line. You can only *trace into* a handler. If you position your cursor in the debugger on a line that's a handler call, then choosing to trace into that line, it takes you into the handler, where you can step line by line through *that handler* (and so on, into any other handler that *it* calls).

The *step over* button is more for when you're comfortable with the behavior of a particular line and don't feel like you need to trace through it line by line. If the line in question is not a handler call, the two buttons behave identically.

The *run* button lets you just run full-speed (that is, not step line by line), until the end of the program or until you hit a breakpoint, whichever comes first.

Breakpoints

The other real joy a debugger affords, besides stepping, is setting breakpoints. Positioning your edit cursor on a line in the script pane and clicking on the breakpoint button (the red-circled one) establishes a breakpoint on that line. Clicking on it again removes it.

Figure 8.7 shows a script window that contains a breakpoint button; there's also one in the debugger window, as shown earlier. The solid red circle to the left of the line indicates that a breakpoint is set on that line.

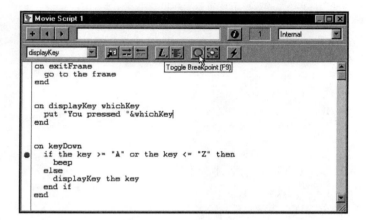

Figure 8.7
A script window with a breakpoint.

What is a breakpoint? A *breakpoint* is a place that you establish in your script where you want the program to stop and the debugger to kick in. You then run the program (in authoring mode only, not the projector). It goes along, doing its merry thing, but the second it trips across a breakpoint, whoa! The program freezes, the debugger window opens, and you're positioned there on the line where the breakpoint is *before the line executes*. You then can step through the program line by line, see what the variables currently are, see where the program goes or why it doesn't go, and basically, *debug* your program.

You also aren't restricted to setting just one breakpoint. You can set multiple breakpoints.

If you suspect a problem in a certain script in a certain handler, put a breakpoint there and run the program. If and when the program makes it to that breakpoint, the program stops, as I said, and you're in the debugger—and you can figure it out (the program, that is) from that point.

Breakpoints also are good on a temporary basis. Take a situation in which you have the following section of code:

```
set total =0
repeat with x=1 to count(myList)
  set total =total + getAt(myList, x)
end repeat
set average =total / count(myList)
```

You might work your way to line 1 or 2, but you soon realize you might not want to keep tracing through the loop. If the list has 100 items, you don't want to keep pressing the step button while it executes each of those three lines (2, 3, and 4), because then you would be looking at 300 clicks just to get the loop.

You're better off just setting a breakpoint on line 5 and letting the program run. It runs quickly and then as soon as the loop ends, it hits the new breakpoint and puts the debugger window back up again. Now *you* can continue on *your* merry way.

Two things to keep in mind are:

✤ Because you can't trace into built-in functions, like the count() function used here, if you want to see the result from that function you need to make a separate line that assigns it to a variable. For instance:

```
set listCount =count(myList)
```

Because if you just have:

```
repeat with x = 1 to count(myList)
```

you don't have any way to know the count, because count() is an internal function.

❖ When you stop on a breakpoint, it *has not yet executed the line.* So, if it stops positioned on:

```
set listCount = count(myList)
```

and you see that listCount is 0, remember that you haven't yet executed the line. If you then step to the next line, you can see that this line gets executed and that the variable is then assigned a value.

Execution History

Another cool pane in the debugger window is the one that gives you the execution history. It shows you how you got to your current handler if, in fact, it had been called by other handlers.

Figure 8.8 shows a modified version of the example handler (modified so that it *works*—I cover that soon). You can see that we're positioned on a line in displayKey and that the execution history window lists displayKey under keyDown, indicating that we came to displayKey from the keyDown handler. If you were to click on the keyDown item, the window would reposition so that you could see the line in keyDown that we launched from. In this particular example, it all pretty much fits in one window, but in a large project, the calling handler could be many scripts away. This is particularly helpful if you've set a breakpoint in a routine that multiple handlers share, but when the breakpoint activates you're not sure just what path it took to get there. The execution history window shows you the way.

Figure 8.8
The Execution History window.

Variable Pane

The variable pane is also an excellent feature, because it enables you to watch the current value of all the global variables, local variables, and properties effective in the handler, which is great for seeing what values your variables have and verifying that what's really happening is what you want to happen.

Note the local variable `whichKey` displayed in figure 8.8. The variable pane makes for easy monitoring of the variables while you use the debugger.

The Debugger in Action

Although your manuals contain further information, I'll just use a brief example to give you a quick run through the debugger. Say you don't want your program to accept letter keys, so if the user presses a letter key, you want to have the machine beep. For all other keys, you'd print them out to the message window. You try a script like this:

```
on exitFrame
  go to the frame
end


on displayKey whichKey
  put "You pressed "&whichKey
end


on keyDown
  if the key >= "A" or the key <= "Z" then
    beep
  else
    displayKey the key
  end if
end
```

But it doesn't work! It *always* beeps, no matter what key you press, letter, number, or anything else. What's going on?

The easiest way to figure out what's wrong would be to set a breakpoint just before the point where you suspect it's going wrong. Here, that would be on the first line of the handler, the `if` statement (see fig. 8.9).

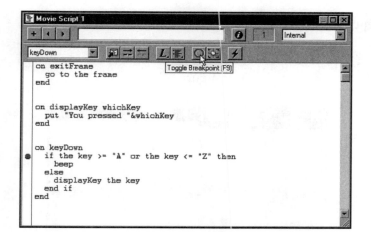

You then close the script window and run the program. The breakpoint is in your keydown handler, so press a non-letter key and see what happens. Press **3**. The debugger window pops up (see fig. 8.10).

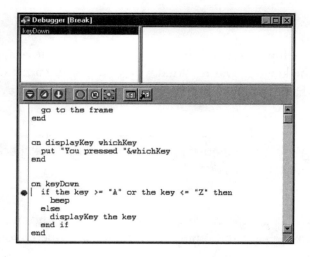

Figure 8.10
The debugger window.

A green arrow to its left indicates the current line. Because the current line also happens to be the line that has the breakpoint, you see a green arrow overlaid onto a red circle (in other words, you're positioned at the breakpoint).

Because the current line simply is an evaluation (that is, it doesn't call any handlers), it doesn't much matter whether you press the *step over* button or the *step into* button—both advance you to the next line. So, you do it, and find yourself at the beep line, as shown in figure 8.11.

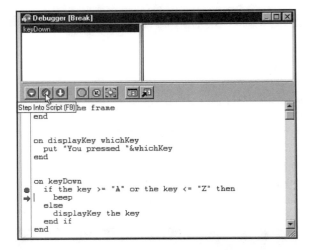

```
on displayKey whichKey
  put "You pressed "&whichKey
end


on keyDown
  if the key >= "A" or the key <= "Z" then
    beep
  else
    displayKey the key
  end if
end
```

Of course, that doesn't tell you much. You knew it was beeping anyway. First, make sure that the key that was reported was what you intended it to be (you pressed **3**, so that's what should have been sent down to the keyDown handler).

Ancient debugger's secret: Before you waste too much time checking your code, make sure your data is what you expect.

You can test to see if you're getting the key you want by pulling up the Watcher window, choosing Add, and typing the variable or property you want to watch, as shown in figure 8.12.

Figure 8.12

The Watcher window.

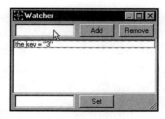

Figure 8.13
The variable or property shows up in the Watcher window.

After pressing Return, the variable or property you want to watch shows up in the window, as shown in figure 8.13.

As you can see, the value is 3, which is what you expected (because you typed 3). Because you can't pin the problem on a bum value, you need to figure out why it keeps triggering the `if` statement. Using the watcher window, you can put in an expression to watch, so put in the components of the `if` statement to see what triggers it. Then add both of the individual comparisons (see fig. 8.14), which, after you finish, give the result shown in figure 8.15.

Figure 8.14
Adding both of the individual comparisons.

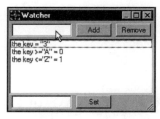

Figure 8.15
Viewing the final result.

By looking at this information, you can see that the key is 3, and that the result of `the key >="A"` is `0`, or `FALSE`, but that the result of the expression `the key <="Z"` is `1`, or `TRUE`. A moment of looking at this and you can see that your `if` statement reads:

```
if the key >= "A" or the key <= "Z" then
```

If the first subexpression *or* the second one is true, the whole thing is true. This is not what you want! You want the key to be >="A" *AND* also <="Z"; in other words, in the range of "A" to "Z." By having it greater than "A" *OR* less than "Z," you create a situation in which the key always qualifies for one or the other, depending on its position on the ASCII chart.

At first look, this example might seem kind of extreme, but it really isn't. This is the sort of thing that debuggers are good for; letting you perform a microscopic examination of your program.

But It's Not Good for Everything

Certain things defy the debugger, however; mainly *real-time operations*. Real-time operations only make sense when they're actually happening—stopping everything and using the debugger is not easy. Most of the real-time operations involve the mouse. Mouse movements and rollovers are very hard to track with the debugger because the very act of using the debugger disrupts use of the mouse. For stuff like this, it's better to use the message window or the alert boxes or beeps.

Alert Boxes

You invoke alert boxes using the Lingo command `alert`, followed by the message you want to print (in which you can incorporate variables). For instance:

```
alert "Unable to open the xtra!"
```

or possibly:

```
alert "Return code " & retCode & " from call to MCI services"
```

The alert box is a basic dialog box that contains an OK button. The big advantage alert boxes provide over the message window, and even the debugger, is that they are available from within a projector, whereas the debugger and the message window are not.

Another advantage or disadvantage, depending on your point of view, is that the alert box stops everything until you respond to the message. For some situations, like being unable to open a file, that might be perfectly fine. For others, such as moving the mouse in a particular region, having an alert box can be disruptive. In such cases, you might want to use beeps.

Beeps

The beep is an underappreciated and often ignored debugging tool. Its advantages are that it's relatively unobtrusive (that is, it doesn't stop everything and demand that you respond to a message), and that it works in a projector.

You can stick a beep command, say, in a rollover test, so that you get a beep whenever a rollover occurs. If you hear beeps, you know the test succeeded. If it doesn't beep after you roll over your sprite, you know that your detection is faulty. Either way, though, you avoid disrupting the flow of the program.

For instance:

```
if rollover(2) then
  beep
end if
```

The major disadvantage the beep poses is that the amount of information that it can convey is severely limited. You can have multiple beeps as opposed to single beeps, but that's about as fancy as it gets. As a result, rather than pepper your code with beeps for various occurrences, just pick one thing and test for it. Otherwise, figuring out what beep goes with what will prove impossible.

Roll Your Own

If a message window proves absolutely invaluable, and you have some problem that shows up only in a projector, you can create your own message window. Make a text field and put it someplace on the stage out of the way. Then, rather than put messages to the message window, you can update the text field. The text field isn't quite as versatile as the message window, but it does prove convenient if you want to monitor the status of something particular, such as the mouse position.

If the field is in cast member "debug info", for example, you could do the following:

```
on idle
  set positionInfo ="Mouse at "&the mouseH&", "& the mouseV
  set the text of field "debug info" to positionInfo
end idle
```

The idle handler gets called when Director has a free moment, so it's a good time to update the field. This particular example gives somewhat sluggish performance, for several reasons:

- It will be called at irregular intervals.

- It has to look up the location of the field cast member each time.

- It updates a field cast member (a slow operation).

- It does text output to the screen.

Still, it works, and you can use it in a pinch when nothing else will work.

Be Creative

Using both the message window and the debugger can really provide you with an extraordinary amount of insight into your program's activities. Instead of scratching your head about what's going on, think about how you can find out everything you can about your problem. Put breakpoints in problem areas and walk them. Make sure your variables are what you expect them to be.

Don't know where the problem is? Put messages in places where you expect things to be right and verify that they are right. Put a breakpoint *before* the place you think there's a problem and then walk through the program to get to that point. Use messages and beeps to give you clues as to what's being executed and what's not.

Be creative.

part **III**

Heartier Stuff

Puppets

Lingo has this concept of a "puppet" and, I think in part because of the actual term *puppet*, that people regard it with some air of mystery. The way the term is applied conjures up an image of some mystical, magically-controlled sprite with special attributes.

In part this comes from the supposed distinction between a "regular sprite" and a "puppet sprite." There's nothing special about a puppet sprite. In fact, there is no such *thing* as a puppet sprite. A sprite is a sprite is a sprite. This whole confusion about puppeting is what happens when you apply weird terminology to an otherwise perfectly simple event.

This Is the Deal

Sprites go in channels in the score. Director looks at the score and takes the sprites and sticks them on the stage. If the score says that a sprite will be at position (120, 42) then Director will put that sprite on the screen at position (120,42). If the score says that a sprite will have member 19 as its cast, then it will have member 19 as its cast. Likewise, if the score says that a sprite will have copy ink, or a backcolor of 3, or a particular blend, or a type, or a visibility value, then Director will put the sprite up on the stage as the score dictates.

So, say you wrote some code to position the sprite to the same place as the mouse if the mouse button was depressed (effectively dragging the sprite with the mouse by adjusting its location to match that of the mouse cursor):

```
on enterFrame
  if the mouseDown then
    set the locH of sprite 1 to the mouseH
    set the locV of sprite 1 to the mouseV
    updateStage
  end if
end

on exitFrame
  go to the frame
end
```

Director's not going to know you changed the attributes of the sprite! How's it going to know that you're making changes? Sure, you could make your changes, but when Director updates the stage again at the start of the frame, it'll use the values it gets from the score to determine what goes where. The net effect is that your changes are only temporary until Director refreshes the stage based on the score.

In fact, if you run this code as is (you'll have to put some sort of sprite in channel 1 first), you'll see that although it does drag the sprite, it keeps flashing and putting the sprite in its original position. This is because Director resets the sprite to its original position, positions it as you requested, and then repeats the process.

So the obvious thing to do is to set up a mechanism to tell Director that it should not bother updating that sprite channel any more because you have control of it.

Through some elaborate process of thinking, the concept of the sprite being your "puppet" arose (it was a puppet because you had control of it, and you pulled the strings, so to speak) which is where the term came from, but please don't read any more into the terminology or the concept than that. Setting a sprite as a puppet sprite makes *you* responsible for its placement and appearance. Not having it set that way leaves Director in charge.

To take control of a sprite, issue the puppetSprite command. It takes two forms:

```
puppetSprite whichSprite, TRUE
set the puppet of sprite whichSprite to TRUE
```

Both do the same thing. The first is more of a convenience, the second is more reflective of what you're actually doing, which is changing the puppet attribute of that sprite and setting it to TRUE. When Director goes to build its screen, and needs to decide if it should take the current attributes of a sprite or base it off the information in the score, it checks the puppet property of that sprite. If the puppet property is set to TRUE, then it leaves it alone. If it's set to FALSE, which is the normal state, it updates it according to the score.

As you might assume, to relinquish control you would make the same kind of call, except that you set it to FALSE instead.

Let's see what the script might look like now:

```
on enterFrame
  if the mouseDown then
    set the locH of sprite 1 to the mouseH
    set the locV of sprite 1 to the mouseV
    updateStage
  end if
end

on mouseDown
  puppetSprite 1, TRUE
end
```

```
on mouseUp
  puppetSprite 1, FALSE
end


on exitFrame
  go to the frame
end
```

The puppetSprite upon the mouseDown puts us in control and the one at the
mouseUp relinquishes it. After we unpuppet it, the mouse will be returned to
its normal score position, effectively "snapping it back."

If, as I mentioned, Director updates the sprite according to the score
unless you've declared that you want control of the sprite through
the puppet command, then you could probably noodle out the
reasoning behind this common problem:

"I have the Lingo commands to move my sprite, or to change its
cast member, but Director keeps setting it back on me!"

Knowing what you know now, it's probably pretty easy to figure
out that they forgot to set the puppet of the sprite in question to
TRUE.

You're in Control

When you've got a sprite puppeted, it's yours. You can change almost any
attribute that can be set from the score. As a matter of fact, I can't think of
anything that can be done or set from the score that you can't also do from
Lingo. As regards a sprite, though, the attributes that you can change are
known as its *properties*.

Sprite Properties

So, if you're in charge, you need to become familiar with some of the properties of sprites. A property is a variable that's tied to a sprite. It contains the
value of some particular attribute of that sprite. For instance, the puppet
property, as we discussed, defines whether or not that particular sprite channel is to be updated by the score or whether it's under Lingo control.

Another popular set of sprite properties to change are the locH and locV properties. The locH property determines the horizontal positioning of the sprite (the *x* coordinate of the registration point, actually). The locV property determines the vertical positioning (the *y* coordinate).

Under Director Help, if you look in the *Lingo Dictionary* section under sprites, you will see a list of sprite properties that you can change. Pretty much anything you need is in there, but there are also some sprite properties that are not in there. As of this writing, for instance, the locH and locV were missing from that particular list, but you could look them up individually. Some of the properties that *are* there, however, are `the backColor of sprite`, `the constraint of sprite`, `the cursor of sprite`, `the forecolor of sprite`, `the height of sprite`, `the memberNum of sprite`, `the scriptNum of sprite`, and `the visible of sprite`, just to name a few.

All properties can be *tested*, meaning that you can see what the property's value is. You can do this either in your code or in the message window. "Testing" is a Director term, because some properties you *would* test, like:

```
if the mouseDown then
```

However, testing really means "read," because you can see what the value is. You can assign the property to another variable for safe-keeping, like so:

```
set originalMouseLoc =the mouseLoc
```

or just put it to the message window:

```
put the mouseLoc
```

All the sprite properties can also be *set*, which means changed; however that's not true for all properties within Director. Some regular Director properties cannot be changed (for instance, you're not allowed to change `the machineType`, which tells what kind of machine you're on, such as a PC or a Mac). To set a sprite property, however, is not any different from changing any other variable. For example:

```
set the locH of sprite 1 to 302
```

This changes the horizontal location of sprite 1 to 302 pixels over.

Other "Puppets"

The puppet name has been applied to other entities that are also under the control of Lingo. If you want to do a transition from Lingo, you'd be interested in the PuppetTransition command. If you want to play sound from Lingo, you'd be interested in calling PuppetSound. Change a palette? Use PuppetPalette. Cranking up the tempo requires the PuppetTempo command.

Unlike the sprite puppet property, these other "puppet" commands are commands for one-time actions that you invoke from Lingo, and they merely supplement the score, not override it. That is, you can use PuppetTransition to set up a transition that's a one-time only transition. It gets used, and that's the end of it. Director will still react to transitions that it encounters in the score.

Not properly understanding the distinction between sprite puppets and other puppet commands can create confusion. Most of this is a result of the dual use of the *puppet* term. In one case, applied to sprites, it means to set a permanent condition and to set it apart from the score. In other cases *puppet* means to do a temporary action.

In both cases, though, it means "under the control of Lingo," so perhaps that's the way to think of it. A puppeted sprite is under the control of Lingo and not the score. A puppetTransition is invoked from Lingo. The easiest thing is to just not think about it too much.

I don't want to delve into the specifics of these features at this time. Some are adequately explained in the manuals; others, like PuppetSound, we'll cover later in Chapter 25 when we get to talking about audio.

Some of these features, though, like PuppetPalette and PuppetTransition, do not take effect until an updateStage occurs. This is a source of consternation for many people the first time they encounter this. They put a puppetTransition in their Lingo, but nothing happens! If, however, they have the stage update, then transitions and the like will take effect.

Mass Puppeteering

If you're working with a combination of the score and Lingo, you'll want to puppet your sprites as you need to. The point at which you need to control a sprite channel from within Lingo is the point at which you will set the puppet property of that sprite to TRUE.

In the prior example of dragging the sprite with the mouse, there was no need to puppet that sprite until we wanted to have control over it from Lingo (to do the dragging). At that point, it was necessary to puppet it and take control. When we were done, we chose to de-puppet it and return control to Director (had we not de-puppeted the sprite, however, the sprite would have remained where we left it, because Director had been told to leave it alone).

If you're doing everything in Lingo though, the easiest thing is to just puppet all the channels in your startMovie handler. Just do something like this:

```
repeat with x = 1 to 48
  set the puppet of sprite x to TRUE
end repeat
```

That way, they're all puppeted and you don't have to worry about them, and you're now in charge of the sprite channels for the remainder of the movie.

In short, there's no real magic or mystery to puppets. Don't make them out to be more of a mystery than they are. Think of them as more of a switch to put you in charge of the sprite channel. Then it's up to you. Kind of like picking the kids up from the baby-sitter. They're yours now.

Symbols

A Universal "Name Constant"

Symbols are something special to Lingo. They're sort of a "name constant," giving you the portability of string names minus the computational and data overhead.

If you come from another language, such as C, you might be tempted to go looking for constants or #defines in Lingo and trip across symbols. Well, they ain't what you're looking for. Lingo doesn't have any constants or #defines. Symbols do, however look like C numerical constants (actually, the compiler #defines), with their pound sign preceding, as in #mySymbol, but symbols are something different entirely.

In C, #defines are used in two ways. One, as a substitution convenience to using literal numbers, like so:

```
#define MAX_CUSTOMERS    9999
```

Anywhere you would normally have hard-coded 9999 you can use MAX_CUSTOMERS instead. Lingo offers no equivalent for this particular use—you just have to use plain old variables.

The other reason to use #defines is to get a text equivalent of a numerical value, where the text part is for convenience and the numerical value is for speed or convenience. Here are some examples:

```
#define SUCCESS          0
#define ERR_BADFILE      1
#define ERR_BADHANDLE    2
#define ERR_NOMEMORY     3
```

The point of using #defines for this purpose isn't so much the actual numerical value you assign as the name of the thing itself. Messages are like this, too. Nobody much cares that the Windows message WM_MOUSEMOVE is #defined as 0x0200, just that it's not the same as WM_PAINT, which is 0x000F. The numbers are arbitrary, it's the name that counts.

Lingo symbols are similar in that regard. When Lingo encounters a symbol for the first time, it re-creates the symbol internally and assigns the symbol a numerical value. Although you can determine the assigned value from Lingo, no one much cares. You can't do anything with the value, and it can change every time you run the program.

The symbol itself, on the other hand, has some unique properties that make it very attractive to a programmer. In fact, if you can forget about your quest for a #define of a value, you might even find that you *like* symbols. A *lot*.

No Declaration Required

Man, not having to predeclare a symbol is such a nice feature that it almost makes up for having to declare your global variables all over the place. Not quite, but *almost*.

The first time you use a symbol, it becomes automatically declared. Unlike locals, though, they're automatically declared on a global basis. This means that you can create support handlers to perform some generic function, and you can pass symbols to those handlers that they automatically recognize.

For instance, suppose you have a handler for playing digital video. It might look something like this:

```
on playVideo whichVideo, whichChannel, specialWay
  if specialWay = #loop then
    .. do the loop stuff
  end if
  if specialWay = #reverse then
    .. do the reverse stuff
  end if
  ... do more video stuff ...
end
```

The calling side, which might even be located in a different movie (depending on how your program is organized), also can use the symbols when it calls the handler:

```
playVideo logoVideo, videoChannel, #reverse
```

The cool thing about it is that neither side has to define the symbol. It's automatically defined by virtue of your using it. #reverse is #reverse; it's not a variable, it's not nothing but #reverse. Use a #reverse over here, and it still means #reverse over there. It's really very neat when you use it as a sort of name constant.

In this manner, the symbol's more like a string than anything else. It works very much like that. Imagine that the preceding example had been done as follows:

```
on playVideo whichVideo, whichChannel, specialWay
  if specialWay = "loop" then
    .. do the loop stuff
  end if
  if specialWay = "reverse" then
    .. do the reverse stuff
  end if
  ... do more video stuff ...
end
```

Then it would all make sense, right? Particularly if the call was made like this:

```
playVideo logoVideo, videoChannel, "reverse"
```

A string is good in one section and instantly understood in the other. Symbols are the same way. The only real drawback with strings is that they take up space and processing them takes time. Symbols, on the other hand, process with the speed of a number, but still retain the power and flexibility of a string constant.

Lingo Breakdown

The very fact that symbols are universally understood can be leveraged in two ways. The first is when you go to write handlers that more than one movie (or more than one person) will share. Rather than have to remember that 1 means this and 2 means that, you can use symbols to specify what you want, just like I did in this example using `#loop` and `#reverse`.

Second, symbols are incredibly powerful when used in conjunction with property lists. I cover property lists in the next chapter, and it's then that you can begin to see the true flexibility and power of symbols shine through. They're also key to many of the examples I present in the later chapters.

The Speed of a Number, The Power of a String

Because symbols are so unusual, the best way to understand just what you can do with them is to test their boundaries and their behavior. In this way, you can reveal their underlying characteristics.

To begin with, a strange, incestuous, relationship exists between symbols and strings. If you did a simple test to see if a symbol and a string were the same, you'd wouldn't succeed. Like so:

```
put (myVar = "loop")
-- 0
```

Used in this way, you don't assign "loop" to myVar, but rather, you evaluate (myVar = "loop") and put out the result. A 0 means that they're not equal. So, a symbol is not a string.

However, try this:

```
put "Hello, I'm a " & #loop
-- "Hello, I'm a loop"
```

Here, it converts #loop to a string and concatenates it to the string you're putting out without blinking an eye. You also can do this:

```
put string(#loop)
-- "loop"
```

This puts out the string value of #loop. If you went to see the numerical value of the #loop, however, you simply get #loop tossed back at you, as follows:

```
put value(#loop)
-- #loop
```

To see the true numerical value, you have to trick it into converting it to a number, which you can do by involving it in a numerical operation. All you need to do is add zero to it to reveal its true value:

```
put #loop + 0
-- 85
```

That trick's purely for intellectual curiosity, because that 85 isn't good for anything, at least as far as we're concerned.

I suspect that what happens when you use a symbol for the first time is that it makes an entry into a table somewhere (probably a hash table, for those of you who majored in computer science), and the numerical value you saw is an index into that table.

Then it seems that the string is used as a way to look it up and give it the same sort of universality that regular strings get. The first definition of the string wins. Consider this:

```
put #KissMe
-- #KissMe
```

Okay, so that uses the symbol #KissMe for the first time. Note the use of case in that symbol: the K and M are capitalized.

Now, print out the string #kissme. It's the same symbol, except notice that I used all lowercase characters when I referred to the symbol as #kissme. However, look at what gets printed out:

```
put string(#kissme)
-- "KissMe"
```

See how it's still capitalized in the pattern of the original use of the symbol? Finally, you can verify that it does retain case, as used by the original symbol, like so:

```
put #kissme
-- #KissMe
```

Now again, this is more for curiosity's sake that anything else, because I'm not yet sure of a good use or value for it; but again, every little bit of insight is a clue you can apply to another little bit of insight in the future, so take 'em where you can get 'em.

Useful in Their Own Right

In any case, #symbols are great things to have around. They offer all the portability and universality of a string, but none of the usage overhead. Plus, in a pinch, you can convert them into a string! What could be better?

They're not #defines, in the sense that C has #defines, and it's mainly the # sign that implies that, but if you stop trying to compare them to #defines and just appreciate them for what they are, you can get a whole lot more enjoyment and use out of them. Sort of a pretty good philosophy for some things in life too, eh?

Lists

My, oh my, it's time for lists. If anything has traditionally served to separate programmers from non-programmers, it's lists. Not because they're hard or anything, just that they've rarely been described very well and consequently, haven't been well-understood. Those with a programming background understand them just fine because they're very similar conceptually to arrays and linked lists. Non-programmers, however, have no such background upon which to draw, and aren't as familiar with the tricks and techniques for putting lists to good use.

Well then, I guess we'll just have to take care of that little problem right now, won't we?

Understanding Lists

A list is an assembled collection of information. Know how you write down your shopping list? That's a list. In Lingo it takes this form:

```
set shoppingList=["milk", "eggs", "butter", "cookies", "beer"]
```

See? Each of the five food groups.

Although the list *per se* consists of the brackets and everything in between, that's sort of unwieldy, so we assign it to a variable so that we can lug it around. From that point on, doing an operation on the variable shoppingList is the same as doing one on the list previously mentioned.

The shopping list contains a collection of items we want to keep around, and keep together. Lingo gives you functions for determining the number of items on a list, finding particular items by name, finding particular items by position, deleting items, adding items, and so on (see table 11.1).

Table 11.1 List Functions	
Name	Description
add(*list, value*)	Places value in list (at proper position, if list is sorted)
addAt(*list, position, value*)	Adds value to list at specified position
addProp(*list, property, value*)	Adds value, indexed by property, to list
append(*list, value*)	Appends value to end of list
count(*list*)	Returns number of items contained in list
deleteAt(*list, position*)	Deletes item at specified position from list
deleteProp(*list, property*)	Deletes item with specified property from list
findPos(*list, property*)	Returns position of specified property in sorted list
findPosNear(*list, property*)	Returns position nearest to property in sorted list

Name	Description
getAt(*list, position*)	Returns value at specified position (item must exist)
getaProp(*list, positionOrProperty*)	Returns value at specified position
getProp(*list, property*)	Returns value at specified property
getPropAt(*list, index*)	Returns property at specified index
getLast(*list*)	Returns last value in list
getOne(*list, value*)	Returns position or property of specified value
getPos(*list, value*)	Returns position of specified value
listP(*variable*)	Returns TRUE if variable is a list
max(*list*)	Returns value of largest item in list
min(*list*)	Returns value of smallest item in list
setAt(*list, position, value*)	Sets item at position to value
setaProp(*list, property value*)	Sets item at property to value
setProp(*list, property, new value*)	Sets preexisting item at property to value
sort(*list*)	Sorts list (list will remain sorted)

Although the order of the items in the shopping list didn't vary, you sometimes *will* want the items to be in a particular order—usually when you're using the list as a *lookup table*. When you use a lookup table, it's the position that counts. The items in the list are *position-dependent*.

Consider this list:

`[28,30,30,30,30,31,31,31,31,31,31,31]`

What's so special about it? Frankly, nothing.

Now consider the same list, but with the items in a special order:

`[31,28,31,30,31,30,31,31,30,31,30,31]`

Same items, different order. This list has meaning: It's a list of the number of days in each month. The tenth item corresponds to the tenth month (October), giving us 31 days. The fourth item corresponds to the fourth month (April), giving us 30 days.

Note that this is not a *sorted* list, at least not sorted in numerical order like the first one. But it is an *ordered* list. The order in which you have the items listed has relevance and value to you.

Items in Your List

You can have any kind of item in your list, as well as any combination of items. Your list can consist of strings, integers, floats, symbols, and even other lists!

Before you scoff and assume I'm exaggerating about having other lists in your list, I'm not. Such a list is called a *list of lists* (assuming that its only contents are lists). For instance, you could have a master list that contains *x* number of other lists, each of which refers to the attributes of a player in a game or something (this way you could effectively have an unrestricted number of players in the game).

Just know this: No rules govern what constitutes the makeup of a list. The members can be anything, or any combination of things.

Accessing Lists

Although you might create some lists beforehand, such as the number of days per month list, you create most lists on-the-fly. Usually you use lists to keep track of something going on in the program.

For instance, you might have a list of sprite channels. A list might contain the sequence of animation commands you want to execute. It might contain items the user wants to look up. It might be a grid for a game like checkers. You rarely would need to create one of these in advance; you can create most of them programmatically using Lingo, and can add to them as you go along.

Initializing Lists

Several functions are available for manipulating lists, but they all require that you already have a list. To initialize a list, take the variable you intend to use and set it to an empty list, like so:

```
set myList =[]
```

It's not so much that you've created a list, as that you've set the variable to be of type `list` by assigning an empty list to the variable. If you don't, you have trouble when you go to work with the list. For instance:

```
add(myList, 22)
```

Had you not initialized it, you would see this error:

```
scriptError: Handler not defined
add(myList, 22)
```

This error tends to mislead many people. Because of its phrasing (`Handler not defined`), the first reaction is "but of course it is; why, `add`'s right here in my *Lingo Dictionary*!" In fact, it's not that there's no `add` function so much as that there's no `add` function that's applicable to the `myList` variable if it turns out that you haven't initialized `myList` as a list. Which, of course, is why it's important to initialize any variable on which you intend to do list operations as a list.

Pitfall

> Suppose you did initialize it but still get this error? You probably have done one of two things. You initialized it in another handler and forgot to declare it as global, or you did declare it as global but forgot to make it global everywhere you referenced it.

Common List Functions

Some list functions give you access to the list. I don't spend much time on them here because you can find all of them in your *Lingo Dictionary*, but I do take a moment here to offer you a quick overview.

The At Functions

At functions let you get at specific elements in the list. They consist of the following:

- setAt. Sets item #x in the list.

  Example: setAt(myList, 4, 8)

  Sets item 4 to the value of 8.

- getAt. Returns the value of item #x.

  Example: set amount =getAt(myList, 4)

  Sets the variable amount to equal whatever slot #4 had.

- deleteAt. Deletes item #x.

  Example: deleteAt(myList, 4)

  Removes item #4 from the list. All subsequent items in the list shift down one position. (Keep this in mind if you delete more than one! You might want to work backward to retain the order!)

- getLast. Returns the value of the last item in the list.

  Example: set amount =getLast(myList)

  Sets the variable amount to equal whatever the last item is.

The Search Functions

These functions enable you to find certain items in the list.

- getOne. Tells you what position in a list a particular value is in.

  Example: location = getOne(myList, 8)

  Sets the variable location to the slot # that contains 8. If 8 occurs more than once, only the first qualifying slot # is returned. For instance, if the list was [24,55,3,8,99,42], then getOne(myList, 8) would return 4 (because number 8 is in the fourth position).

- getPos. Works the same as getOne. The difference is that getOne will also work on a special type of list called a *property list* (we haven't covered these yet). On regular lists, however, the two functions are functionally identical.

✤ max. Returns the highest value in the list.

Example: `set highScore =max(scoreList)`

Note that this is not the *position* of the highest value, but the highest value itself. If the list was `[24,55,3,8,99,42]` then `max(scoreList)` would return 99.

✤ min. Similar to max, but returns the lowest value in the list.

Really Working with Lists

In many of these little examples, I use actual numbers to demonstrate stuff, like `SetAt(myList, 4, 8)`. Aside from rare occasions, however, no one in his right mind does this. You nearly always combine lists with variables and loops. For instance, to set store someone's name in the list you might do the following:

```
set userName = the text of member "UserName"
  add userList, userName
```

Then later you can print out the user names you collected:

```
repeat with x=1 to count(userList)
  put getAt(userList, x)
end repeat
```

See? In the first example, I collected the name I wanted in a variable (there are many ways to do this, I just picked one) and then added it to the list. Later, I looped through the list, retrieved each item in turn, and printed it out to the message window. In reality, you don't have your final products do anything with the message window, but it's an easy example here.

Rarely, as I said, will you do operations on lists with exact locations. It's almost always a combination of loops and variables.

Tandem Lists

You can have more than one list going at a time. It's a good way to keep a lot of related information together.

For instance, suppose you had to keep track of a bunch of items the user selected for purchase. You decide that you want to track the following information:

- ✤ Item name

- ✤ Cost each

- ✤ Quantity

The easiest angle to take would be to make three separate lists. When you get an order, update all three together to keep them in sync.

For instance, you might start off like this:

```
global itemList
global costList
global quantityList

set itemList =[]
set costList =[]
set quantitylist =[]
```

Then, to accommodate adding an item, you can create a handler to add the order to the list. Like so:

```
on addOrder whichItem, cost, howMany
  global itemList
  global costList
  global quantityList

  add itemList, whichItem
  add costList, cost
  add quantityList, howMany
end
```

So now when you call it, each of the lists has one more entry than it did before. If you call the handler 100 times, each list will have 100 entries.

It's important when adding or deleting an entry that corresponding operations be done on all the accompanying lists, otherwise they'll get out of sync and not match up. Imagine that you had to delete an item, and you did the following:

```
deleteAt(itemList, itemToDelete)
```

If you fail to delete the corresponding entry in each of the other two lists, then `itemList` would have one less entry than the other two and the set would be out of whack. So, if you need to delete one item, make sure you keep all three lists in sync:

```
on deleteItem whichItem
  global itemList
  global costList
  global quantityList

  deleteAt(itemList, whichItem)
  deleteAt(costList, whichItem)
  deleteAt(quantityList, whichItem)
end
```

You can apply the concept of tandem lists to many things. You can use it in a game; for instance, you can keep track of each player's name, where their piece is, what color it is, what their score is, how many frogs they have left, and so on. Just remember that if you're adding or deleting entries to add or delete all the corresponding entries as well.

Property Lists

Remember Chapter 10 on symbols? You *don't*? Go back and read it!

If you did read it, then here's where you get to put symbols to use. A property list is like a regular list, except that you get to assign a tag to each entry in the list. It's sort of like the tandem list concept, but inverted.

Here's the deal: In a regular linear list like we've been using, each slot contains an entry (the value). In a property list, each slot has two parts: a property *and* a value. The property is another word for the tag that goes along with the value. The tags can be anything you want—strings, numbers, even lists, I guess. In reality, though, most people use symbols, numbers, or strings as tags.

I use symbols a lot, because they facilitate a mini-database within my list. Consider:

```
set myPurchase =[#item: "Snowboard", #cost: 400, #quantity: 1]
```

That's a list that's self-contained in the information it holds. Recall how we were using tandem lists? Property lists are one way to eliminate them (tandem lists are still good for other things, though). By making a property list and adding the list to a list of lists (remember those?) we can get the same effect. Our prior example would now look like this:

(First, though, we need make sure we've initialized the master list somewhere along the line.)

```
global salesInfoList

set salesInfoList =[]
```

Now, to add to our order we just do this:

```
on addOrder whichItem, cost, howMany
  global salesInfoList

-- First, create a property list for this order
set thisOrder =[:]
  addProp thisOrder, #item, whichItem
  addProp thisOrder, #cost, cost
  addProp thisOrder, #quantity, howMany

-- Then add it to the total list of sales
add salesInfoList, thisOrder
end
```

The net effect is that we just carry around one list, `salesInfoList`, which is nothing but a list of many other lists. *Those* lists, however, happen to be property lists that contain information about each order in them. In database terms, `salesInfoList` is our database, the individual list entries are the records, and the individual property entries are the fields.

Lingo Breakdown

The one thing I'd like to point out is how the property list was initialized. A regular list initializes by setting it to empty brackets, like so: `set salesInfoList = []`, but a property list has a colon separator in it to denote that it's a property list: `set thisOrder = [:]`.

Accessing Property Lists

Similar to the regular linear lists, a number of functions are available for accessing property lists, as follows:

* ✤ addProp. Adds an entry to a property list.

  Example: addProp(myList, #myTag, 4)

  Adds the value 4 to the list with the tag #myTag.

* ✤ setaProp, setProp. Adds and/or replaces an entry in the list.

  Example: setaProp(myList, #myTag, 5)

  If #myTag was already in the list, its corresponding value would now be set to 5. If it wasn't in the list, it would be added, at least using setaProp. SetProp is similar, except that if the property doesn't exist, it puts up an alert box and complains. Why anyone would prefer this over setaProp eludes me. I think what happened is that SetProp was the original function, and then, owing to popular demand, it was modified to create new entries without dying, but was called setaProp so as to not screw up the existing products out there. That's just conjecture, though.

* ✤ getaProp, getProp. Gets the value from an entry in the list.

  Example: set howMuch =getaProp(thisOrder, #cost)

  These get the value associated with the specified tag and return it. Similar to the setProp/setaProp pair, getProp complains if it can't find the entry, whereas getaProp simply returns <VOID>. Chances are, you just want to use getaProp and forget all about that pesky getProp variant.

* ✤ getPropAt. Returns the property at the specified index.

  Example: set mainFeature =getPropAt(movieList, 1)

  This one's a little different. Whereas all the other functions return the value associated with a property, this one returns the property itself, if you give it the position in the list to look for it.

If you were doing a flexible database of some kind, or who knows what else, this could be a helpful feature. Put it this way: You may eventually know that this is exactly the feature you need. And when that time comes, why, here it is!

* deleteProp. Deletes the entry associated with the property.

    Example: deleteProp(thisOrder, #cost)

    Deletes the entry associated with #cost (both the property itself and the value from the list).

Numbers Rather Than Symbols

Although symbols and property lists go hand-in-hand, property lists also are great for working with widely scattered numbers. For instance, I use them a lot for working with cast members. I might use a list of cast members for some purpose, whether in a game or whatever, and I might need to keep track of whether I've used that cast member yet. In such a case, using numbers as the tag values helps considerably.

A list of 3 cast members might look like this:

```
[75:#played, 95:#new, 522:#played]
```

In this case, I can look up the property, because the property represents the member number, and see if I've played that member yet. If I was using a traditional linear list, I'd have to have perhaps a few thousand entries, to represent all the possible cast slots, and just filling in the ones I needed. Or, I'd have to have tandem lists, one for the numbers and one for the status. This way's much easier.

Sorted Lists

Sorting the lists is the final variant. You can sort both a linear list and a property list, using the sort function:

```
sort memberList
```

A regular linear list gets all its entries sorted by value. A property list, on the other hand, sorts by property. This means that if you decide to use strings as your property that you could have a list with all your strings sorted automatically. Very cool. Plus, as an added bonus, when you add new items they go into their correct, sorted position automatically. Very cool again.

When to Use Lists

If you've got more than one item to keep track of, consider using a list. If you've got a whole *list* of things to keep track of, the word list should come to mind (see the connection?).

For instance, if you find yourself writing Lingo like this:

```
if card1 = 1 then
  put "Card 1 is the ace!"
else if card2 = 1 then
  put "Card 2 is the ace!"
else if card3 = 1 then
  put "Card 3 is the ace!"
else if card4 = 1 then
  put "Card 4 is the ace!"
else if ...
```

and so on, then you should be using a list. And don't think I was making this up, because I wasn't. I've actually seen code like this (actually, it was worse).

A good combination of repeat loops and lists would solve this puppy's problem in a hurry:

```
repeat with thisCard =1 to count(cardList)
  if getat(cardList, thisCard) = 1 then
    put "Card " & thisCard & " is the ace!"
  end if
end repeat
```

The great thing about lists and loops is that all you have to do is change a number or two and you can support 500 items just as easily as you can support 2 items. Just try writing 500 if statements and you quickly learn to appreciate lists for what they're worth.

chapter 2

Objects

What Is an Object?

Objects once occupied some sort of mystical, gurus-only plane in the programming world. As time went by and more and more developers began to work with objects, and object-oriented programming concepts, they found that objects weren't really all that hard to deal with.

However, for many newcomers, that mystique still lingers. There's a feeling that objects are only for real programmers and that without a degree in Computer Science there's no understanding them.

Not so.

True, you need a good foundation in the basics of scripting, but you should have that by now, if you've made it to this chapter. Objects are perceived as complicated because people have a hard time describing the concept of an object. In reality, objects are extremely easy.

Of course, in order for you to believe that, I have to take my obligatory turn at describing objects. I'll try a couple of different ways, and you can latch onto the one that suits you the best.

The Highly Conceptual Description

In the Highly Conceptual Description, an object is an entity, a member of a class. All the objects in the class share the same capacity for similar behavior, but each one can have its own unique properties that might cause it to act differently.

Highly Conceptual Descriptions have a lot to do with the mystique of objects, because for many years that's all you could find. Whole books would be written about objects using Highly Conceptual Descriptions, and reading them, your mind would just swim. Consequently, most people conceded it was too much work to understand objects, and that was the end of that. Plus, there weren't a whole lot of compilers that could handle objects, so you had to roll your own, and not too many people tried.

As a result, it took a long time for objects to work their way into more common use in software. Even now, I wouldn't say that their acceptance rate is particularly high. Not because they're not worthy, just because of the big understanding bugaboo.

Frankly, you either instantly understand and can relate to a Highly Conceptual Description or you don't. I usually need something more concrete if I'm going to wrap my mind around it.

The More Concrete Description

For the More Concrete Description, I'll start by picking apart the Highly Conceptual Description:

✤ **"An object is an entity, a member of a class."** The *class* is the operative term. In Lingo terms, a class is a script. The script has handlers in it, just like all scripts do. An object is an implementation of this script. We'll discuss this more in just a second.

✤ **"All the objects in the class share the same capacity for similar behavior."** A script has a defined set of handlers. An object, because it is an implementation of this script, automatically has those handlers incorporated into it. If the script had five handlers:

New, which is called when the object is created
Move, which makes the object change its position on the screen
Reset, which resets its position
Grow, which makes the object resize itself larger
Shrink, which makes the object resize itself smaller

then any object based on that script has those five handlers too. In fact, that's all they have.

Because each object is an implementation of a script, wouldn't all objects borne of a script be the same in behavior? Perfect clones? Not necessarily, as the next line of the Highly Conceptual Description points out:

✤ **"...each one can have its own unique properties that might cause it to act differently."** In addition to the handlers that it gets from the script, each object has the capacity (if you, the programmer, determines it to be so) to have properties. Properties are variables, but they stay with the object.

Putting It Together

I've left you hanging on a couple of points, most notably that the object is implemented from a script and that it has properties (or variables) that stay with the object.

Let's see what a script of an object might look like. You create a script like you normally do, but you change the type of the script to *Parent*. You can do this through the Script Cast Member Properties window (see fig. 12.1), which is accessible when you have your script window open.

Figure 12.1

*You can use the Script
Cast Member
Properties window to
change the type of the
script to Parent.*

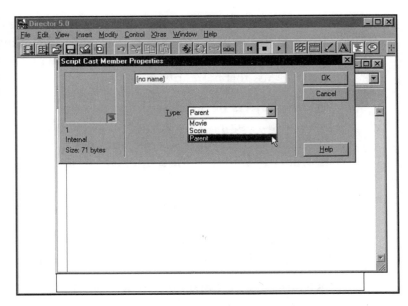

A parent's role in life is to define the behaviors for the children that are created of it. So, too, in Lingo.

The parent script is written as a generic script for the individual objects. We'll do a 1-2-3 step-through later in the chapter, but here's an example so that you can see what I'm talking about:

```
-- Parent script for person object.
property myAge
property myGender
property myHeight
property myWeight
property myEyeColor
property myHairColor
property mySkinColor

on new me, age, gender, height, weight, eyeColor, hairColor,¬
skinColor
    -- This is called when the object is first created
    -- You can set the initial starting values here
    set myEyeColor = eyeColor
    set myGender =gender
    set myHeight =height
    set myWeight =weight
    set myEyeColor =eyeColor
```

```
    set myHairColor =hairColor
    set mySkinColor =skinColor
    return me
end


on haveABirthday me
  set myAge =myAge + 1
  if (myAge < 16) then
    set myWeight =myWeight + 10
    set myHeight =myHeight + 4
  else
    set myWeight = myWeight + 2
  end if
  if myAge = 55 then
    set myHairColor =#grey
  end if
end
```

Although we won't pick this apart, if you study it you'll see that we have a handler called new, and one called haveABirthday. This object can't do much; it can just be created and have a birthday. That's all we arranged for it to do. But, there are some interesting points.

First, you will notice that at the top of the script we have listed the properties. These are the variables that will stay with the object.

In the new handler we accept some parameters and then assign them to our properties. This is how we get some starting values. See, not all objects have to be perfect clones. In fact, the power of objects is that each one can be different, yet share similar templates of behavior.

In the haveABirthday handler, there's some rudimentary code for changing the properties of the object. The age goes up by one, which was easy, and then there's some unrealistic formula for adding on height and weight if you're under 16, and just adding on weight if you're over 16 and, finally, getting grey hair when you hit 55.

The key point is that an object based on this script can vary, depending on what you set the starting values out to be. If you set the starting age at 20, and the weight at 300, you'll get a different result than if you started with an infant's height and weight.

A script like this is good for demonstrating how objects can be the same, yet different. This leads us to the Behavior Analogy.

The Behavior Analogy

I like to describe objects by making an analogy to objects in nature. One criticism of that approach is that it bears little resemblance to programming, and it is hard to make the connection. I disagree. It's important to understand how objects can share the same script and yet retain different but similar behaviors.

The Person object we just went over is a fine example of this sort of thing. We're all people, and we all share identical properties: arms, legs, eyes, hair, gender, skin, and so forth, but their actual values for each of us differ. In fact, over our lifetimes they differ.

Those properties vary in value from one human implementation to another. My mother's gender is #female, but my gender is #male. My dog's gender is #male too, but he's from a different parent script.

There are certain values that don't change for an individual implementation. For instance, unless you've undergone some very specific surgery, the gender you start off with is the gender you retain throughout your life. On the other hand, your height, weight, age, and hair color can vary through the years, or even from day to day.

We all share a script with handlers for walking, talking, ducking, bending, jumping, running, and so on, but the scripts themselves might have code that causes those handlers to execute differently based on the values of our properties. For instance, imagine that we have a running handler like so:

```
on startRunning me
    -- First check to see if we can run
    if (numLegs <> 2) then
     alert "Unable to run"
     return
    end if

    ... do the rest of the handler
end
```

Now if due to some accident or other cause our *numLegs* is not two, but merely one (or none), then our *running* handler would put up an error message and return. Our real life object could not run, because the number of legs property was not two.

Likewise, a Lingo object should have all the necessary handlers in its parent script to perform the functions it needs to perform. Those handlers, however, might decline to run, or might behave differently, depending on what the values of certain properties are.

Anatomy of an Object

The simplest script for an object would be this:

```
-- Minimum parent script

on new me
   return me
end
```

Heck, you can type that with your eyes closed! Let's see what the components are.

First, there's only one thing in the script and that's a handler called new. new is a specially named handler—it's a Lingo keyword actually, which means that it's a reserved word with a special purpose. When you create an object, Director immediately searches the parent script for the new handler.

The me parameter is a variable that's passed in to the handler. It represents the ID number of the object. Director always passes in the object's ID number, so you need a variable to pick it up. Even more important, you need the variable so that you can return it to the caller.

The ID Number

Recall when we talked about objects deriving from the same script, but not necessarily being identical clones? When you create an object from a script, that object is given a unique identification number. Then, from that point on, referring to the identification number allows you to refer to that object.

This is how each object can have its own property values that are different from those of another object derived from the same script. (That is, each object from the same script can have a remainingCards property, but for one object the remainingCards value is zero, and for another it's 38.) The way this is kept straight is by using an ID number for each object.

Other Terms You Might Have Heard

When you create an object from a script, that's called *instantiation*, or creating an *instance*. Also, the ID number that you get back is sometimes called a *handle* or a *pointer* to the object.

I try not to use the terminology when describing what's going on, but if you hear it used elsewhere, now you'll know what they're referring to!

P.S. In Director 4.0, the new handler was called birth, and creating an object or instantiating it was sometimes called *birthing* an object. You might read some older articles or books that refer to birthing an object; it's the same thing, just the terms changed.

Creating the Object

To create the object, you have to tell Lingo to make a new object from some parent script that you will specify. You do it like this:

```
set myManObj =new(script "parent: Man")
```

Naming Your Cast Members

This is as good a place as any to talk about naming cast members. To distinguish between types, I usually have the beginning of the name be the type of cast member that it is. For instance, in the example on these pages I use:

```
"parent: Man"
```

where "parent" refers to a *parent script*. For sound files I usually do "audio: xxxx", for video "video: xxxx", for plain scripts just "script: xxxx", for pictures, "image: xxxx", and so on. For the start of a series, I use: "start: xxxx". This practice lets me make a distinction between "video: man" and "audio: man".

Whatever you choose, try to be consistent with its use throughout your program. I don't always manage this myself, but I give it a good shot. In this book I might take liberties with this practice in order to not complicate a point I'm trying to make, but in real life I do it whenever possible. In general, you'll find it makes your life easier if you have a simple but consistent system.

When we call new(script "parent: Man") we are specifying that an object be created from the script "parent: Man".

It's very easy to forget to specify script, and just have new("parent: man"). Not only won't this work, it'll have you scratching your head while you swear it's correct.

At this point Lingo will invoke the script "parent: Man", create an object ID number, and pass that ID number into the new routine. The new routine picks it up as the me variable:

```
on new me
  return me
end*
```

You will notice that it turns around and returns the *me* variable back to the caller. This is so that the caller can get its fingers on the ID number:

```
set myManObj =new(script "parent: Man")
```

In other words, myManObj becomes set to the same thing as the me variable.

The ID number, as we discussed, is what distinguishes your object from all other objects made from the same script. Every time you use the new command, Lingo will create a new instance of the object and give it an ID number.

But if you're going to refer to that object, you're going to need to know what that ID number is. Lingo passes it into your new handler, and your new handler can pass it right back out to the calling routine. You then save it in a variable, like we did here with myManObj, and then you can refer to that object from that point on by using your myManObj variable.

Creation-Time Parameters

When you call new is the time to pass in any parameters you may have written your new handler to accept.

In our original example we defined our new handler like this:

```
on new me, age, gender, height, weight, eyeColor, hairColor,¬
skinColor
```

so when we create it we can pass in our variables like so:

```
set myManObj =new(script "parent: Man", 33, #male, 67, 165,¬
#brown, #brown, #green)
```

(his skin is green from spending too much time in front of a computer monitor).

This is how you can have similar objects from a similar code base but with different property values. They get specified at runtime.

That's not to say that the object can't have its properties change at any time, though. We saw in the haveABirthday handler how internally it changed a parameter. Likewise, your object may have handlers that allow new values to be set for properties. For instance:

```
on changeEyeColor me, newColor
  set myEyeColor =newColor
end
```

This can be called from outside the script like so:

```
changeEyeColor(myManObj, #blue)
```

Likewise you can write a handler to return the value of a property:

```
on getEyeColor me
  return(myEyeColor)
end
```

and you would use it like this:

```
set currentEyeColor =getEyeColor(myManObj)
```

Pretty darn easy, huh?

Calling Handlers in the Object

Without realizing it (or maybe you did), we just did a demonstration of how to invoke a handler from an object. Normally, with a non-object, you'd specify the name of the handler you wanted to call, like so:

```
showSplashScreen()
```

But if it was in an object, you'd have to pass in the object ID number so that Lingo would know where to go:

```
dealCards(dealerObj)
```

In this case, dealerObj is the object ID that we would have gotten when we created some fictitious dealer from some object that we wrote to deal cards.

If you have any parameters to pass into the objects handler, you do so after you specify the object, like so:

```
dealCards(dealerObj, 3)
```

This would assume that the handler was set up to receive a parameter, like so:

```
on dealCards me, howMany
```

The object ID is always specified first when you call, because that's the way it is in the handler. It has to be that way in the handler because Lingo always passes in the object ID as the first parameter.

A common mistake is to forget to specify me on the parameter line for the handler. This is particularly problematic because everything ends up shifted and doesn't get filled the way you want it to. Consider:

```
on registerPlayer me, playerName, age, money
```

This is properly written for an object handler. However, if you forgot to include the me parameter you'd end up with:

```
on registerPlayer playerName, age, money
```

This is easy to do, because it's how we write handlers everywhere else *except* in objects. However, it'll screw things up if you leave the me parameter off. Because parameters are *position dependent*, the object ID will still be sent in as the first parameter, the name will still be sent in as the second parameter, and so on. The net effect is that the player name has the value of the object ID. The age has the value of the player name, the money has the value of the age, and nothing works the way it should.

Releasing the Object

When you're done with the object, whether it's only a few lines of code later, or not until the end of the program, you should release the object in order to free up the memory. An object is considered freed when there are no more variables that refer to it.

Whenever a variable contains an object ID, and you're all done with that variable, assign it to something else:

```
set myManObj =0
```

This makes it so that there's one less thing that refers to the object. When no one refers to the object any more, it'll be released from memory.

Reference Counts

Lingo keeps track of how many variables are referring to an object by its *reference count*. Each time an object is assigned to a variable, its reference count goes up. When that variable is set to something *other* than the object, the reference count goes down.

If you made a little parent script like this:

```
on new me
   return me
end
```

and named the script `"test"`, you could see what happens when you create it and then print the return value. If you just print the return value *without saving it to a variable*, you get:

```
put new(script "test")
-- <offspring "test" 1 3a7702f0>
```

The `offspring "test"` shows that it's a child of the script `"test"`. The number 1 that you see shows that it's only got one thing referring to it (the instance itself), and the last number (which is in hex) is the actual ID.

Now, had we assigned it to a variable, which should be your practice, we would have seen:

```
set myObj =new(script "test")
  put myObj
  -- <offspring "test" 2 3a7702f0>
```

The reference count is now 2, which means that something else now refers to the object besides the object itself (that is, the variable `myObj` now refers to it). If we then copy `myObj` to another variable, we see:

```
set myCopy =myObj
put myObj
-- <offspring "test" 3 3a7702f0>
put myCopy
-- <offspring "test" 3 3a7702f0>
```

Although they still have identical ID's, you will see that the reference count has been bumped up by one, no matter which variable you look at (they all show the current reference count).

So you can't delete an object until you bring that reference count back down one, where the only reference to the object is by the object itself. At that point, because no variables refer to it, it'll be released.

The Chameleon Misunderstood: Using Objects as Tools

When I described objects in terms of people and genders and nature, it wasn't so much an example of what objects are used for as to show an example of how objects can be of the same script and yet still retain individual properties.

Objects often are used, particularly in animation, as a convenient way to encapsulate individual behavior in a nice self-contained module. For instance, there very well could be a person script, or an alien script, or a dog script, or a ball script, or whatever, that models the behavior of that object. However it's very easy to get into the rut of thinking that's all objects can be used for. In reality, objects are very useful even when they don't have anything to do with what goes on the screen.

Later on in this book I'll give you some demonstrations of writing some tools you'll need as objects. For instance, you'll look at a non-repeating random number generator. This is a tool that gives you a list of all numbers in a certain range (say, 1 to 100), but mixed up without repeating any. This is good for, say, insuring that you play all the selections of a jukebox in a random order, without repeating any, until you've done them all (and then you start over again).

The reason why the generator was written as an object is that in a game, say, you might have a few different things that you need in a non-repeating random order (for instance, the cards in a deck, and the sound effects, and something else). Each requires a script to regenerate the list, keep it around, hand out the new values when they are asked for, and so on. This is perfect for an object—the behaviors are identical, but the values of the actual properties (that is, the list itself and where you are on it) will vary. Each time you need a new non-repeating list, why, make a new object! It doesn't matter if you already have ten, just make one more!

To be honest, I use objects more for utilities like non-repeating random-number generators than I do for imbuing screen objects with personalities. The same holds true for a lot of other developers I know, too. Objects are great for behind-the-scenes stuff.

Using Ancestors

The one thing we haven't touched on yet in our discussion of objects is the subject of *inheritance*. Recall when I said that the handlers in the script are all the handlers the object will ever have? Well, I lied.

Okay, okay, I didn't *really* lie, but I did fudge the truth just a little teensy, weensy bit in the pursuit of not burdening you with more details than necessary. It was actually more of an omission. Think of it as my saving the best for last.

You can, if you want, have objects incorporate the handlers and properties of *other* objects. You don't *have* to, mind you, but the ability is there. There are terms that apply to this capability, such as inheritance, which I mentioned, and *subclassing*. But from the point of view of Lingo, and just to keep things simple, you can think of it as embedding one script into another. That's a bit of an oversimplification, but it is a starting point.

To establish that your script utilizes the properties and handlers of another script, you declare an ancestor. First, you declare a special variable as a property:

```
property ancestor
```

This literally creates a property called `ancestor`. By itself, there's nothing magical, except that when Lingo goes to handle calls to your object it will also check to see if you have an `ancestor` property declared. If you do, Lingo will refer to the ancestor if it needs to.

So, declaring an ancestor is a start, but it doesn't do much. It's like saying, "I have a relative!" Well, big woof. Everyone has relatives. The question are, who is it, and what is he like?

At any point, though most typically when your object is created (that means, in your new handler) you need to establish just who's going to be your ancestor. You do this by creating an object and assigning it to your ancestor property.

Too Simple

Yes, I know—it sounds too simple. In fact, it sounds like a cop-out: Create an object, store it in an ancestor property. Then, whenever a call is made to your object, and it turns out that you don't have a handler to accommodate the request, Lingo will check to see if you have an ancestor object assigned and, if so, give *it* a shot at handling the call.

But, honestly, that's all there is to it.

Why Use Ancestors?

You should use ancestors because there's power in simplicity. Your object can incorporate (possess) handlers and properties of another object, almost as if they belonged to your object alone. Your object can refer to the properties of the incorporated object, too.

The cool part is that your object can *change its ancestor at any time.* That's cool part number one. Some people do a lot with this capability. Remember, the ancestor property is just a property like any other, and it can be changed at any time. Its specialness comes from the fact that Lingo will reference it when trying to resolve a request to use a particular handler that your object's script doesn't have. But beyond that, there's no real restrictions. Feel free to get rid of the old ancestor and pick a new one.

Cool part number two is that the ancestor can have an ancestor of its own (and so on and so forth, until you lose track). This is very powerful. You can use this to build from a root object with certain basic, fundamental features, so that each object that declares that root as its ancestor can add its own features, thus increasing the power, and other objects can branch off from them. With a variety of offspring, you can build a family tree of functionality, as shown in figure 12.2.

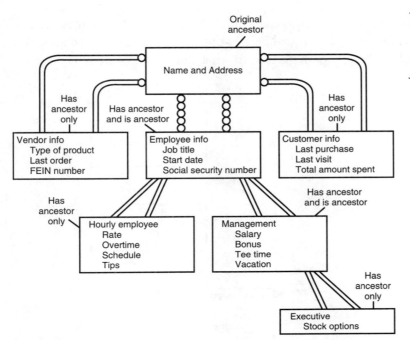

Figure 12.2
You can use objects to build a base of functionality.

The potential here is enormous. For instance, you could create a database that has a base record (keywords, actual data). That's a script with properties that can be made into an object. Good enough, but very simple. However, it can incorporate basic database functionality, whatever you want to give it.

You can then create various object scripts that use the previous one as an ancestor. They build on that object. One might be an employee script, with employee information. One might be a customer script. One might be a vendor script (see fig. 12.3).

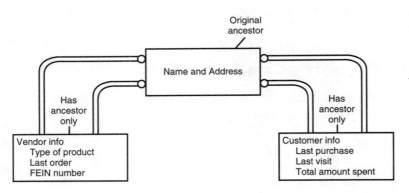

Figure 12.3
You can leverage off an ancestor and build from there.

Then there might be other scripts that build off of those. For instance, there might be a low-end worker script that uses the employee script as an ancestor. It includes an hourly rate, perhaps info for tips, and so on (see fig. 12.4).

Figure 12.4

You can have ancestors that leverage off of their own ancestors.

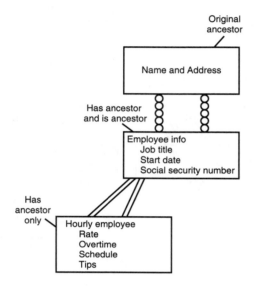

Likewise there might have been another script also using the employee script as an ancestor. This script, though, is for upper management, and has things like salary, bonus, perks, reserved tee time, color of Lexus, and so on (see fig. 12.5).

In each case, the later objects leverage off the previous one.

This, to my mind, is more useful on a regular basis than changing ancestors mid-stream, which, I'm sure, has plenty of uses too. It's just that you can do an incredible amount with just the simple ancestry feature to make your life easier.

Calling Your Properties and Handlers

You can, as discussed previously, refer to your own properties by name. For instance, if you had a parent script like this:

```
property occupation

on new me, whichJob
    set occupation =whichJob
```

```
    return me
end

on showOccupation
  put occupation
end
```

Whenever the script refers to the property occupation, it just does so, without having to specify the owner. It's *assumed* to refer to the property of the object, because the object has one by that name.

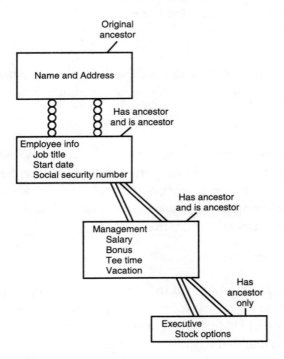

Original ancestor

Name and Address

Has ancestor and is ancestor

Employee info
Job title
Start date
Social security number

Has ancestor and is ancestor

Management
Salary
Bonus
Tee time
Vacation

Has ancestor only

Executive
Stock options

Figure 12.5
As in a tree, there can be more than one branch deriving from the same limb.

Properties of Ancestors

To refer to the property of an ancestor you need, of course, to know what the name of that property is. Using our employee example, we'll pretend that the root ancestor looks like this:

```
property empName
property empAddress
property empIDNumber
```

No Conflict

There are two ways to refer to those properties from other scripts that have this as their ancestor. The first way is if there is no conflict in names between the root script and the later script. Imagine that the later script looks like this:

```
property empJobTitle
property empStartDate
property ancestor

on new me
  set ancestor =new(script "root: Employee")
  return me
end
```

Obviously I've skipped some parts, but you get the drift. Now, the later one can refer to properties that belong to its ancestor just by doing this:

```
the empName of me
```

It can't refer to just `empName`, because Lingo can't resolve the name as belonging to the script (because it doesn't belong to the script). However, because ancestry is dynamic and can change at any time, if you specify the `empName of me`, it knows you're referring to the `empName` of the object me. This is because property references can take the form:

```
the property of object
```

In this case, the property you're interested in is `empName`. The object you specify is represented by the object ID contained in (in this case) me. Lingo will search through the object chain starting with that object, and hitting up its ancestors, until it finds one that has that property.

Conflict

At times the ancestor might have a property of the same name as an object that inherits from it. This is a design decision that you have to think carefully about if you're going to have overlapping and conflicting properties. It's not a big deal if each object refers to its own properties, but if you want to start reaching back through the object chain to ancestors with similarly named properties, you should have a good reason for doing so.

But, assuming you do, how would you do it?

You can use the format `the property of object` with other object IDs than just `me`. Why not use `ancestor`?

In fact, that's the solution. Because by default a reference to either the property by name alone or `the property of me` will land squarely on the property of the current object, in order to hit up the property of the same name, but belonging to the ancestor, you have to refer to the ancestor specifically, like so:

```
the property of ancestor
```

Then, when Lingo goes to resolve the `property` value, it will start with the ancestor object that you specified and then hit up any or all of *its* ancestors as necessary to resolve the name.

It should occur to you that if you can refer to a property in an ancestor by specifying that ancestor's object ID, then you should be able to refer to a property in *any* object by specifying that object's ID instead. And so you can. Likewise, as you'll see when we talk about calling handlers in your ancestor, you can call handlers in totally unrelated objects by using the same techniques.

Handlers of Ancestors

Similar to referring to properties, a handler somewhere else in the object chain is called by giving passing in the object ID.

No Conflict

To have Lingo call the first handler of a given name that it comes across, just specify the handler name and the object it should start with and Lingo will try that object, and then try each ancestor in turn:

```
handlerName(objectToStartWith)
```

Let's pretend our later employee script looked like this:

```
property empJobTitle
property empStartDate
property ancestor

on new me
  set ancestor =new(script "root: Employee")
  return me
end

on displayEmpName me
  put the empName of me
end

on showName me
  displayEmpName
end
```

You will notice that the there are two ways to show the name. I did it this way to demonstrate handler calling. First, you could simply call displayEmpName from somewhere else in Lingo, like so (pretend that the object ID is in myEmployeeObj):

```
displayEmpName(myEmployeeObj)
```

Or, you could call showName, which is also in the script:

```
showName(myEmployeeObj)
```

They both will do the same thing. ShowName just calls displayEmpName to do the work. I only split it up to show that a handler in the object script can call another handler in the same object script just like normal.

However, you will notice that when showName called displayEmpName it passed in me. This wasn't so much because we needed it to find displayEmpName (we didn't—it's part of the script), but because displayEmpName itself needs it in order to make this statement:

```
put the empName of me
```

Had you not passed it in, displayEmpName wouldn't have had anything to refer to.

Rather than passing me back and forth through all your handlers in the object script, you might consider storing the object ID in a property in the beginning. Like so:

```
property myID
property ancestor


on new me
  set myID = me
  return me
end
```

Then, any time you need to refer to me, instead of passing it down you can instead refer to myID. The only catch I can think of is that you need to create some sort of a *dispose* routine to unassign the ID so as to drop the reference count, and you would need to call the dispose routine before getting rid of the object.

Conflict

Just as you can call a handler in the object, you can call a handler in an ancestor just by giving the object ID of the starting object (in this case, your ancestor), and Lingo will search back until it finds the handler:

```
showEmployeeID(ancestor)
```

Other Ideas for Objects

An object hierarchy like this is great for doing a mini-database like I've alluded to here. You can also use it for other functional objects, or for doing stuff on the screen. What'd I'd love to see someone do is make a kid's game where they could create monsters or aliens or weird animals from scratch by taking objects with individual properties (head of man, body of cheetah), and combining them, using ancestry to relate them all. There could be some really interesting combinations, I bet.

end if
end

on exitFrame
--Loops intil 10
if the timer < 1
ramNeeded (_,_)
put 1000 into
put msgla "Test
1000

chapter 13

Movies in a Window

A movie is a .DIR file, and a movie is a movie is a movie. What you do with it is up to you, but all movies are authored the same. They all have casts, a score, and a stage.

You can open up a .DIR file and run it from a projector. You can also jump from one movie to another and start playing the other movie. Furthermore, while one movie is playing you can start up a second one and have it play simultaneously.

If you choose to do the latter, then the way you do it is by opening a window, assigning a movie to it, and telling that window to start playing its movie. What you see happen is that a window appears on the stage, with a separate movie playing inside it. This, my friends, is the aptly named *movie in a window*.

So, it should be clear that there's nothing magical about the *movie* that you play as a movie in a window. In fact, we won't even really discuss the movie itself much. What we're *really* going to talk about is the *window*.

As you've probably noodled out, MIAW stands for movie in a window. In writing (that is, on forums and newsgroups online), most people eschew the longer movie in a window for the simpler MIAW. Besides, it makes it seem like the writer is technically knowledgeable. Well, either that, or they just hate to type (which is quite possible).

MIAW is spoken with the letters individually pronounced as M-I-A-W. Phrases are tossed around like, "I can't get my MIAW to appear." A long time ago it was pronounced phonetically, like "meow," but as soon as programmers started saying things like "I made a meow today" they got even stranger looks than normal. Rather than risk having their caffeine supply shut off, they opted for the equally accurate, and more satisfyingly cryptic, M-I-A-W, and there it stands today.

Putting the W in MIAW

An MIAW can take several forms. It can be a full-sized window that obscures the current stage and effectively is the only one playing. It can be a partial window that is off to the side, like a chart, control panel, or a display area. Or it might not be visible at all.

Not Visible at All

We'll get this one out of the way right off, because it's shortest. In Director 5.0, what with multiple casts and all (particularly because they can be external) you can keep your code in one cast, your graphics in another, and so on. In 4.0, however, this wasn't the case. You only had one cast, and it was contained in the movie. There was an external "shared cast," which could be shared among the different movies in the project, but only one was allowed at most, so it wasn't quite as flexible as what we now have in 5.0.

As a result, if you wanted to make code portable and modular (that is, pack it up in a self-contained file and reuse it so that you weren't cutting and pasting all the time), you had to stick it in its own movie file. Then you'd open that movie up and run it as an MIAW. Of course, consisting only of code, there wasn't any visible component, so there was nothing to see, but it was there to receive commands and perform services. I called this a *services movie*.

In Director 5.0, you lucky ducks, you don't have to fiddle around with services movies. With external cast members, you can keep favored Lingo code in an external cast member and share it among projects. So, although you can still use the services movie technique, it's not really necessary anymore. However, you should know that it *can* be done, it *has* been done and, who knows, you might have to do some work on a 4.0 movie that used this technique! Now, with that out of the way, we can move on to the more typical uses of the MIAW.

Fully Visible

A fully visible MIAW is one that takes up the whole screen. The prior movie is fully obscured.

Why would you do this? Good question. I don't know. However, I must confess that I do it a lot, or at least I used to.

I had been using a combination of services movies and MIAWs to manage my projects. My common routines (ported from project to project) were in a services movie, and then I'd have a root movie that got things fired up and rolling. The root movie, however, didn't have the main interface (a different movie did). It would launch the other movie, whose window was full-screen and fully visible, and a scheduler in the services movie would load the submovies in turn (each of which was also full-screen and fully visible) (see fig. 13.1). This was great for multi-part games where every room was something totally different.

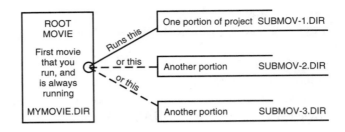

Figure 13.1

One movie can be used to launch various MIAWs.

This technique of using a root movie and various submovies was also very nice because each movie was self-contained but didn't need to burden itself with common services that I had written (those were kept in the services movie). I could also replace the individual movies in a sort of plug-n-play fashion.

This whole MIAW method of scheduling movies began because I started using an MIAW to contain the services movie. The MIAW stuff sort of took on a life of its own and MIAWs seemed like a reasonable way to handle the individual modules. Now, with 5.0, it's not necessary to have such things as services movies and, as a result, I'm not convinced that my prior movie-swapping-scheduling thing is all that necessary anymore. Certainly, MIAWs aren't very complicated, but when you start scheduling them in and using them like I was, things do tend to get a little involved.

With all that in mind (whew) I'm not inclined to worry about full-screen MIAWs. They're no different from any other MIAW anyway, with the exception of their size. We'll just focus on the more typical use of an MIAW, which is that of a partial window, or subwindow.

The Partial Window

The partial window, or subwindow, sits somewhere on the stage and has a movie assigned to it. The submovie, or MIAW, and the main movie share equal air time—that is, the computer gives them both equal time and they both are running.

You have a lot of control over how this subwindow, or MIAW, appears. You get to create the MIAW, to say which movie will be played in it, how big the MIAW window is, and where it's located on the stage. You also get to say if the MIAW has a border around it, whether it has a title bar, and whether the

MIAW itself is visible (it could be hidden, temporarily or permanently). And, you get to get rid of it when you want to.

Let's see how you do it.

Making an MIAW

Making an MIAW consists of declaring a window, assigning a filename (that is, the movie you want to play in it), setting up any other constraints or settings, and then finally opening the window. From that point on, you have an MIAW.

Declaring the Window

To declare a window, you give it a name. By default, when you go to open the window, Director will look for a file by the same name, unless you've specifically overridden the filename (I'll show you how to do that). If you do choose to override it, then you can give the window any descriptive name you choose, much in the same way you give cast members a name.

So, let's say we're going to make a little clock. We'll call the window `"clock"` and that'll be our name for it. Whenever we refer to the window, we refer to it as:

```
window "clock"
```

For instance: close window "clock"

However, it can get tedious to go writing `window "clock"` all over the place. Not only that, but it requires you to put the name in quotes everywhere. I'm usually against that practice because it makes changing the program difficult—should you decide to rename the window, you have to go around and change everything in quotes. Also, it makes it hard to make generic routines that handle more than one window for you.

Although you could assign the word "clock" to a variable, you can also assign, and this is the method I prefer, the whole identifier to a variable, as in:

```
global clockWindow
```

```
set clockWindow =window "clock"
```

Then, whenever you would have referred to window "clock" you can simply refer to *clockWindow* instead, as in:

```
close clockWindow
```

Assigning the Movie

Normally Director will look for a movie of the same name as the window, as I just described. In the example of the clock, if we had our window named "clock" then Director would go looking for a "clock.dir" file. However, you can override this and set any filename you choose. This allows you to refer to the window by a descriptive name that helps you, but still reference any particular file you want. This is especially useful if the filename is not known in advance.

However you work it, the filename assigned to the window is the filename of a movie that will be opened up and played in that window. The format of that would be:

```
set the filename of window "clock" to "clock.dir"
```

You should note again at this point that the name of the window has nothing to do with the name of the file. It could easily be:

```
set the filename of window "Magic TimeTeller" to "clock.dir"
```

Now in this particular example, the setting of window "clock" to "clock.dir" was a little redundant because "clock" would automatically default to "clock.dir" anyway. However, suppose the user could choose the *type* of clock they wanted? Then you might want to choose between "clock.dir", a default clock of some kind, "grndfthr.dir", for a grandfather clock, and "digital.dir", for a digital clock. By having a separate filename from the window name the code stays a lot more flexible.

> Whether or not you actually want to specify "clock.dir" over "clock" is up to you. You'd actually be better off specifying just "clock". Director will attempt to open up the first file with the "clock" name, whether it be a .DIR or a .DXR (or any other file, for that matter).

This makes it easier to test your movie with .DIR files but release them with the protected .DXR files (which you do via `Update Movies`—read about this more in your manuals).

Warning, though, on leaving off the extension: Because Director will open up the first file of that name it comes to, it will also attempt to open up a non-related file, or even a subdirectory folder should there be one. To play it safe, make sure the only thing with that name in the directory is the file that you want Director to open.

Setting Attributes

Still, just assigning the filename doesn't get your movie to play. The next step would normally be to open the window; you can first, however, take this opportunity to set up a few other attributes of the movie.

Size and Location of the Window

You have control over the size of the window, and where it's placed. You do this with the `rect of window` statement, as in:

```
set the rect of window "clock" to rect(0,0,200,100)
```

Break down

The rect coordinates of a window define the area it occupies upon the stage. If the stage is 640×480 then coordinates of `rect(0,0,639,479)` would take up the whole stage (remember that the upper left corner is (0,0), so the lower right corner is (639,479) because the coordinates start at zero).

Rect coordinates are given as `rect(topX, topY, bottomX, bottomY)`, where X is the number of pixels *across*, or horizontal, and Y is the number of pixels *down*, or vertical. Thus, a `rect(0,0,199,99)` as given in the example is a 200×100 box (200 across, 100 down) that's located in the upper left corner (see fig. 13.2). Had the dimensions been `rect(42,50,241,149)` it would still be the same sized box (200×100), but would be located at offset (42,50).

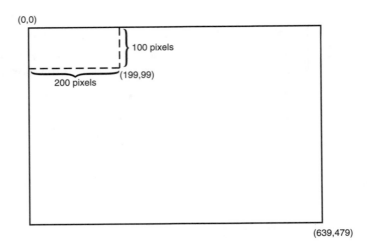

Figure 13.2
Window coordinates start in the upper left-hand corner.

(0,0)

100 pixels

(199,99)

200 pixels

(639,479)

Scale of the Window

This attribute's an interesting one. Normally your subwindow's contents are at a 100% (actual size) view ratio. However, you can change the view scale of it by changing the drawing rectangle of it.

For instance, if you were to see what the normal drawing area for a window might be, you might get a 640×480 area, as in:

```
put the drawrect of window "clock"
-- rect(0, 0, 640, 480)
```

However, an interesting effect is if you set the rect to something smaller, like this:

```
set the drawrect of window "clock" to rect(0,0,320,240)
```

this forces the window to render itself into half the space, thus making everything smaller, as if you had zoomed out. Likewise, the reverse (using larger coordinates, such as `rect(0,0,1280,960)` would zoom in).

It's an interesting effect. You have to fool around with it a bit, and I'm sure some deviant mind will come up with a use for it.

Setting the Style

If you used the default window settings, you'd end up with a window with a thick dialog-style border and a title bar, as shown in figure 13.3. This may or may not be desirable, depending on your needs, so you can change it if you want.

Figure 13.3
The default window frame.

To change the window style itself you want to change the `windowType` assigned to the window. The default type is `-1` which, as far as I know, stands for "default type" (I *told* you this wasn't rocket science).

There are other types, however, but not many. They're listed in your *Lingo Dictionary* under "WindowType". They vary from platform to platform, so you might have to experiment. The `windowType` I prefer is type 2, which is pretty much no border and no title. I say *pretty much* no border because there is still a thin one-pixel line border around the window. Unfortunately, you can't totally *eliminate* the border. This, to my mind, is a grievous omission, but one that we're stuck with.

On the Macintosh, windowType 2032 will sometimes give you the much vaunted borderless window, but it's not cross-platform and, I'm given to understand, not even valid on all instances of Mac. Further, 2032 windows will not necessarily respond to user input. You should consider just sticking to the official types and cursing the design of it under your breath, like the rest of us do.

What you might want to do is open up a window from the message window and just sit there trying the different window types and seeing how they look. To experiment with `"clock.dir"`, all you'd have to do would be this:

```
open window "clock"
set the windowType of window "clock" to 2
```

and go on changing the windowType to see what they're like on your machine. Or, make a handler and do it in a loop. It's up to you.

The Title

The window can have a title if you want (assuming the windowType allows for it). To change the text in the title, you can do something like this:

```
set the title of window "clock" to "Precision Swiss Timing"
```

Or, maybe you don't *want* a title. In that case, get rid of it:

```
set the titleVisible of window "clock" to FALSE
```

Displaying the Window

Okay, *now* we're ready to display the window. We do this by *opening* it, like so:

```
open window "clock"
```

Pretty darned easy, eh? This displays the window. Had you specified any settings, they'd be in effect now. Otherwise, default settings would be used.

In fact, had you not specified *anything* at all and that was the one and only command you gave, it would open up a window called "clock" using the file "clock", with default size attribute and style. So, at the most basic level, this is all you need to do to open a window. However, most people *want* to do more, which is why I took you through the other stuff first.

Removing the Window

To get rid of a window you close it (opposite of open, so it'd be easy to remember). You'd do it like this:

```
close window "clock"
```

That removes it from your sight, but it's still around, internally. What you then want to do is forget about it:

```
forget window "clock"
```

And, poof, it's gone, like it was never there! If only everything were that easy.

The Lifestyle of the Window

Now, after opening a window, but before closing it, the window is displayed. It has a life.

To begin with, remember that the window is a window that contains a playing movie. That movie *may have* a `startMovie` handler, `mouseDown` handlers, and whatever else. It's an honest-to-gosh Director movie that you could have opened up by itself. As a result, you have to understand that it will execute its `startMovie` handler, its loops and events, and all that fun stuff.

Globals

But the movie doesn't operate in a vacuum. For one thing, it shares the global pool with the window that opened it (and any other window you might have opened). This allows you to pass information back and forth. If you have a global variable in your main movie and have a global variable of the same name in the MIAW, they're one and the same.

Usually this is good, but make sure you don't have one movie's global screw up the values of another. For instance, if each movie had a global variable called `lastSectionUsed`, and each changed it, they'd both be working on the same variable. This would mess up the first movie that set it. For this reason, make sure you don't use the same global names in different MIAWs unless it's intentional that the variable be accessed in more than one movie.

the WindowList

When a movie is added to the system it gets added to a list called `the windowList`. If you put `the windowList` in the message window it will show all open windows.

You can use this to your advantage if you need to by looping through `the windowList` (you treat it like any other list) and doing what you want with it. For instance, it may look like this:

```
put the windowList
  -- [(window "clock"), (window "calculator")]
```

When you refer to a window, you can refer to it by name, as we have been doing, or by its position in the windowList. That is, as window 1, say. Normally you wouldn't want to do this explicitly, but most likely in a loop. For instance:

```
repeat with x = 1 to count(the windowList)
  close window x
  forget window x
end repeat
```

would shut down all the windows.

Talking to Your Window: Executing Instructions from the MIAW

Bored? Been hanging around your computer too long? Saying *meow* when you should say MIAW? Just wait until you start talking to your window.

Just as a window, in its startMovie handler (or any of its other handlers, for that matter), can execute a Lingo instruction, you can have your MIAW execute an instruction for you. That is, you can tell your window to run a handler, or create an object, or go to another frame. This is a sort of remote control, and it has a tremendous amount of potential to be powerful.

In fact, combine this with score generation (which we'll talk about in the next chapter) and you've got something incredibly powerful at your disposal.

The way you communicate with the window is to use the tell command. For instance:

```
tell window "clock" to puppetSprite 3, TRUE
tell window "clock" to set the memberNum of sprite 3 to 8
tell window "clock" to updateStage
```

Of course, it's clear that trying to send a series of tell windows in this fashion would quickly become cumbersome. That's why there's a nice alternative for the volume consumer:

```
tell window "clock"
   puppetSprite 3, TRUE
   set the memberNum of sprite 3 to 8
   updateStage
end tell
```

The `tell` block makes all the commands between the `tell` and the `end tell` statements execute in the context of the window you're telling it to, as if the window itself issued the commands.

You need to be acutely aware of which window's context the commands are being issued in. For instance, if you did this:

```
tell window "clock" to set the memberNum of sprite 3 to 8
updateStage
```

you'd find that nothing would happen in the MIAW. That's because although you set the sprite properly, the updateStage command you gave will execute in the context of the current movie, not the MIAW. To get the MIAW to update its stage you need to tell it to do so, like this:

```
tell window "clock" to updateStage
```

Local variables that you set during a tell, however, are kept in the local pool of the current movie. For instance:

```
tell window "clock" to set timeField =the number of member "time"
put timeField
```

Here we didn't have to tell the MIAW to put *timeField*, because that variable is local. Likewise we can do this:

```
repeat with x = 1 to 48
   tell window "clock" to puppetSprite x, TRUE
end repeat
```

Here *x* is our local variable, and we refer to it, but it's still valid within our `tell` call. It's the commands themselves (puppet commands, updateStage commands) that are executed in the context of the other movie. This actually is a good system because it lets you easily control it. Otherwise, there'd be no way to intermix them.

Experimenting with Your Window

You can experiment with your MIAW by using the message window. One way is to make a movie and save it. Then, starting fresh (choosing New | Movie from the File menu) open up the message window.

Or, you could cut corners and just use our little `clock.dir` as found on the CD that comes with this book.

Let's say the movie was "clock" and you had some handlers in it. From the message window you could do:

```
open window "clock"
set the windowType of window "clock" to 2
```

which would let you see the MIAW go to a thin border. You could give it commands like:

```
tell window "clock" to set the visible of sprite 1 to FALSE
```

Of course, you need to have a movie "clock", but you can do this with any movie you create. You can tell it to run a handler. Let's say that "clock" had a handler that counted from 1 to some number:

```
on countUp howFar
   repeat with x =1 to howFar
      put x
   end repeat
end
```

If that handler was in the movie "clock", you could do this from another movie:

```
open window "clock"
tell window "clock" to countUp 100
```

And then "clock" would call the handler *countUp*, passing it in 100, and it would count up to 100, spitting the results out to the message window.

Storing Your MIAW

Your MIAW, if you plan to use it along with your projector, can be stored in the projector if you want, along with the main movie. You specify this in the Create Projector dialog box (see fig. 13.4) where you add movies.

Figure 13.4
The Create Projector dialog box.

Make sure you don't specify the Play Every Movie option, which can be set using the Options button (see fig. 13.5). This will run the movies in sequence (do all the frames of the first movie, then all the frames of the next, in the order in which you have them listed). Instead, you should leave the option unchecked if you intend to open up these additional .DIR files as MIAWs. That way you can just store them in the projector. Your program's more self-contained this way, but larger (because everything's all in one unit).

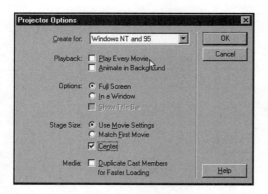

Figure 13.5
Options for the Create Projector dialog box.

If you don't bind them into the projector, the MIAWs will have to be external files on your disk, preferably in the same directory as the projector (Director seems to be happiest when this is the case; it saves you the trouble of fooling around with paths and whatnot). If stored on disk they can be protected as .DXR's or unprotected, though I suspect you'll want them protected if you're distributing them. Your manuals discuss the use of the Update Movies option to protect movies. As far as your Lingo code goes, as I mentioned, if you specify your movie without an extension, like "clock", Director will open up whatever file it comes to with that main name. This allows you to test without protected movies, but distribute *with* protected movies, effectively the best of both worlds.

Score Generation

Director 5.0 enables you do something that no other version of Director did—change the score from within Lingo. Oh sure, you could always puppet a sprite and control *that* from within Lingo, but the score you came in with was the score you went out with. The best you could do with Lingo was to override it. Well, now, with Director 5.0, you actually *can* change the score directly from Lingo. In Director 5.0 this is called *score generation*.

And you can do it pretty easily. You tell Director you're going to start making changes, you make them, and then you tell Director you're done. The changes then become part of the score.

Modifying the Score with Lingo

To make changes to the score with Lingo, you first need to tell Director that you intend to modify the score. You use the `beginRecording` command, which tells Director that from that point on, the changes you specify are to change the score, not to be immediately acted upon.

The recording session ends with an `endRecording` command, like so:

```
beginRecording
  go to frame 1
  set the locH of sprite 4 to 50
  go to frame 4
  set the locH of sprite 4 to 60
  go to frame 5
  set the locH of sprite 4 to 70
endRecording
```

A recording session isn't where you want to puppet sprites. You don't need to in a recording session; you're not overriding the score with Lingo, which is why you use puppeting. You're actually *changing* the score, and the `beginRecording` statement is all you need to get going.

Some of the commands specific to score generation are things like `clearFrame`, `deleteFrame`, `duplicateFrame`, and `insertFrame`. I don't waste time on them here because they're fairly self-explanatory and you can just look them up in your *Lingo Dictionary*. I did want to mention, however, `updateFrame`, which the help text says "enters the changes that have been made to the current frame and steps to the next frame. You must issue an `updateFrame` command for each frame that you are updating."

With all due respect, this isn't necessarily true. Not that it doesn't work (it does), but the statement that you must issue an `updateFrame` is incorrect. Try this quick-and-easy experiment:

1. Start up Director with no movie selected.

2. Bring up the score window and position it to the right.

3. Bring up the message window and position it so that channel 1 of the score window remains visible.

4. Type the following in the message window:

```
beginRecording
set the type of sprite 1 to 1
go to frame 2
set the type of sprite 1 to 1
go to frame 4
set the type of sprite 1 to 1
go to frame 6
set the type of sprite 1 to 1
endRecording
```

Each time you do a "go to frame", the score automatically updates the previous frame. Plus, when you use endRecording, the final frame (6) gets updated. Nowhere in the preceding little experiment did you use updateFrame.

I'm not disputing the efficacy of updateFrame, just the necessity for always using it. Using it certainly doesn't cause any harm, so for completeness' sake you might want to use it anyway. If you decide to forgo it, and live the wild life, just be alert for a situation when your frames are not being updated. If they're not, then you know where the problem might lie!

In order to add a sprite to the score and have it be visible on stage, it's important to set its forecolor to 255. For instance:

```
set the forecolor of sprite 1 to 255
```

This is not documented much (if at all), but it's a key ingredient to success with score generation.

When using Score Generation, the stage will update as you modify the score. You can control this behavior using the updateLock command. Setting it to TRUE locks the stage and prevents it from reflecting changes to the score. Example:

```
set the updateLock =TRUE
```

Don't forget to change it back to FALSE when you're done.

Permanent or Temporary?

The changes you make are part of the score. What you do with them then is up to you. Should you just leave the program normally, you lose the changes and the next time you run the program you start anew—which might be exactly what you want.

Or, you might want to save the changes. This would most likely be if your program was a tool to create or modify other programs (or itself permanently). If so, you must use the Lingo `SaveMovie` command, which tells a movie to save itself out to a file. For instance, the following line directs the movie to save itself as a .DIR file:

```
saveMovie "mymovie.dir"
```

If it's a movie in a window (MIAW) that you want to save, you need to tell that window to save itself, as in the following:

```
tell myWindow to saveMovie "myMovie.dir"
```

Now you should note that these will save to external files. If you try to save your main movie and it's in a projector (which of course it would be), you can't update the projector. All you might end up with is an external file that simply matches the projector's contents. If you intend to save the main movie, then you need to make a little stub movie that goes into the projector. That stub movie then invokes the main movie, which would be an external file. Being external, you can then write it out and reload it next time. Of course, it's unprotected, so you might or might not want that, depending on your situation.

Using Score Generation

It's so often true that tools themselves aren't necessarily hard to learn, but their potential and how you use them can be tremendous. The same applies to Score Generation.

You can use Score Generation to modify your own movie on-the-fly, should you want. One likely scenario would be to use it to create some permanent logo that shows up upon the user entering their serial number or something; another use might be to build some modifiable game (for example, create your own dungeons). Of course, someone's going to go away thinking of some incredible non-obvious use, and I hope they do. I'm just dying to know what it is.

However, I can think of plenty more reasons to modify *another* movie. We've just finished going over MIAWs, and it's there that I see the greatest potential. Your Director program can use Score Generation to create other programs—perhaps it's a logo designer, or kid's animation maker!

Consider this scenario. Suppose you have an empty template movie. By *template*, I just mean a shell of a movie; nothing in it. Under the control of the main movie, you open up the template movie as an MIAW. You let the user select cast members or artwork from some menu and import what's necessary into the submovie's cast. You get certain things from the user, say, the name of their company. Using Score Generation and MIAW commands, you tell the submovie to begin recording, and then you lay out a score to display the company name or whatever. Finally, after you finish and you end recording, you tell the submovie to save itself out to disk.

At this point, you've custom created a Director movie from under the control of another one. If you have a stub projector that opens up only a specific movie, you can have it open up the one you just created and then you've effectively made a custom executable, distributable program for your user.

Again, time will tell what people come up with. It's a powerful tool, with powerful potential.

Idles

> *It is impossible to enjoy idling thoroughly unless one has plenty of work to do. There is no fun in doing nothing when you have nothing to do. Wasting time is merely an occupation then, and a most exhausting one. Idleness, like kisses, to be sweet must be stolen.*
>
> *Jerome K. Jerome (1859–1927)*

Nowadays, most computers have too much time on their hands. And it's a real shame, too—all these high-end processors just sitting around doing nothing.

This situation stems from advances in technology—not just faster processors (which get the work done more quickly) but also from the capability to pass off some of the workload onto the lesser chips.

The CPU used to do almost everything. If something needed to be moved from one place to another, the CPU did it. Computers have gotten much faster, not just because the CPU is faster, but because secondary chips can perform many of the services that the CPU used to do. Now the CPU can just direct the traffic and use the remainder of its time for computation.

Director is a lot like today's CPU. It spends a certain amount of time getting a frame ready, then compositing the video buffer and moving stuff out to the screen. While some of the secondary chips are doing the work, Director and the CPU both get to sit back, relax, put their feet up, crack a cold one, and sit there tapping their fingers until the alarm goes off that it's time to do the next frame.

Lazy bums! Put them to work!

Actually, you can do just that. During the dead time when Director has nothing to do, you can arrange for it to call one of your handlers rather than just sit around.

What you want to do, to pull this off, is create a handler called on idle. It needs to be in a movie script. What happens from that point forward is that whenever Director has a free moment, like when it's waiting between frames, it sends out an *idle* event. If you have an idle handler declared, Director uses it. For example:

```
on idle
  put "I'm idle!"
end

on exitFrame
  go to the frame
end
```

This handler, when placed in a movie or frame script, will be called whenever Director issues an idle event (the exitFrame handler is necessary to keep looping around). If you have the message window open when you try this out, you'll see a stream of "I'm idle!" messages while this handler exploits Director's free time.

Impact of Idles on Performance

The things that you do in your idle handler should be short and quick, if at all possible. The idle handler is called between frames when Director has nothing else to do for the moment; however, if you spend *too* much time in an idle handler, you could make Director late for its next appointment for the next frame update—which could bring down your frame rate and, consequently, degrade your overall performance.

Also, keep in mind that you might not get *any* idles. Don't expect that functions in your idle handler are guaranteed to be called, because they're not. Test your particular program to see if it gets called (placing a `beep` statement in the idle handler is a good way to test it). Also, try to test on the lowest machine on which you expect the program to be run. If you always develop on a top-of-the-line ThunderBolt Computing 986, and have tons of idle time, that doesn't mean that Joe and Jane Consumer with a refurbished Packard-Bell 386 are going to see the same sort of idle time, if indeed they see any at all.

One good way to work around this problem is to stick calls that *must* be done at least at some regular interval not only in the idle handler, but in an `exitFrame` handler, too. That way, they're guaranteed to get called at least once per cycle.

Possible Uses of Idles

An idle handler is a good place to check for rollovers. Although I haven't covered rollovers in this book yet (see Chapter 23, "Rollovers"), you should be familiar with them to at least some degree from reading the manuals. A *rollover* is a situation in which the mouse is over a sprite. To detect a rollover, you need to look at the mouse position as often as possible. An idle loop is a great way to do so, because it's not very intrusive and should have very little, if any, performance impact. By being in an idle handler, it checks as often as possible without unnecessarily impacting performance.

Another good example for an idle is updating an on-screen clock. If you make an on-screen clock, you want to update the time as often as possible, but you don't want to be so hung up just keeping your clock up-to-date that you don't get anything else done. An idle handler, therefore, becomes great for this sort of thing. If you get a free moment, you can update the clock. Otherwise, you don't worry about it.

For instance, if your clock uses a text field named "clock", your handler might look like this:

```
on idle
  set the text of field "clock" to the short time
end
```

A third thing: If you use the custom timers I talk about in Chapter 18, you can check to see whether any of your timers have expired.

Availability of Idle Cycles

Because idles are generated when Director has nothing to do, things that keep Director occupied or slowed down can reduce the number of idle events that your handler gets called on.

For instance, the CPU suckage level of digital video is extremely high. Digital video (like QuickTime) sucks about every available cycle out of the CPU to provide the best video performance possible. The net result is that you can expect very little, if any, idle time.

Also, a high frame rate can reduce the number of idles you get. If you think about it, this makes sense. If you have a relatively low rate, say, 10 fps (frames per second), then each frame has 1/6th of a second in which to do its work. If it takes only 1/12th of a second to actually do the work, the rest of the time is idle time. If you schedule a frame rate of 100 fps, however, then although it might still take 1/12th of a second to do the work, the amount of time available per frame now is only 1/60th of a second. Thus, Director becomes perpetually behind schedule, and you see precious few, if any, idles available, depending on what you've got going on.

Other things that constantly demand Director's, or the CPU's, attention also can drag things down. Heavy CD disc access, perhaps. Playing audio? Lots of image changes?

As mentioned, sticking a beep statement in your idle handler can give you a good feel for how much time your program has between tasks. The handler need be no more than the following:

```
on idle
  beep
end
```

Then run the program and see how many beeps you hear. Hear many beeps? That's good. Hear very few beeps? Well, that represents the amount of idle time you apparently have.

Know what you've got to work with before you try to do something with it and you won't be disappointed.

Limiting Idle Cycles

On the other end of the spectrum is the capability to limit the idle cycles. This is done by Lingo's `idleHandlerPeriod` property. This property is used to specify the minimum amount of time (specified in ticks) that passes between idles. At its default value of 0, Director sends idle events as often as possible. However, you could choose to ensure that idles occur no more than once a second (or once per minute, whatever). The following example limits idles to no more than once every five seconds:

```
on startMovie
  set the idleHandlerPeriod =5 * 60
end

on exitFrame
  go to the frame
end

on idle
  put "Idle event!"
end
```

If you put this in a movie script, run it, and watch the message window, you'll see that the "Idle event!" message shows up no more than once every five seconds.

Why would you do this? Why not just have them show up as often as possible? This feature would most likely be used when you have some sort of housekeeping function to do during idle periods, but that you don't want to do too often because it happens to be time consuming. Another reason to use it might be to run some sort of entertainment animation when nothing has happened for a while, but you don't want to run it if Director is busy doing something, and you don't want to run it all the time (which it might if the `idleHandlerPeriod` was set to 0).

Remember, though, that this is no guarantee of having an idle event during the requested time period; it just ensures that if they do occur that they will occur no more often than the time period specified by the `idleHandlerPeriod` property.

end if
end

on exitFrame
--Loops intil 10
if the timer < 10
loop
end

chapter 16

Text

String Operations

Text in Director takes the form of string variables. A string is a group of characters, such as:

```
"Your life now belongs to Lingo"
```

Strings can be assigned to variables, and then further manipulated. Often it's necessary to extract or isolate different parts of a string, such as words or letters, from the complete string itself. Dissecting strings in Director is actually fairly easy. Director views strings as consisting of chunks. A chunk might be a letter (or char, short for character) or a word. You might use the chunk feature to extract words, such as a first name or a telephone number, or to manipulate letters (for instance, to uppercase all the letters, or perhaps encrypt them).

There is no "chunk" command per se, but the Lingo documentation makes reference to the term in a number of places. Whenever it does, you should know that it means you can use any of the chunk specifiers, such as `word x of y` or `char this of that`.

The string `"Developer's Guide to Lingo"` has 26 characters in it (the quotes don't count), as well as four words. Director considers something to be a *word* if it's delimited by white space, white space being a space or a tab character. According to Director, the phrase `"Developer's Guide to Upside-Down Lingo"` is a string that contains five words, where you or I would probably assert that it contains six words. Director considers `"Upside-Down"` to be one word because it has no white space, whereas `"Upside Down"` *would* count as two words.

Using Lingo, you can specify exact portions of words. If you did the following, for example, you'd get the letter `"d"`, because it's the fourth character of the second word of the string:

```
set bookTitle ="Developer's Guide to Lingo"
put char 4 of word 2 of bookTitle
```

You also can specify `the last word`, and get a count of `the number of words` in a string. Another helpful feature is that you can obtain the length of a string, given as a character count:

```
set numChars =length(bookTitle)
```

I often combine this with a loop to manipulate the characters in the string, such as, for instance, to encrypt them.

Encryption

Encryption, in its simplest form, utilizes letter-shifting. If you were to shift all letters up five slots, for example, *A* would become *F*.

On computers, all characters occupy a slot on the ASCII chart (pronounced ASS-KEY, without snickering). The ASCII chart has been around for years, and was intended to insure that a byte #65 that meant letter *A* on one computer also meant letter *A* (and not something else) on a second computer.

Every byte #65, to computers that honor the ASCII chart (pretty much all of them nowadays), means the letter *A*. Characters 0 to 127 are standardized; 128 to 255 are more up in the air.

Some of the characters on the chart have functional purposes; for instance, character #10 is a line feed character, #13 is a carriage return (generated when you press Enter), #8 is backspace, #9 is the Tab key, and so on. Any printable character on the keyboard is somewhere on the chart. A quote mark (") is character #34, for instance; a space is #32.

In Lingo, to get the numerical position on the chart from a character, you use the Lingo charToNum() function. To go the other way you use numToChar(). For instance:

```
put charToNum("A")
-- 65

put numToChar(65)
-- "A"
```

If numToChar(65) is "A", what do you think numToChar(65 + 5) would be? It'd be "F". And therein lies the basis of simple encryption.

```
on encryptString whichString
  set secretString =""
  repeat with x = 1 to length(whichString)
    set bumpedValue =charToNum(char x of whichString) + 10
    set secretString =secretString & numToChar(bumpedValue)
  end repeat
  return secretString
end
```

This handler is pretty representative of common string functions. The idea is to make a copy of the string, but to move every character ten positions up on the ASCII chart, rendering it gibberish.

To build a string, I often take a temporary string and set it to empty. You can use the Lingo keyword EMPTY or you can just use what's called a *null string*, (two quotes with nothing in between):

```
set secretString =""
```

Then, subsequent uses of the string can add onto it like so:

```
set secretString =secretString & thingToAdd
```

This line then takes the previous contents and concatenates to it the thing you want to add.

The following lines look at each character one by one, bump their value, and then add it back into the secret string:

```
repeat with x = 1 to length(whichString)
  set bumpedValue =charToNum(char x of whichString) + 10
  set secretString =secretString & numToChar(bumpedValue)
end repeat
```

The net effect is that you can call the handler and get an encrypted result:

```
put encryptString("Developer's Guide to Lingo")
-- "No_ovyzo¦1}*Q sno*~y*Vsxqy"
```

Making a decryption algorithm would be the same, except you'd subtract 10.

A variation would be for you to choose the value by which it changes; just make sure that you encrypt and decrypt with the same value. Also, make sure that the value isn't huge (keep it to 25 or less, so that you don't go off the charts). Another variation would be to have fluctuating values, using a source string as a template. This would be much harder to decrypt casually—you'd have to use the same sequence of encryption characters, and you'd have to start the sequence in the same place for both encryption and decryption.

Changing Case

Using the same technique, you can change the case of a string. The uppercase letters start with *A* at position 65 and the lowercase ones start with *a* at position 97. They're 32 positions apart.

So, to lowercase a string, you'd add 32 to each valid letter:

```
on lowerCase whichString
  set newString =""
  repeat with x=1 to length(whichString)
    set thisChar =char x of whichString
```

```
      if (thisChar >="A" and thisChar <="Z") then          -- Is¬
it uppercase?
    set thisChar =numToChar(  charToNum(thisChar) + 32  ) --¬
Add 32 to lowercase it
    end if
    set newString =newString & thisChar                    --¬
Add char into newString
  end repeat
  return(newString)
end
```

It's very similar to the encryption routine in the way it goes through the string (that's actually about as standard a technique for strings as you're going to find). In this case, it plucks off a character, thisChar, and checks whether it's in "A" to "Z". Any other character is of no interest; it might already be lowercase, or a symbol, and the program would just turn it into gibberish— which in this case isn't what you want.

If this code finds a valid letter, it converts it to its numerical form, using charToNum(thisChar), then adds 32 to it, and then converts it back and adds it on.

You can make an upperCase function by doing the same thing, but with two changes. You'd want to *subtract* 32, which is easy to noodle out, and you'd want to check for "a" to "z" rather than "A" to "Z", because now you'd be interested in the *lowercase* ones.

Other functions you can use enable you to see if one string *starts* with another, if one *contains* another, and so on and so forth. All of that is documented in your *Lingo Dictionary* and your other manuals. The next trick is to do something with the text, like put it up on the screen.

Displaying Text

Displaying text has never been a strong point in Director, but now in Director 5.0, it's much better than ever before.

For instance, Director now supports RTF (rich text files) and anti-aliased text. Unfortunately, these formats really are supported only during import. When your movie makes its way into a projector, these text members become bitmapped, which is good for performance, but means that you still can't have rich text fields. The overhead involved in editing rich text, however, makes this perfectly understandable.

The end result is that Lingo's capability to manipulate text hasn't changed a whole heck of a lot, although Director's capability to display that text certainly has.

Fields

Fields are the workhorse of Director text support—editable fields, scrollable fields, wrappable fields, and so on.

Because they're rendered dynamically, or on-the-fly (as opposed to being bitmapped ahead of time), they utilize the fonts that the user has installed in his system at the time that he runs the projector. As a result, it's usually a good idea, unless you plan to go supplying fonts, to only use fonts that you understand to be system standard. On Windows, for instance, Arial is a standard font. Everyone should have it. If they've deleted it, they've got problems with all their programs, not just yours. Don't go using some obscure font you got from Freddy's Font Factory, 'cause chances are, your users won't have it.

You control most of the features concerning fields the same way you control most things in Director, by setting the properties of the member or sprite. Some of the more popular properties are as follows:

editable of sprite	wordWrap of member
textAlign of member	alignment of member
height of member	lineHeight of member
textFont of member	dropShadow of member
textHeight of member	font of member
textSize of member	fontSize of member
textStyle of member	fontStyle of member

Changing Field Text

One of the most important properties, though, is the capability to set the field's text. You change the contents of the field via:

```
set the text of field whichField to whichText
```

as in:

```
set the text of field "HelpBar" to "Press the blue key"
```

You could use this example to create a help bar that appears and changes the field's text as you pass the mouse over some sprite.

Changing Field Color

Another powerful property is the capability to change the color of a text word. Normally, I would just lump this in with the other field attributes you can set, but for some reason the question of how you set the color of a particular word keeps cropping up in the online forums. Anyway, it's easy:

```
set the forecolor of word 2 of field "Description" to 3
```

The above would set word 2 to be color 3 (blue, on my system). You can do separate words, or a bunch of words:

```
set the forecolor of word 2 to 5 of field "Description" to 3
```

You could even do individual characters. The very way you specify chunks when you refer to strings is how you do it in fields, because a field basically is one big string.

If you wanted to, you could do this:

```
on rainbowText whichField
  set textlen =length(field whichField)
  set color =0
  repeat with x=1 to textLen
    set the forecolor of char x of field whichField to color
    set color =color + 1
    if (color > 255) then
      set color =0
    end if
  end repeat
end
```

It changes each character to a different color, up to 255, at which point it cycles around to 0 again. It won't win any awards for speed or readability, but it's just fun to try.

Locating Words

Setting the color of a word is the first step in creating *hypertext*, which is where you can rig things up so that clicking on a word takes you to further information that the word references.

So, how do you locate a word? A few different tools are available. First, Lingo lets you identify which word, character, line, or item is under the mouse at any given time, by using the functions the mouseWord, the mouseChar, the mouseLine, and the mouseItem.

As an exercise, make a large field full of text and put it on the screen. At the same time, make a smaller field for status purposes and put it in the corner.

Now, say the status field is called "status". You could make an idle handler such as the following:

```
on idle
  set whichLine =the mouseLine
  set whichWord =the mouseWord
  set whichChar =the mouseChar
  set statusText ="Line: "&whichLine
  set statusText =statusText && "Word: "&whichWord
  set statusText =statusText && "Char: "&whichChar
  set the text of field "status" to statusText
end
```

When you try this, you should notice that a line is not a *displayed* line, but a line of text in the field until a carriage return (the Enter key) was hit. On one hand, this is good for calculations that depend on the content of the text. On the other hand, it makes it hard to know from Lingo what's where on-screen.

By trying this, you also can see that changing text in a field member isn't the fastest thing to do in the world. It's kinda slow.

Variants

New to 5.0 is the capability to map a screen point to a character, and the other way 'round. That is, you can use:

```
locToCharPos(member, position)
```

and

```
locToLinePos(member, position)
```

to provide a point or a vertical pixel location and see what character or line that would be in the specified member. For instance:

```
put the locVToLinePos(member whichMember, the mouseV)
```

It's not so much that you might want to use the mouseV because you can use *any* value, not just one that comes from the mouse, as you are so restricted by using the mouseLine. These values are calculated from the top, though, so they give different results from the mouseLine because they measure different things. Don't think they're the same, 'cause they're not.

Moving Stuff Around

A very nice addition to 5.0, however, is the capability to scroll the text yourself, from Lingo:

```
scrollByPage member, numPages
```

and

```
scrollByLine member, numLines
```

These will let you shift the cast member up or down a number of lines or pages.

Providing negative numbers makes it go backward. Unfortunately, you need to have set the field's scrolling attribute. This makes sense, but it also causes those ugly scroll bars to appear. Otherwise, it would be really easy to make your own custom scroll bar that just tied into these functions but, alas, it's not to be.

chapter 17

Menus

Just as you can set up menus in Director, so too can you set them up with Lingo.

As a quick review, in Director you can create a *field* cast member and put in menu commands that define a menu. For instance, a menu bar that looks like figure 17.1:

Figure 17.1
A sample menu bar.

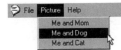

might be defined as this:

```
Menu: File
  Exit            /X  | stopMovie
  Menu: Picture
  Me and Mom          | showPicture "me and mom"
  Me and Dog          | showPicture "me and dog"
  Me and Cat          | showPicture "me and cat"
  Menu: Help
  Help                | doHelp
```

The menu format requires that you first define the main menu heading and then follow it with any submenu items.

Each submenu item takes the following form:

  SubmenuName attributes | lingoCommand

SubmenuName represents the part that appears to the user; for instance, "Print". *lingoCommand* represents the Lingo command that you want to perform if that menu item is chosen. If you need more than one command performed, you need to put those commands in a handler and make the *lingoCommand* simply be a call to that handler.

The *attributes* are optional. You can specify a Command/Control key equivalent to the command, and you can format how it appears (italic, bold, and so on), regardless of whether it has a check mark on it, and so forth. The complete attribute collection is documented in your "Using Lingo" book and your *Lingo Dictionary*.

Changing Attributes

You can go through and examine and modify the names of the menu items and their enabled state, their check marks, and their script text (the script text being the Lingo command I referred to), all from Lingo. For instance, the following loop would disable all the submenu items:

```
repeat with topMenu = 1 to the number of menus
  set numSubitems =the number of menuItems of menu topMenu
  repeat with thisItem =1 to numSubItems
    set the enabled of menuItem thisItem of menu topMenu to FALSE
  end repeat
end repeat
```

As you might notice, the syntax does get a bit unwieldy. I broke it up *a little* by pulling `numSubItems` out, but you still end up with mouthfuls like `set the enabled of menuItem thisItem of menu topMenu to FALSE`. What you're doing here is setting a property of an item of a menu, but specifying all that can get to be a somewhat excessive.

Changing the Associated Lingo Command

The capability to change the script text is very helpful, in that it basically allows you to change the behavior of the menu on-the-fly by letting you change the command that gets executed when a user selects the menu item.

For instance, the following changes the Lingo for one of the menu items:

```
set the script of menuItem "Exit" of menu "File" to "askIfOkay"
```

It then executes the Lingo command `"askIfOkay"`, which apparently is a handler we've written.

Changing the Menu Itself

Although you cannot directly change the overhead menu categories (File, Edit, and so on), you *can* easily change the names of the subitems. *Why* you're not allowed to change the names of the top menu categories is beyond me, but that's the way it is. All is not lost, though, as you'll see in a bit (I'll show you how to create a menu in Lingo from scratch).

This is how you change the name of a submenu item:

```
set the name of menuItem 3 of menu "Help" to "Help on Printing"
```

As your program changes into different areas, you might want to modify your help menu or other menus to match.

Creating Your Own Menu in Lingo

The one thing you cannot do directly through Lingo is change the overall menu structure. That is, you can't add attributes, add top menu categories, add menu items under those categories, and so forth.

You define the menu structure in a *field* cast member which, supposedly, you're supposed to create at author time and fill with your menu definitions. That shouldn't stop you, however, Lingo stud or studdess that you are; we'll do it from Lingo.

Basically what you're going to do is change the text of that field cast member. If you change it in a format acceptable as a menu definition, then you can effectively change your menu structure on-the-fly.

To begin with, you need at least one sacrificial field cast member. Click on an empty cast member and choose *Field* from the *Window* menu, just as you would to create a menu. Then just type a space, or anything else, and close the window. All you want to do is generate a cast member of the *field* type. Its contents don't matter, because you're going to replace them anyway.

Now, I have some routines for creating menus on-the-fly. These aren't incredibly comprehensive, and if you have some time on your hands, you might want to make a really fancy menu-building object or something instead. In lieu of that, though, you can use these. Make a movie script and put these handlers in it:

- ✸ `CreateMenu(whichCastMember)`

- ✸ `AddMenuHeading(whichCastMember, whichHeading)`

- ✸ `AddMenuItem(whichCastMember, whichItemName, whichFunction, attributes)`

Let's see what they're made of...

CreateMenu()

The CreateMenu function simply wipes out the cast member text, so we can start from scratch with a brand-new menu.

```
on CreateMenu whichCastMember
  set the text of member whichCastMember to ""
end
```

Obviously, if you're going to wipe out the text, make sure you don't have anything in there that you're going to need later.

You call the function like so (say, for cast member 5):

```
CreateMenu(5)
```

All of these functions take as a parameter the member number to change. That member is expected to be of type *field*. It's up to you to ensure that you perform these operations on a *field*-type member.

AddMenuHeading()

The AddMenuHeading function adds a top-level menu category (like "File"). Because a menu definition for a top-level menu looks like this:

```
menu: File
```

you might as well just put your additions in this format too, as follows:

```
on AddMenuHeading whichCastMember, whichHeading
  set currentText =the text of member whichCastMember
  set currentText =currentText & "Menu: " & whichHeading & RETURN
  set the text of member whichCastMember to currentText
end
```

This takes the current text and adds to it "Menu: " plus the heading, then places the text back in the cast member.

The handler adds the menu heading to the existing text (thus preserving it) because it's possible, and likely, that there will be more than one menu heading. This is why it's important to call CreateMenu() at the beginning to clear out any existing text before you add the first menu header.

You also add a RETURN character because the menu format expects each definition to be on its own line. This ensures that we start a fresh line for the next entry.

You call the function like so:

```
addMenuHeading(5, "Surprise")
```

AddMenuItem()

After adding the menu category, it's time to add the individual menu items.

This handler will accept, as parameters, the name of the menu item and a Lingo string to serve as the Lingo command to be invoked. Finally it'll also accept some optional attributes, if you want to add them. The attributes must conform to the format given in the manuals for specifying attributes (like "/C>B" for bold, with Ctrl+C as a command key). You can leave the attributes off if you want; the function detects that the attributes weren't supplied (they show up as <Void>) and substitutes an empty string.

```
on AddMenuItem whichCastMember, whichItemName, whichFunction,
attributes
  set currentText =the text of member whichCastMember
  if voidP(attributes) then
    set attributes =EMPTY
  end if
  set currentText =currentText && whichItemName && attributes¬
&&"|"&&
                                    whichFunction & RETURN
  set the text of member whichCastMember to currentText
end
```

Again, this retrieves the current text of the cast member. It then builds the string in the following form:

name attributes | lingoCommand

that's defined for creating menu items, and it adds it back into the cast member.

Giving It a Whirl

Okay, now's the time to give it a shot. We'll test it by making a handler to use our menu creator to create a brand new menu. This example requires only that one of the cast members (here we use #5) be of type *field*. You create this cast member ahead of time.

Creating the menu is always done in the following order:

1. createMenu   To start things off

2. addMenuHeading   One of these for the first category

3. addMenuItem   One of these for each menu item

Repeat the *heading-item-item-item* sequence as necessary for each category.

Here's an example of how a build process of a silly menu might appear:

```
on testMenu
  createMenu 5

  addMenuHeading 5, "Surprise"
  addMenuItem 5, "Birthday","beep","/B<B"
  addMenuItem 5, "Anniversary","beep 4","/A("

  addMenuHeading 5, "No surprise"
  addMenuItem 5, "Bills", "alert "& QUOTE & "Pay me!" & QUOTE
  addMenuItem 5, "Death", "beep"
  addMenuItem 5, "Taxes","","/T"

  installMenu 5
end
```

The sequence begins with createMenu() and adds menu headings and items in turn until complete. At the very end, we install the menu. The installMenu() function is a built-in Lingo command that you can find in the *Lingo Dictionary*. Basically, it sets the current menu to be the one as defined by the cast member you specify.

Something to Think About

The functions available now make it possible to rewrite your menus on-the-fly and provide custom menus that change as appropriate with your program.

You should use menus wisely. Disable invalid items, enable valid items, and keep pace with your program. The example of changing one of the help items to match where you are in a program is a good one; it's nice to find help on exactly what you need without having to go searching for it.

You might want to modify the routines here (goodness knows they could stand it!). It might be interesting to write a handler that modifies an existing menu without having to rebuild it from scratch. You could give some thought as to how to do that.

Unfortunately, no Lingo function can tell you which cast member you're currently using as a menu, but because it's your program, it wouldn't be that hard to rig one up. Then try to write some Lingo to allow you to add or delete menu items at will. Hint: Maybe you want to keep the current menu structure in a list (or lists) and then add to or delete from it as necessary, and then generate the cast member from that list—a good project for a rainy day.

part **IV**

In the Laboratory

Timers and Timeouts

Although you can get the current system time out of
Director in the form of hours:minutes:seconds
(1:30:24 PM), doing so isn't particularly helpful for
the sort of high-end, real-time cutting-edge sort of
work you want to do, right? To begin with, such time
is accurate only to the nearest second, and furthermore, you have to parse it out of a string each and
every time you need to retrieve the current time.

Fortunately, you do have an alternative. Each computer maintains a set of internal system clocks and
timers, which the timer chips update continuously.
Director enables you to retrieve the value of the
internal timer, which it returns to you in the form of
a tick count.

Director reports ticks at a ratio of 60 ticks to a second. In other words, 60 ticks represent 1 second, 120 ticks represent 2 seconds, and so on.

Director provides three timing mechanisms you can use, each with a different purpose: the ticks, the timer, and the timeoutLapsed. After I go over these mechanisms, I'll talk about making your own custom timer as well.

the ticks

The grandpappy of all the timing mechanisms is the ticks property, which contains the tick count of the time that has passed since the computer was first turned on. the ticks is based on the computer's own internal tick counter, although Director adjusts the value so it appears to have a 60 tick per second tick rate (the actual rate might be more or less than 60 ticks per second).

You can't change the tick's value; it's ever increasing—sort of like the grand mileage odometer on your car. It only goes up, and you can't reset it (except by rebooting). For what it's worth, your car's odometer can't be reset at all (except by buying a new car).

the timer

The child of the ticks is the timer. the timer increments at the same pace as the ticks but, unlike the ticks, you can reset it. In this way, the timer is more like the trip odometer on your car. You can push the button at any time and reset it, by calling the Lingo function, startTimer.

If you never call startTimer, the value of the timer represents the number of ticks since Director was started, not that you can really do much with this number. Actually, what happens is at startup, and whenever you call startTimer, Director internally records the value of the ticks. Then, any time you want to know the current value of your trip odometer, the timer, Director returns the difference between its current setting and the tick's value at the point at which you called startTimer. In the end, you really only have the one timer.

I mention this mainly because you use a similar technique for your own timer mechanism.

The `timeoutLapsed`

The `timeoutLapsed`, the third variation, has a more specific purpose in life—to keep track of the time elapsed since the last user event. If enough time goes by, it can trigger an alarm or an event, letting you do cute things like somehow remind the user to wake up, put some whimsical thing on screen, or whatever.

The `timeoutLapsed` is just a timer. You can set it if you want; for instance, as follows:

```
set the timeoutLapsed to 0
```

To set the alarm, you need to establish the expiration time. For instance, 30 seconds would be 30 * 60 ticks:

```
set the timeoutLength =30 * 60
```

You do need to establish just what will happen when the timeout occurs, and to do so, you set the `timeoutScript`. You set the `timeoutScript` to a string that you want to execute at timeout. It could be a simple statement, like "beep" or, more than likely, you would use the name of a handler you want to call; for instance, as follows:

```
set the timeoutScript to "wakeUpUser"
```

`wakeUpUser` would be a handler you wrote to do something to wake up the user.

Canceling the Timeout

If you want to cancel the timeout or make sure it doesn't keep timing out on you, set the script to nothing:

```
set the timeoutScript to EMPTY
```

Don't try setting the `timeoutLength` to 0. Although a commendable idea on the surface, all it does in the end is cause the timeout to expire and reexpire instantly. If you set the script to EMPTY, Director doesn't waste any more time monitoring timeouts; it's the best way to do it.

Rather than continue to do math to figure out the seconds, or stick little *60s everywhere, you can make a handler to do the conversion for you:

```
on seconds howMany
  -- Converts seconds to ticks
  return (howMany * 60)
end
```

You then can use it whenever you have to specify a value in seconds (just make sure you put it in a movie script or some other place where you can find it):

```
set the timeoutLength =seconds(30)
```

The other major advantage is that your code is abstracted from the Director-specific feature of having 60 ticks to the second. If you ever go to Super Director or some other thing that has 1,000 ticks to the second (measured in milliseconds), you would only have to change this one handler, not all the occurrences of x * 60 in your code.

Resetting the Timeout

The purpose of the timeout is to have the program do something if the user fails to do something (as discussed). A timeout can also keep the program from doing something if the user *did* take some action.

Perhaps you want your program to automatically go on to the next screen *unless* the user presses a key or clicks the mouse. Well, you could rig it up so that the user could play on a particular screen to their heart's content. At whatever point they stopped interacting, the program could move ahead automatically.

Regardless of the timeout's purpose, you still end up needing to have a user activity reset a timeout. You do have some control over which activities reset it. By *reset*, I mean zero out the timeoutLapsed to start counting over again. For instance, suppose the user was two seconds away from having the timeoutScript executed when he clicks the mouse. The timeoutLapsed could reset back to zero and the timeoutScript wouldn't execute until he waited the full period of time.

You can set one or both of the following to TRUE if you want them to reset the timeoutLapsed:

- the timeoutKeyDown. Resets if user presses a key.

- the timeoutMouse. Resets if user clicks the mouse (a mouseDown event).

- the timeoutPlay. Resets if user plays a movie.

Setting them to FALSE means that such an event has no impact on the timeoutLapsed.

Simulating a timeoutMouseMoved Feature

One particular timeout I'd like to see supported, that isn't, is a timeout that occurs if the user hasn't moved the mouse. Although the current features let you see if a user has clicked the mouse or not, there are times that you might want to know if the user hasn't even moved it, possibly because the user is at a loss as to what to do. In such a case you might want to provide some sort of hint. Of course, it's also possible that the user has left his desk and gone to lunch. Still, regardless of how you want to interpret it, it's not too hard to rig up this capability even though Director doesn't specifically have the feature.

Mainly, you need to determine whether the mouse has been moved and, if so, to reset the timeoutLapsed to 0. You can do it like this:

To begin, put the following in your startMovie handler:

```
global lastH
global lastV

set lastH =the mouseH
set lastV =the mouseV
```

This code records the initial position of the mouse at the start of the movie, and uses it as the last known position of the mouse.

Next, you need to make an idle handler or stick the following in an existing idle handler:

```
on startmovie
   global lastH
   global lastV
   set lastH=the mouseH
   set lastV=the mouseV
end
on idle
  global lastH
  global lastV

  if (lastH <> the mouseH) or (lastV <> the mouseV) then
    set the timeoutLapsed =0
    set lastH =the mouseH
    set lastV =the mouseV
  end if
end
```

What we've done here is if, during an idle moment, we see that the mouse has moved (either vertically, horizontally, or both) from its last known position, we reset the timeoutLapsed. Then we record the current position as being the last known position so that we can tell if it moved again.

This, in effect, would give you a timeoutMouseMoved feature—a perfect example of "If you don't like the Lingo, change it!"

Timer Resolution

The resolution of a timer represents how often that timer gets updated. A watch typically has a resolution of 1 second, which means that the time displayed is updated at 1 second intervals. A stopwatch, on the other hand, might have a resolution of 1/100th of a second (or better). The computer's different internal timers, too, can have different resolutions.

On the PC, for instance, there's more than one way to measure ticks, and it varies from operating system to operating system. Under DOS, the resolution is something like 18.2 ticks per second. Windows 3.1 has the same resolution, because it uses the DOS timer.

Because Director reports ticks at 60 to a second, how does it do it? Is it overriding the timer?

No, sadly, it's doing nothing so exotic. Under Windows, at the end of a second, Director's counter reads 60, but it updated the counter not at 1/60th of a second intervals, but only about one third as often (that is, 18, rather than 60, times). If you could watch the timer, it would sort of look like this:

```
1 1 1 4 4 4 7 7 7 10 10 10 13 13 13
```

If you had true 60th-of-a-second resolution, the same 15-second period would look like this:

```
1 2 3 4 5 6 7 8 9 10 11 12 13 14 15
```

See, at the DOS timer resolution, the test got only 5 updates during that 15-second period, as opposed to 15. The count went up accordingly, just not as often.

Under Windows 3.1, the Windows internal tick count function (I'm talking about the Windows tick count, not Director's tick count) was supposed to be 1,000 ticks to a second, but because it uses the DOS timer, it updates only 18.2 times per second—not exactly split-second timing.

Under Windows 95, however, the internal tick count function behaves differently. Windows 95 changes the way it behaves so as to have a true millisecond resolution. Because the internal count under Windows 95 updates 1,000 times a second, Director easily gets its chance 60 times a second. The net effect, then, is that Director under Windows 95 has true 60th-of-a-second resolution, whereas under Windows 3.1 it has a resolution of only 18.2 ticks per second.

If you're interested, you can test this yourself with this quick-n-EZ timer resolution checker:

```
on testTimerResolution
  put "Testing..."
  set lastTick = 0
  set differentOnes =0
```

```
      set maxTicks =600
      startTimer
      repeat while the timer < maxTicks
        set currentTime =the timer
        if currentTime <> lastTick then
          set lastTick =currentTime
          set differentOnes =differentOnes + 1
        end if
      end repeat
      set tickRatio =float(maxTicks) / differentOnes
      set resolution =60 / tickRatio
      put "Resolution: "&resolution&" ticks per second."
    end
```

Type this little handler into a movie script and then call it from the message window:

```
testTimerResolution()
-- "Testing..."
-- "Resolution: 17.4000 ticks per second."
```

Because this was run under Windows, it shows a low resolution of 17.4 ticks per second, as opposed to something closer to 60 ticks per second.

The reason it shows 17.4 ticks and not 18.2 no doubt owes to my low-tech way of measuring. Basically, I looped around for a set number of ticks (10 seconds, or 600 ticks), and if I found that the tick count was different from the last one, I incremented a counter that keeps track of how many different tick readings I get.

At the end, I figure out the ratio of actual tick changes to expected ticks, and use that to find the ratio. Although low-tech, it's close enough for horseshoes and government work, so it should be good enough for us, right?

Creating a Multiple-Timer Facility

I like to have a variety of timers at my fingertips. In games, particularly, I like to set one timer to remind the user to do something when a certain time expires (sort of like the timeoutLapsed). I like to have timers so I can kick in a sound effect or display the next animation frame after a certain point.

Because I often need more than one timer and Lingo only offers one (or two, I guess, if you want to commandeer the timeoutLapsed), I had to create a little multiple-timer facility.

General Theory

The basic theory in making a single timer is that to establish a timer, you get to give it a name and say when you want it to expire. Suppose you want your timer to expire in 1,800 ticks (30 seconds). You start by looking at the current tick count—say it's 400,527—and then figure that if it's 400,527 ticks now, then your timer will expire at 400,527 + 1,800, or when 402,327 rolls around.

So, you store that result, and then later you can just check to see if the tick count has passed it yet. If it has, then the timer has expired!

Making it handle multiple timers is very easy. You just accept a name for the timer from the caller and stick it in a list along with the expiration point. If you use symbols for the names, it becomes really portable. If you use a property list, it becomes really easy to look up the requested timer and see if it has expired.

Using the seconds() function described in the sidebar, you can set your timer as follows:

```
setTimer(#soundTimer, seconds(5))
```

#soundTimer is the name I've given this timer, in the form of a symbol, for speed and portability. This call sets up #soundTimer to expire in 5 seconds.

setTimer()

Now, take a look at setTimer:

```
on setTimer whichTimer, numTicks
  -- Set the expiration time of a timer
  global timerList

  set expirationTime =the ticks + numTicks
  setAProp(timerList, whichTimer, expirationTime)
end
```

What this does is figure out what the expiration point would be (numTicks away from the current tick count) and store it in the list, using the timer name as the property by which to look it up.

initTimer()

If you recall from the discussion on lists (see Chapter 11), you need to initialize timerList if you intend to use it as a list. Consequently, you need to make a little initTimer routine and call it from startMovie:

```
on initTimer
  global timerList
  set timerList =[:]
end
```

Otherwise, any calls will fail when you go to set and check your timers.

timerExpired()

Now, you need to have a way to see if the timer has actually expired. You also need a way to kill the timer so it doesn't keep reporting that it has expired after it has served its purpose.

So, let's consider an expiration time of zero to be a killed timer that is not to be checked any more. Setting it to zero is a good way to do this because it's obviously not a valid expiration time *anyway*.

Keeping that in mind, you would call the check to see if it has expired as follows:

```
if timerExpired(#soundTimer) then
   ... do the stuff we need to do when it's expired ...
  killTimer(#soundTimer)     -- and kill it so it stays expired
end if
```

The actual handler would look like this:

```
on timerExpired  whichTimer
  -- Check to see if a given timer expired
  global timerList

  set expirationTime =getAProp(timerList, whichTimer)
  set expired =expirationTime and (the ticks >= expirationTime)
  return(expired)
end
```

This first extracts the expected expiration time from the list, then sets the *expired* variable to be true only if there's a non-zero `expirationTime` *and* the current tick count has walked past the expiration time.

I put the more complicated check last in the expression, because if we fail the check of there even *being* an expiration time at all (that is, it was set to 0) then I didn't want to waste any time doing the actual tick comparison.

Finally, you return the determined value, which is either zero (FALSE, didn't expire) or non-zero (TRUE, expired).

At this point, you might want to kill the timer. I left it out of the expiration check because it gives me more flexibility to call it manually, but that's up to you. You could easily stick in the following three lines:

```
if expired then
  killTimer(whichTimer)
end if
```

I just do it differently. But regardless of your preference, you need to kill the timer one way or another so it doesn't keep coming up as expired.

killTimer()

Killing the timer, as described, is as simple as setting the expiration time to zero. You can do it like this:

```
on killTimer whichTimer
  -- Force a timer to be dead
  global timerList

  setAProp(timerList, whichTimer, 0)
end
```

Of course, another way to kill the timer would be to take the timer out of the list altogether. The only problem with that technique is that when you go to get the expiration time for a timer and the timer's not even in the list, you get a <Void> back. Everything should still work, but it offends my sensibilities as a programmer for some reason. But you can do it that way if you want to, I guess. I won't tell.

chapter 9

Random Numbers

Sometimes you don't need your world to operate in
such an orderly fashion. A degree of unpredictability
can liven up many applications, and is intrinsic to
game programming.

Picking numbers at random is harder than you might
think, particularly if you want them to be truly
random. Fortunately, most languages, Lingo included, provide a *random* function whose sole purpose
in life is to make up random numbers. In this chapter,
I show you how to put this and other functions to
use, and to make a non-repeating random number
generator that you can use for slide shows, billboards,
or whatever.

Where Would You Use Random Numbers?

This question isn't as silly as you might think. In games, it's obvious. In real life, it's less obvious, and less necessary.

In games, you use random numbers to order the cards in a deck, determine whether a monster will appear, determine how hard a level will be or whether a shot fired at an opponent's ship actually destroys it, or whether the prize is behind door #1 or door #2.

In real life, you don't have as much call for it, but you can still use random numbers to decide which background picture to show next, which song to play next, which billboard sales-info pitch to show next, or which greeting to give the user.

Generating Random Numbers within Lingo

Lingo provides a function, random(upperLimit), that returns a random number between 1 and the specified upper limit. For instance, random(10) returns a number between 1 and 10.

You should realize that, true to the nature of random numbers, each call to random() is a new one. Just because the last call returned a 4 doesn't mean that you won't get a 4 this time. In fact, it's entirely possible (and likely) for certain numbers to appear more than once while other numbers don't appear at all. Certainly, if you make enough calls, they all eventually show up—but with plenty of repetition in between.

For instance, I made a little routine to generate *x* instances of random numbers with a specified upper limit:

```
on genRandomNumbers upperLimit, numTries
  repeat with x=1 to numTries
   put random(upperLimit)
  end repeat
end
```

I called it to see what would happen if I specified an upper limit of 10 (meaning I would get numbers from 1 to 10). If I just call random(10) once, I get one number back. However, I am interested in the results of random(10) when called 10 times (the point being to demonstrate that you don't get all ten numbers). Here's the result of ten calls to random(10) via genRandomNumbers():

```
genRandomNumbers(10,10)
-- 10
-- 8
-- 10
-- 1
-- 10
-- 4
-- 8
-- 1
-- 3
-- 7
```

Then I tried it again:

```
genRandomNumbers(10,10)
-- 3
-- 7
-- 2
-- 5
-- 8
-- 7
-- 9
-- 9
-- 2
-- 7
```

Missing some numbers out of each set, eh? Not only did I get many multiples of some numbers, certain other numbers (like 6) didn't even show up once!

The lesson to learn here is that random numbers are just that—*random*. There simply are no guarantees that each and every number will show up, or that certain numbers won't show up multiple times.

Not that that can't be arranged, though. Soon, I'll go over a nonrepeating random-number generator that lets you get a set amount of numbers in a particular range ordered so as to give each number once before repeating.

Determining Your Random Number Range

Random(x), as shown, generates random numbers between 1 and x. The bigger the x, the less likely you are to get consecutive repetitions. For instance, random(1000), which generates a random number between 1 and 1,000 each time you call it, is unlikely to repeat a number from one time to the next, although it could happen.

Random(2), however, which generates a 1 or a 2 each time you call it, is *very* likely to repeat the number, and perhaps even give you a whole series of repeats.

But what if you *don't* want a number between 1 and x? What if you need a number between, say, 500 and 599? Or between 0 and 9? Or between −5 and 5?

Just add to or subtract from the result as necessary. For instance:

To get a random number between 0 and 9:

```
set myNumber =random(10) - 1
```

To get a random number between 500 and 599:

```
set myNumber =random(100) -1 + 500
```

To get a random number between −5 and 5:

```
set myNumber =random(11) -1 -5
```

For each example, I figured out what the range would be. For 0 to 9, for example, the range would simply be 1 to 10 but subtracting 1. You always have to work from the first number being 1.

For 500 to 599, I first figured that 0 to 99 is random(100) -1, so for 500 to 599 it would be random(100) -1 + 500. I could have also done random(100) + 499, but doing it as random(100) -1 + 500 makes the steps involved clearer.

For −5 to 5, random(11) -1 gets 0 to 10, and subtracting 5 gets you −5 to 5. You have to use random(11), not random(10), because you have 11 numbers between -5 and 5 inclusive, counting 0.

Chances are that you might not be doing anything so involved, and that you might just need some random number between 1 and *x*. But if you do need something different, it's important to be able to figure out how to get there.

Pitfall

If you're going to need to use the random number more than once (not need more than one number, but need to use the same number more than once), for gosh sake's, stick it in a variable. It might sound simple, but I've seen more than one person try to evaluate a random number like this:

```
if random(6) = 1 then
  ...
else if random(6) = 2 then
  ...
else if random(6) = 3 then
  ...
else if random(6) = 4 then
  ...
else if random(6) = 5 then
  ...
else if random(6) = 6 then
  ...
end if
```

The person is sometimes amazed that sometimes, *nothing happens*! Can you figure out why? I can understand their misconception. They consider `random(6)` to be *the random number that they requested*, but it's not. Each time they call `random(6)`, they get a different number! Consequently, whether they hit anything at all is a real crap shoot.

`if random(5) = 5` evaluates to TRUE, and therefore works, only if `random(5)` happens to generate a 5 that time through. And that's not very likely! What you should do (and what they should've done) is this:

```
set myNum =random(6)
if myNum =1 then
  ...
else if myNum =2 then
  ...
```

continues

continued

```
else if myNum =3 then
   ...
else if myNum =4 then
   ...
else if myNum =5 then
   ...
else if myNum =6 then
   ...
end if
```

See the difference?

Testing with the `randomSeed`

Each time you call the `random()` function, you get a different number. The random series is a numerical series that derives from some seed number that is based on a huge body of mathematical formula and theory. As far as you and I are concerned, though, all we need to know is that each seed number generates the same series of numbers.

When Director starts, it normally picks a seed number to use. I don't know exactly what it uses, but if it's like most programs, it uses the number of ticks since the computer was turned on, the date and time, or some combination of all three.

A unique seed number promotes a unique series of random numbers. Sometimes, though, you might want the same series of random numbers for testing purposes.

Suppose, for example, you have an application that uses random numbers but for some reason you keep coming across a bug in your code. If you can ensure generating the same set of random numbers each time through the program, you can make your debugging job much easier, because you know what to expect.

To generate the same set of random numbers each time through the program, you can set a variable called the `randomSeed`. As I said, the `randomSeed` initially is set to some large number most likely derived from the ticks and the date and time, but you can set it to something yourself or just record it in case you need to reproduce a bug.

To see what it is, you can just print it to the message window:

```
put the randomSeed
```

or, you can set it to your own value for ease of testing:

```
set the randomSeed =41281003
```

If you always use the same value, you always get back the same random numbers in the same order!

> If you *do* set your own random number seed for testing purposes, make sure you remove it before you ship the product. You might laugh, but it's not as far-fetched as you think. It's easy to forget you've put one in there.

A Nonrepeating Random-Number Generator

If you can't rely on the random() function to give you nonrepeating numbers, what *do* you do if you need a set of numbers, but just in random order? Suppose you want to display all 15 pictures in your gallery. You want to do it randomly, so it doesn't seem like the same show *every* time you run it, but you also don't want the picture of the barnyard showing up three times in a row while the picture of the sunset doesn't show up at all.

For that sort of scenario, you need a nonrepeating random-number generator. Try this one (put it in a parent script and name it "randomListMaker" or something):

```
-- Parent script for randomListMaker
property randomList
property listSize
property nextItem
```

```
on new me, howMany
  set listSize =howMany
  generateList()
  return(me)
end

on getNextRandom
  if nextItem > listSize then
    generateList
  end if
  set thisNumber =getAt(randomList, nextItem)
  set nextItem =nextItem + 1
return(thisNumber)

on generateList
  set randomList =[]
  repeat with x=1 to listSize
    addAt(randomList, random(x), x)
  end repeat
  set nextItem =1
end
```

To use it, you create the object like so:

```
set pictureDisplayList =new(script "randomListMaker", 15)
```

This passes down 15 as a parameter, because what you want are numbers from 1 to 15, in random order. The 15 passed down lets the object know how many to generate in its list.

Calling new creates a new instance of an object based on the script "randomListMaker". The object stores the list in properties, which means that each object can be different. By using objects for this, you can set up many different random lists at a time.

The objectID is returned in pictureDisplayList, which serves to refer to the object from this point forward. Now, to get the next number out of the list, use the following:

```
set pictureToDisplay =getNextRandom(pictureDisplayList)
```

This calls the getNextRandom() function in the object and returns the next random number, and stores that number in pictureToDisplay so you can use it to look up that picture in the sequence, or whatever you want to do with it.

How Does It Work?

The random list maker, if told how many items the list needs to contain, generates a randomly ordered list that contains the specified number of elements. In other words, if 15 items are to be on the list, it generates a list of 15 elements, numbered 1 to 15, in random order.

That list is stored with the object in the property randomList. Then, each time the user wants a new item from the list, we give it to them. We keep track of our position in the list with the property nextItem. nextItem represents the next item in the list that is to be returned to the user.

New( )

In the new handler, we accept a parameter that specifies the size of the list. We store that in listSize, because generateList() needs that in order to work. We then generate our initial list and return.

GenerateList( )

To generate the list, we first initialize it to an empty list, as follows:

```
set randomList =[]
```

Then there's a loop to add each of the elements to the list. This loop uses a little trick by taking advantage of Lingo's addAt() function. addAt() adds a specified value to a specified list at a specified position.

By looping from 1 to listSize, we take each of the numbers in that range and add them to the list. The position we specify to addAt(), however, is random—this is the unusual part. If you wanted to add just 15 numbers, say, you could do this:

```
repeat with x=1 to listSize
  addAt(randomList, x, random(x))
end repeat
```

This would add to `randomList` at position *x*, a random number in the range 1 to *x*. This won't work for us, though. We'd get repeating numbers, particularly at the beginning, when we're doing numbers from 1 to 1 or 1 to 3.

You need to make sure that you add each number only once, and you can do it by reversing the way you do it:

```
repeat with x=1 to listSize
  addAt(randomList, random(x), x)
end repeat
```

The third parameter of `addAt()` is the value to place in the list. In this case we're first putting 1 in the list, then 2, then 3, and so on up until we've put all 15 items in the list.

What's random is the order in which the 15 items fall in the list. The position we add it to, you will notice, is not a set position, but a *random* position. So the first number, 1, might be placed into position 12. The second number, 2, might be placed into position 7. And so on.

You might figure out that we could end up repeating the position; that is, position 12 might show up more than once. And you'd be right. But it wouldn't matter, because the way `addAt` works, it puts the new number in that location and pushes the rest aside (what was in 12 is now in 13, whereas the new entry goes to 12). If it merely replaced it, this solution wouldn't work, but because it inserts the new number and relocates the rest, everybody gets a slot.

The net effect is that you can get a randomly ordered list out of the deal.

Finally, `generateList()` wraps up by setting the `nextItem` to be 1, so that on the next call from the user, the first item in the list is returned. This is necessary because you want the user to start from the beginning of the new list each time the list is generated.

GetNextRandom()

The next step, now that the list has been generated, is to provide a way for the user to get the next item out of that list. The idea is that the user will call to create the object once and then keep calling `GetNextRandom()` every time he needs a new number.

The beginning of the getNextRandom() function checks whether the prepared list has been exceeded:

```
if nextItem > listSize then
  generateList()
end if
```

If you *have* blown over the limit, it generates a new list. We know that the generateList() function resets nextItem to 1 as one of the last things it does, so this statement assures that one way or another, a value that can be returned to the caller. Whether you have to make a new list to do so is your problem, not the caller's.

Then it extracts the specified next item from the list:

```
set thisNumber =getAt(randomList, nextItem)
```

Finally, we have to advance the next item up one, so we don't continually return the same darned item (which would look pretty silly):

```
set nextItem =nextItem + 1
```

We wrap up by returning the number we extracted to the caller.

Possible Enhancements

I can think of two things you might want to do to improve on this script.

The first would be to have it return the actual generated list. You can do this by making a function that simply returns randomList, but then you'll want to manually regenerate the list, unless you want that to happen automatically when you give out the randomList. It depends on your specific needs.

The second is to make sure that there are no repetitions across regenerated lists. By this, I refer to a situation in which one list ends with, say, 8, and the next list starts with 8. What you would want to do is to have a little loop that determines what the last item of the current list is and keeps regenerating the list until it gets one that starts with a number that isn't the same as the last number of the previous list. I never bothered doing this, but if you think it'd be appropriate for your situation, go ahead. It would be a good exercise.

chapter 20

Stacks

Ever notice how hypertext programs enable you to click on a word; take you to a definition for the word you clicked on, where you can then click on another word, for which it takes you to related text for *that* word; and so on down the drain, until you start clicking on the Back button?

How does using the Back button take you back? How does the program keep track of where you've been?

The secret, my friend, lies in the stack.

Stacks in Real Life

If you've been in an institutional cafeteria, such as one in a hospital or school, and have used one of those pushable dish dispensers (you know, the ones where you take a plate off and the next one pops up), you've used a real life stack.

Imagine that hypertext links are plates on the stack. When the user clicks on a link, you would have the program write down the current location (page, paragraph, and word number) on a plate and put that plate on the stack. The topmost entry on the stack therefore contains the most recent departure point.

Figure 20.1

By saving your departure points you can keep track of where to return.

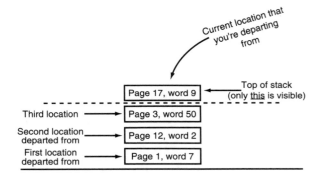

The program can then display the new page. Now, if the user clicks the back button, all you need to do in order to return is take the top plate off the stack to see what the last departure point was. Then you can go to it. The stack's now empty.

If, instead of going back, the user kept moving forward and clicking on links, he would have built up a large stack of places "departed from." There's nothing wrong with this—the user doesn't *have* to move back. In fact, he can keep clicking, move back occasionally, and then move forward more.

At the new page, when he clicks on a word, he needs to have the program write down the current location and put *that* on the stack. This can be repeated, and he can put as many plates on the stack as he likes.

Well, that's not literally true. A stack, like any other data item in Director, has a 32 KB limit. If you store, say, just a numerical location, that's 4 bytes, limiting you to storing just over 8,000 departure locations before you blow the stack. If you're storing a 20-byte string, however, you can only store slightly more than 1,600 locations (32,000 bytes available divided by the 20 bytes each use).

If yours is a "typical" user, he will do a combination of forward and backward movements, and the stack will probably get no more than a couple dozen departure locations deep at the most, so you should probably be safe. A good engineer, however, is aware of both the expected and extreme uses of their software and plans accordingly, so if you are expecting something that will come close to these limits it might be necessary to start thinking of organizational alternatives.

When it's time to go back, just take the top plate off, read what's written on it, and position yourself accordingly. If you need to go back another level, repeat the process with the next plate.

If, when halfway back, the user decides to start going forward for a while, just write down the new location and put it on the stack before you continue. In this manner, clicks into the hypertext are stored on the stack, and use of the back button retrieves from the stack.

Even though I say "go forward," I just mean continuing to click through the hypertext. It is possible, however, to implement a forward button as well, as some Web browsers do. These enable users to return to their previous locations in *either* direction.

To implement such a button requires that you have a second stack to record the forward locations. When a user clicks the back button, you would then record the current location on the forward stack and enable the forward button, thus enabling movement in both directions.

Stacks in Lingo

You can create a stack machine in Lingo very easily. The primary parts consist of something to handle the pushing part (putting something on the stack) and something to handle the popping part (popping something off the stack).

The stack itself, being just a bunch of items that you add to a pile, ought to suggest to you a Lingo *list*. And so it will be. You add to the end of the list when pushing an item and remove from the end of the list when popping an item off. It's that easy.

So, at a minimum, assuming you've initialized your stack as an empty list, your routines could look like this:

```
on push whatItem
  global stack

  append(stack, whatItem)            -- Add to end of stack
end


on pop
  global stack

  set thisItem =getLast(stack)       -- Get item at end
  deleteAt(stack, count(stack))      -- Delete end of stack
  return(thisItem)                   -- Return retrieved item
end
```

In this section of code, the *push* routine adds to the end and the *pop* routine first retrieves the item from the end of the stack, saves it in a variable, then deletes it from the stack itself. Finally, it returns the retrieved value.

An Improved Version

Of course, I'm not going to let you off that easily. What would be really nice would be to have *multiple* stacks—stacks of current pages, stacks of favorite colors, whatever you like.

So I'm going to show you how to make a property list. When a caller wants to push something on a stack, that caller needs to provide the name of the stack to which to add it. He then checks whether his master list currently has a stack under that name. If so, he retrieves it and add to it. If not, he creates it and adds to it.

Basically, this is an example of a list of lists.

The naming trick (using symbols) is the same one I showed you in Chapter 18 on the multiple timers, so you can use that as a reference if necessary.

Initialization

First, you would need to initialize your little master property list like so:

```
on initStacks
  global stackList
  set stackList =[:]
end
```

What this does is create an empty property list. That's all. No stacks are defined yet.

Pitfall

> Make sure you call the `initStacks` routine from your `startMovie` handler or *somewhere* before you start using the rest of the stack facility. Otherwise, the list won't be initialized and you'll get a `"Script error: Handler not defined"` complaint from Director.

The actual stack data doesn't go here. Whenever you create a new stack, all you do is add that stack into this master stack list. The data gets added to the stack, the stack gets added to the master stack list. Everybody's happy.

push()

You would need to revise the *push* handler to accommodate the fact that you now have a master stack list:

```
on push whichStack, whichItem
  global stackList
```

```
  set whichList =getaProp(stackList, whichStack)
  if (voidP(whichList)) then
    set whichList =[]
    addProp(stackList, whichStack, whichList)
  end if
  append(whichList, whichItem)
end
```

You would call the previous function like this:

```
push #webPageStack, currentLocation
```

The push() function starts by doing a getaProp() to see if the requested stack (in this case, #webPageStack) is in the master stack list. If so, getaProp() gives back the list. If *not*, which you know by the fact that the retrieved list is <Void> and therefore not a list, then a list can be created and added to our master stack list, so it'll be there for reference in the future.

You would then append the newly pushed item to the end of the list.

pop()

To get an item out, you do it in reverse—sort of. You retrieve the stack from the master list, suck off the value like in the original pop, and delete it. The only difference is that you can be nice and do a little checking to make sure you actually have such a list and actually have such an item. This is more important to do here than when pushing. When pushing, it's not a problem to *create* a new stack, but when popping, trying to return a value from a non-existent stack is another story altogether. For instance, the following code is one way to perform these checks:

```
on pop whichStack
  global stackList

  -- Get the stack. If it's missing, complain and go back.
  set whichList =getaProp(stackList, whichStack)
  if (voidP(whichList)) then
    alert("Attempt to pop from non-existent stack #"&whichStack)
    return 0
  end if
```

```
  -- Since it's here, see how many items are on it
  set stackSize =count(whichList)

  -- If nothing on it, then complain and go back
  if not stackSize then
    alert "Attempt to pop from empty stack #" & whichStack
    return 0
  end if

  -- So now we have a stack and the size.
  -- Get the item, delete it behind us, and return it
  set thisItem =getLast(whichList)
  deleteAt(whichList, stackSize)

  return(thisItem)
end
```

As described, you verify that you have a stack and that it actually contains something you can pop. If so, you get the item, delete it from the stack, and return it.

The only place this varies (apart from the error checking and the master list stuff) is that I separately get the count of the list. I did it separately here (in the original example, I just called count(stack)) because I reference the count more than once, and I wanted to cut down on unnecessary calls to do something for which I already have the answer.

closeStacks()

If you want to be kosher, you really should call to dispose of the lists after you finish using them:

```
on closeStacks
  global stackList
  set stackList =[]
end
```

Trying Out Your New Stack Routines

To try your new routines, you can push anything you want on the stack (you even can have different types of items on it):

```
initStacks

push #myStack, "One"
push #myStack, "Two"
push #myStack, "Three"

put pop(#myStack)
-- "Three"

put pop(#myStack)
-- "Two"

put pop(#myStack)
-- "One"
```

You don't have to go all the way back to the beginning. You can push, push, pop, push, pop, pop, push, push, push, push, pop, pop, push, and so forth, as long as your pops don't exceed your pushes. Same as in hypertext. You can go forward, forward, backward, forward, backward, backward, forward, forward, forward, forward, backward, backward, forward, as long as you don't go backward more than forward.

The point at which your stack is empty is the point at which you have nowhere left to go backward, and that's the point at which you should gray out your *back* button.

Extending Your Stack's Error Checking

Although this implementation of pop() just puts up an alert box and returns 0 when the stack is empty, you could skip the alert box and have the calling side check for a 0 return value and react with a dialog perhaps, or just no action at all. In addition, you might want to make handlers to return the size of the stack, or even just indicate whether items are still left on the stack. Then you can use that information to determine whether you should even have a *back* button enabled. For instance, if there are no items left on the stack, there's nowhere to go back *to*, so you might want to have the back button disabled (dimmed out).

Arrays

Common to many languages, the array is an ancient programming concept. In one-dimensional form it represents a linear list. In two-dimensional form, with rows and columns, the array is the electronic implementation of a grid. Used for everything from board games to representing the pixels on a screen, the two dimensional array is the workhorse in the programmer's tool chest.

Unfortunately, Lingo doesn't support arrays.

Fortunately, we can make them ourselves!

Understanding Arrays

Because a two-dimensional array is a grid, we can simulate it using lists. There are actually two ways to do so—one messy, one not so messy. The messy way entails making one list for each row in the array and then a column list to tie them all together (see fig. 21.1).

Figure 21.1

Making one list for each row in the array, and a column list to tie them all together.

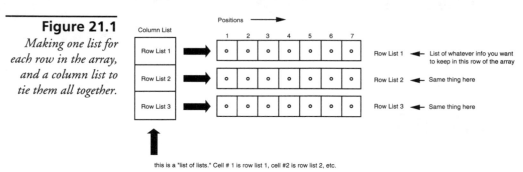

But actually, there's no need to go to all that trouble. We can make our array the same way computers do it internally.

The Ancient Array Technique

Memory in the computer is linear. You start at location A and just advance A+0, A+1, A+2, A+3, on through memory.

To simulate an array in memory you need to know the dimensions of the array. Let's say it's 5×5. 5 columns across, 5 rows down (see fig. 21.2). As long as you know how many columns across, it's very easy to simulate a two-dimensional array in memory.

If you advance through the array like this (given as row,col):

(1,1) (1,2) (1,3) (1,4) (1,5)

and then

(2,1) (2,2) (2,3) (2,4) (2,5)

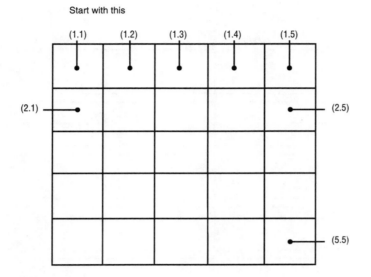

Start with this

Figure 21.2

An array that is 5 columns across and 5 rows down.

and on down to the next row, and so on...

(3,1) (3,2) (3,3) (3,4) (3,5)

(4,1) (4,2) (4,3) (4,4) (4,5)

(5,1) (5,2) (5,3) (5,4) (5,5)

...it's easy to figure what cell (2,3) is. It's in the second row, so it's one complete set of 5, which is one complete row, and then it's three cells into the second row. Second row, third column (see fig. 21.3).

If our array has 5×5 cells, then it has 25 cells in all. Internally we can reserve 25 cells in memory, so to speak. Or, in Lingo terms, 25 items in our list. The first five are for row 1, the next five are for row 2, the five after that are for row 3, and so on (see fig. 21.4).

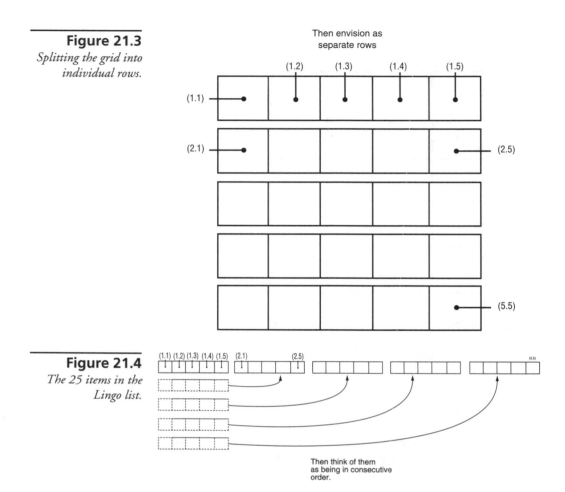

Figure 21.3

Splitting the grid into individual rows.

Then envision as separate rows

Figure 21.4

The 25 items in the Lingo list.

Then think of them as being in consecutive order.

If we think of it this way, it becomes really easy to simulate an array.

An Array Object

Basic array functionality should let you create an array, specify the dimensions, and set any cell in the array to any value you want. It also should let you get the value of any cell in the array. If you can't do at least this, it's pretty useless as an array.

The only other functions that immediately come to mind as valuable are functions to dump the contents of the array (so you can see what you've got), and to set all the cells in the array to some particular value—whatever value you want.

I'll show you how to create a basic 2D (two-dimensional) array object that does all of this except the last (to set all cells to a particular value). I'll leave that as an exercise for you (in case you feel you're not getting enough exercise).

The following is the array object. You should put this in its own parent script (because it's used for creating objects). I decided to do it as an object because objects are most appropriate: You can keep the information you need about the array (dimensions, the array itself) in properties in the object, and have handlers to manipulate that data.

My example parent script is named "Array Script".

The Script

```
-- Array object script

property array
property numRows
property numCols

on new me, rows, cols
  set numRows =rows
  set numCols =cols
  set totalCells =rows * cols

  set array =[]
  addAt(array, totalCells, 0)
  return me
end

on dispose me
  set array =[]
  return 0
end
```

```
on cell row, col
  -- Internal function to locate cell in list
  set cellLoc =((row -1) * numCols) + col
  return(cellLoc)
end

on setCell me, row, col, whichValue
  -- Sets the specified row and col to value
  setAt(array, cell(row, col), whichValue)
end

on getCell me, row, col
  -- Returns value at specified row and col
  set cellValue =getAt(array, cell(row, col))
  return(cellValue)
end

on dump me
  -- Dumps out the array
  repeat with row =1 to numRows
    set thisRow =row && "--"
    repeat with col =1 to numCols
      set thisRow =thisRow && getCell(me, row, col)
    end repeat
    put thisRow
  end repeat
end
```

The Properties

We only store three properties with the object. The array itself and both the row and column dimensions.

New()

The new() routine initializes the array and fills it with zeros. It does this by means of a trick. The list addAt() function will add an element into a list at a specified position. Now if the position you're adding to is beyond anything that's in the list already, it'll put it in the proper position, after filling the intervening positions with 0s.

So, if you wanted something in position 10, and the list was either empty or smaller than 10 cells, it'd put it in the tenth position, and fill any before it with 0 in order to pad it out to 10 cells.

This will work out great for us. If we put something in the very last position in the array, all the intervening positions will automatically be created for us. To take advantage of this, we'll need to know what that last position will be. It's very easy—the last position is rows×cols. On a 5×5 array, the last cell would be the 25th cell.

So when we do this:

```
set totalCells =rows * cols
set array =[]
addAt(array, totalCells, 0)
```

we're creating an array, dimensioned rows×cols, that's filled with zeros.

Dispose()

The other feature we want to get out of the way is the one to dispose of the array when we're done with it. The dispose() routine will release the array by setting it to empty contents. It also will return a zero to make things easier, as described in Chapter 12 on objects.

Cell()

The next function is not meant to be called from the outside world, but is just for internal use within the object. Its purpose is to convert the (row,column) location of a cell to its true position in a linear list. I just put it in a handler so we don't have to stick this math everywhere in the script that we need to do these calculations.

```
on cell row, col
  -- Internal function to locate cell in list
  set cellLoc =((row -1) * numCols) + col
  return(cellLoc)
end
```

If, on a 5×5 array we want cell (2,3), the third one over in the second row, that can be determined as the number of cells in the complete rows plus the number of cells into the current row.

The number of complete rows is one less than the requested row. For cell (2,3) we have only one complete row, because we're asking for row 2, column 3. Row 2 is incomplete (we're not going all the way through).

So, (row - 1) represents the number of completed rows. To find out how many cells that represents, we have to multiply it by the number of cells in a single row, or *numCols*.

Therefore, ((row - 1) * numCols) represents the total number of cells in completed rows up to, *but not including*, the current row. And if we're only asking for row 1 to begin with, it comes out to 0, because there'll be no completed rows before row 1.

To get the current cell position, all that's left to do is add in the number of cells in the current row. And that's how we end up with this:

```
set cellLoc =((row -1) * numCols) + col
```

SetCell()

To set a particular cell at a particular row and column location, we can use the list SetAt() function. We give it the list to use (which is *array*), the location (derived from our call to *cell*), and the value we want to set it to.

GetCell()

To get the value of a cell, we have the *cell* function determine the actual location in the list, and then we call the list function GetAt() to give us back the value that's stored there.

Dump()

This is the only non-essential function, but it's very valuable for seeing what's going on with your array.

In it we use a nested loop to scoot through all the elements. First we set a row, and then we loop through each column within that row.

Because we're trying to dump the contents of the array, we want it to *look* like an array. This means having all the items in a row on the same line.

To do that, we build a string variable. It starts off with the row number and a couple of dashes:

```
set thisRow =row && "--"
```

Then, each column that we do, we add to the string until we get a string that represents all the cells in that row. Of course, this will only work with small arrays. If you're going to have 2,000 columns across, you'll want a different way of dumping the array information.

```
set thisRow =thisRow && getCell(me, row, col)
```

Wrapped up in a nested loop, this allows us access to every cell in the array.

```
on dump me
  -- Dumps out the array
  repeat with row =1 to numRows
    set thisRow =row && "--"
    repeat with col =1 to numCols
      set thisRow =thisRow && getCell(me, row, col)
    end repeat
    put thisRow
  end repeat
end
```

Taking It for a Spin

To use it, you need to create an instance of the object. All you need to do that is to know the dimensions you want the array to have.

```
set myArray =new(script "Array Script", 10, 10)
```

This creates a 10×10 array object. I should probably mention at this point that although I use things like 5×5 and 10×10 for illustrative purposes, nothing says your array has to be square. It could easily be 100×2.

At any rate, let's see what our array looks like:

```
dump(myArray)
-- "1 -- 0 0 0 0 0 0 0 0 0 0"
-- "2 -- 0 0 0 0 0 0 0 0 0 0"
-- "3 -- 0 0 0 0 0 0 0 0 0 0"
-- "4 -- 0 0 0 0 0 0 0 0 0 0"
-- "5 -- 0 0 0 0 0 0 0 0 0 0"
-- "6 -- 0 0 0 0 0 0 0 0 0 0"
-- "7 -- 0 0 0 0 0 0 0 0 0 0"
-- "8 -- 0 0 0 0 0 0 0 0 0 0"
-- "9 -- 0 0 0 0 0 0 0 0 0 0"
--"10 -- 0 0 0 0 0 0 0 0 0 0"
```

All zeros! Pretty darned neat. Well, we can change that easily enough:

```
setCell(myArray, 5, 5, "X")
dump(myArray)
-- "1 -- 0 0 0 0 0 0 0 0 0 0"
-- "2 -- 0 0 0 0 0 0 0 0 0 0"
-- "3 -- 0 0 0 0 0 0 0 0 0 0"
-- "4 -- 0 0 0 0 0 0 0 0 0 0"
-- "5 -- 0 0 0 0 X 0 0 0 0 0"
-- "6 -- 0 0 0 0 0 0 0 0 0 0"
-- "7 -- 0 0 0 0 0 0 0 0 0 0"
-- "8 -- 0 0 0 0 0 0 0 0 0 0"
-- "9 -- 0 0 0 0 0 0 0 0 0 0"
--"10 -- 0 0 0 0 0 0 0 0 0 0"
```

Now we've got an "X" in cell (5,5). You'll note that we were able to mix a string ("X") with numbers (the zeros).

Let's make sure our array formulas work properly at the extremes. Let's set the first element in the array:

```
setCell(myArray, 1, 1, "*")
dump(myArray)
-- "1 -- * 0 0 0 0 0 0 0 0 0"
-- "2 -- 0 0 0 0 0 0 0 0 0 0"
-- "3 -- 0 0 0 0 0 0 0 0 0 0"
-- "4 -- 0 0 0 0 0 0 0 0 0 0"
-- "5 -- 0 0 0 0 X 0 0 0 0 0"
-- "6 -- 0 0 0 0 0 0 0 0 0 0"
-- "7 -- 0 0 0 0 0 0 0 0 0 0"
-- "8 -- 0 0 0 0 0 0 0 0 0 0"
-- "9 -- 0 0 0 0 0 0 0 0 0 0"
--"10 -- 0 0 0 0 0 0 0 0 0 0"
```

The first element is now an asterisk. Let's set the last element as well:

```
setCell(myArray,10,10, "*")
dump(myArray)
-- "1 -- * 0 0 0 0 0 0 0 0 0"
-- "2 -- 0 0 0 0 0 0 0 0 0 0"
-- "3 -- 0 0 0 0 0 0 0 0 0 0"
-- "4 -- 0 0 0 0 0 0 0 0 0 0"
-- "5 -- 0 0 0 0 X 0 0 0 0 0"
-- "6 -- 0 0 0 0 0 0 0 0 0 0"
-- "7 -- 0 0 0 0 0 0 0 0 0 0"
-- "8 -- 0 0 0 0 0 0 0 0 0 0"
```

```
-- "9 -- 0 0 0 0 0 0 0 0 0 0"
--"10 -- 0 0 0 0 0 0 0 0 0 *"
```

So far, all's well!

Loops

Two-dimensional arrays and nested loops go hand in hand. The outer and inner loops walk you through the rows and columns, and you can set whatever you want. Or, use just single loops to change just single rows or columns.

For instance, this would change row 7 to all asterisks if in a handler:

```
repeat with col = 1 to 10
  setCell(myArray, 7, col, "*")
end repeat

dump(myArray)
-- "1 -- * 0 0 0 0 0 0 0 0 0"
-- "2 -- 0 0 0 0 0 0 0 0 0 0"
-- "3 -- 0 0 0 0 0 0 0 0 0 0"
-- "4 -- 0 0 0 0 0 0 0 0 0 0"
-- "5 -- 0 0 0 0 X 0 0 0 0 0"
-- "6 -- 0 0 0 0 0 0 0 0 0 0"
-- "7 -- * * * * * * * * * *"
-- "8 -- 0 0 0 0 0 0 0 0 0 0"
-- "9 -- 0 0 0 0 0 0 0 0 0 0"
--"10 -- 0 0 0 0 0 0 0 0 0 *"
```

A nested loop would change rows 7, 8, and 9 to a -1:

```
repeat with row =7 to 9
    repeat with col = 1 to 10
      setCell(myArray, row, col, -1)
    end repeat
  end repeat

dump(myArray)
  -- "1 -- * 0 0 0 0 0 0 0 0 0"
  -- "2 -- 0 0 0 0 0 0 0 0 0 0"
  -- "3 -- 0 0 0 0 0 0 0 0 0 0"
  -- "4 -- 0 0 0 0 0 0 0 0 0 0"
  -- "5 -- 0 0 0 0 X 0 0 0 0 0"
  -- "6 -- 0 0 0 0 0 0 0 0 0 0"
  -- "7 -- -1 -1 -1 -1 -1 -1 -1 -1 -1 -1"
```

```
-- "8 -- -1 -1 -1 -1 -1 -1 -1 -1 -1 -1"
-- "9 -- -1 -1 -1 -1 -1 -1 -1 -1 -1 -1"
--"10 -- 0 0 0 0 0 0 0 0 *"
```

When You're Done

When you're done using your array, make sure you dispose of it properly! By returning a zero from the dispose routine I make this really easy:

```
set myArray =dispose(myArray)
```

Not only did it call the `dispose()` routine, but it set it to zero automatically.

Enjoy

Arrays can be used for almost anything you can think of. In cards, a 4×13 (or 13×4, as you prefer) array can represent the four suits of 13 cards in a deck. In chess, it represents the board. A 2×16 array could also represent the pieces.

In more practical matters it can be part of a database, a graphics library, an audio collection (rows represent music, columns represent categories), or whatever you want to bother doing with it. If you have arrays available, you have a lot more options open to you.

chapter 22

Preloading

How do you fit a 14 MB movie into a machine that has only 8 MB of memory (especially considering that not all of those 8 MB are available anyway)? After you account for the operating system, your fax monitor, and your Dilbert screen saver, maybe you have 5.5 MB left over.

Obviously, not all 14 MB are going to fit. Even if you use virtual memory, you come across some movies whose sizes exceed your physical memory.

If Director can't fit the whole movie into memory, the best it can do is load in the parts you need when you need them. It enables you to specify for each member one of the following three choices of when you want that member loaded (which you can see by pulling up the Cast Properties dialog box for your cast member, shown in figure 22.1):

❖ **When Needed.** When Director comes across a frame that has that cast member in it, Director *needs* the cast member and loads it.

❖ **After Frame One.** After Director moves beyond frame 1, it loads the cast member, the purpose being, I assume, to delay loading while some sort of introductory "wait while I get ready" screen appears in frame 1.

❖ **Before Frame One.** When you want to utilize the cast member *in* frame 1. Why *When Needed* wouldn't suffice for this, I don't know.

Figure 22.1

A Cast Properties dialog box.

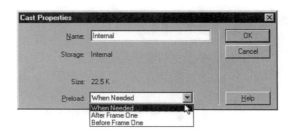

Regardless, these are your loading options. Big woof.

Okay, let me amend that statement. These are your loading options *without using the incredible power of Lingo that can revolutionize your program and turn your life into a blissful state of ecstasy.* Yes, that's what I meant to say.

But, in fact, it's true. Lingo gives you precise control over loading, unloading, and purging cast members.

Loading

When a cast member is loaded, it's in memory, ready to be used—as opposed to being on disk. A cast member in memory, if audio, can be played instantly; if graphics, can be displayed instantly.

The time it takes to load a cast member is a factor of both its size and the speed of the media from which you load it. A 256-byte cast member probably loads very quickly, no matter where it is, but a 256-KB cast member takes significantly longer. Loading from a fast hard disk is one thing, loading from CD-ROM is another. Loading a big file from a slow CD-ROM is excruciatingly slow.

The differences between hard disk and CD-ROM cannot be underestimated. If your program is destined for CD-ROM, be sure to test it at various points. Performance can be drastically different between the two.

Once I was working on the CD-ROM version of a popular game program (a children's title). This was quite a few years ago, when custom CD-ROM burners were only for large companies or anyone with at least $10,000 to spend. As a result, it wasn't until our alpha release that I was able to get a copy of it on CD-ROM, at which point I realized it had to be significantly reengineered.

There were two main problems. First, that CD-ROM was so incredibly slow that the program just crawled. Instead of just loading stuff when I needed it, I had to implement a preloading scheme that would transfer the stuff off the CD-ROM to the hard disk and preload it ahead of time in an effort to achieve animation that even began to approach the performance of the disk-based program.

The other problem was that the CD-ROM loading and my file transfers took so long that time-dependent things like MIDI were left hanging while the file transfer took place. So, unlike when I ran the program from the hard disk, running off CD-ROM was not only slower, but single notes would hang (play continuously) for four seconds while the loading completed. Needless to say, there was a lot of revision done to accommodate those problems.

That program might have been done with a single-speed drive, I don't recall anymore, but even now I only use a double-speed drive even though I can purchase 4X and even 6X or higher drives. I figure, if I can get my program to run well on a 2X drive, it'll run great on a 4X drive.

continues

---

continued

With CD-ROM burners now affordable to the small developer, there's no real excuse for not having tested your program many times on CD-ROM before releasing it. Further, you should make sure you test it on your minimal-requirement platform. Also, test it early. You might find that an animation you never considered troublesome before suddenly is embarrassingly slow. Here is when you need to start taking control and managing the preloading of your cast members.

The trick, then, is not just to wait for Director to load stuff when needed. If you're in Lingo, and the user clicks on a button (and you intend to play some audio and change the member of the button), do you, at *that* point, want to sit and wait for Director to load the sound effect and the replacement cast member from disc? Of course not—you want instant response to your click, not a two-second delay.

When products are released that weren't tested on CD-ROM or don't take advantage of preloading, you end up with a situation in which a user clicks the mouse and then has to wait two seconds before anything happens. This sort of thing contributes to the perception that products made with Director are slow, and that you, as a developer, make slow products. You can avoid such perceptions simply by taking the time to test your product and adjust it accordingly.

The other thing to keep in mind when testing is the kind of test environment you have. Do you have a heavily cached 4X CD-ROM? Will your program be played on a non-cached 2X CD-ROM? *Caching* is the way drives prepare for the future. The theory is that if you asked for a whole bunch of data from a file, chances are that you're going to want some more. Consequently, the caching software reads in more than it needs to, anticipating your wants and needs.

For instance, you might just ask for 4 KB of data. The caching mechanism, however, might just load in 32 KB of data from that location because it's just as easy. It gives you your 4 KB of data, with the normal loading response.

When you then ask for another 2 KB, however, you get it instantly—the reason being that it's already loaded in the drive's cache, so it can just give it to you. The danger is that you don't perceive any loading time associated with loading that particular data. However, run it on a machine with different caching (or no caching) and you might be surprised by the performance hit in a place where you didn't think you had any problems.

It's something to keep in mind.

Basic Preloading

Lingo offers basic preloading functions. You can just issue a request to preload *everything*, and it attempts to cram as much stuff into its mouth as possible, until it runs out of memory. The only problem is that this is appropriate only with small movies.

If you want to try this, you can give the Lingo commands to either `preloadMember`, which tries to do what I just described, or to `preload`.

The latter differs in that it preloads all cast members that appear in the current frame and in each frame to the end. Unfortunately, if you use Lingo heavily and refer to cast members not in the score (that is, setting the sprites directly from Lingo), this particular command won't know about it and won't preload it. For score-oriented programs, plain old `preload` is okay, but for Lingo-oriented ones, it's not.

You can, however, be a little less grand in your requests for preloading. As the documentation on `preloadMember` and `preload` states, you can specify a range of cast members or frames to preload. Or, you can specify just *one* frame or cast member. Because I do most of my stuff only in Lingo, I don't really have any "frames" to preload, so I usually preload certain cast members that I know I'll be needing. So, for me, the `preloadMember` command with a member or member range specified is the one I tend to use if I'm doing any preloading at all. `PreloadMember whichCastNumber` preloads the specified cast member. Use it the same way you should use spicy peppers on your nachos—liberally.

When do you use it? Director, left to its own devices, loads it when you finally set the membernum of sprite x to y. You, on the other hand, might want to load your cast member before then. *When*, however, is a question only you can answer, because only you know your program's behavior.

The best way to determine when to use it is to examine respective behavior you anticipate out of the user and out of your program. You might have certain sprites or hotspots on your screen from which you want instant reaction if a user clicks on them. That reaction might be to make a click sound and to make the sprite glow (by replacing it with a glowing cast member). If you want instant reaction, you want those cast members preloaded. Upon entering the movie, frame, or screen, you want to preload those cast members.

If, say, the screen shows items you can select and then click a button to initiate action, after the user selects an item, you can preload the thing it goes to, even if they haven't pressed the "go" button yet. This is *anticipation preloading*. You have a pretty good idea that the user's going to select such-and-such an item, so you preload it in anticipation of them using that item.

Variations

As well as the basic preloading functions, Lingo also offers some properties and functions that enable you to vary your preloading scheme. These variations are examined in the following sections.

the preloadEventAbort

Director has a cute little property you can set called the preloadEventAbort. This property, set to TRUE (default is FALSE), will have a mouse click or keypress interrupt the preloading. I assume the intention is to let you provide instant reaction to a keypress or mouse click. Of course, if the thing you're preloading is what you'll go to as a result of the click, well, that would sort of be self-defeating, wouldn't it?

Anyway, it's there if you need it.

preloadMovie()

There's one more preload function worthy of mention—the new
`preloadMovie whichMovie`. Just as you can `play whichMovie`, so too can
you preload it; and this helps the movie run faster, play harder, and live
longer.

the preloadRAM

`the preloadRAM` is a property you can set. Its purpose is to limit the amount
of memory that a digital video can utilize when being preloaded. Digital
video can be very large, and all your other preload operations could fail if it
turns out that some digital video cast member is a pig and has taken all the
memory for itself. You might want to restrict the amount allocated to each
digital video cast member to some manageable amount (no, I don't have any
numbers for you—it depends on your program).

the preLoad of Member

This actually should be called `the preload of video`, because it only has to
do with digital video, but that's not the way they named it. All it does is
indicate whether the specified digital video cast member can be preloaded
into memory. In fact, at least on Windows machines, it mainly refers to the
digital video header. The video *does* play faster if preloaded, but it plays even
if it isn't preloaded, so you might want to pay attention to your settings here
and make sure it's set to be preloaded. Note that this setting doesn't actually
preload the video; you still have to do that separately.

Return Value

The `preloadMember` and `preload` functions return the number of the last
member loaded. This can be very valuable for seeing if you managed to get all
the cast members you asked for (or even *any* that you asked for). Just because
you issued a `preloadMember` to preload members 5 through 25 doesn't mean
that it actually worked or that they all got loaded. Check the return value to
ascertain the last one loaded.

It's important to note, though, that you can't check the return value directly,
but that you have to check `the result`. As in:

```
preload 3
if the result =3 then
  put "Successfully preloaded!"
else
 put "Failed to preload cast 3"
end if
```

Unloading

The converse of preloading is unloading. After you finish using something, get rid of it.

Both the preloadMember and preload functions have their partners in unloadMember and unload, both of which work the same as the preload versions, but in reverse. You can unload everything, a range of cast members, a range of frames, or a specific frame.

Use unloading when you *know* that you no longer need a particular cast member. Was it a one time animation? A screen that you put up? Text? Get rid of it if you're not going to use it any more, so you can make room for some new stuff.

The reason is that before Director can accommodate new load requests, it might get rid of loaded items you haven't touched for a long time, on the assumption that you don't need them any more. Rather than let Director decide what you don't need, *you* should decide. Unload your unwanted chaff and avoid Director having to decide for you.

Purging

When Director *does* decide for you that it needs to make room for a requested cast member, it looks at the cast members you have in use and the ones you've used lately. It then unloads the ones you've used least recently, on the assumption that if you haven't used it in the last 20 minutes then you probably aren't going to use it in the *next* 20 minutes. On the other hand, it has this cast member that you want to use *now*.

This *Least Recently Used* purge criteria is a commendable philosophy, and usually the most appropriate. You always have exceptions, though. You might have some cast members that you want to protect. Even if you haven't used them in the last 20 minutes (or at all), you still want them kept in memory. One of them might be the audio click for a particular button. Just because the user hasn't clicked that button yet doesn't mean that you don't need that sound around. In fact, you *don't* want that puppy purged *at all*.

You can specify where each cast member stands in the way of purge priority, by setting the `purgePriority` property of that cast member.

To do so, you'd say something like this:

```
set the purgePriority of member "clickSound" to 1
```

The values you can provide are:

- **0 - Never purge.** You should use *Never purge* very judiciously, if at all. If you do use it, use it sparingly. If you were to set all the cast members to *Never purge*, Director would be hamstrung and couldn't make room for new cast members in memory. Chances are, the program would die a miserable death or lock up.

- **1 - Purge last.** You also should use *Purge last* judiciously, although it's not as dangerous. It specifies that this particular cast member should be purged only as a last resort, after all other efforts to free up room via purging have been used. Setting all your members to *Purge last*, however, defeats the purpose of using the feature. You can set a few to be last, but not *everybody* can be last. That would just make them all equal again.

- **2 - Purge next.** *Purge next* means that, rather then look at the Least Recently Used cast member, this particular one should be the next to go. It's sacrificial, because you don't need it any more or you don't give two hoots whether it needs to be loaded.

- **3 - Purge normal.** *Purge normal* is the default Least Recently Used technique. All cast members normally are set to *Purge normal*, unless you change them.

Idle Loads

Idle Loads are a gift from the 5.0 Macromedian gods, and a close runner-up to the debugger in the category of pleasurable additions to 5.0. The concept of an idle load is that you can arrange for preloading to take place in the background, during idle cycles.

> You should be aware that idle loading only works to prefetch from movie or cast files—you can't use it to preload linked members.
>
> Idle loading also keeps cast members in their compressed state. The upside is that you can preload more when they're compressed. The downside is that they still need to be decompressed when you go to use them, so there won't be an absolutely instant response. Of course, this is still faster than if you *hadn't* used idle loading.

the idleLoadMode

By default, Director does no idle loading. You can *turn on* idle loading, however (and I suggest that you do). The global property the idleLoadMode governs idle loading. It can have the following values:

0 - No idle loading performed

1 - Idle loading during free time between frames

2 - Idle loading during idle events

3 - Idle loading as much as possible

It undoubtedly defaults to 0 (no idle loading) to make Director as backward compatible as possible with prior versions, but I see no reason not to crank it up as long as doing so doesn't cause problems. I'd go right ahead and set it to 3, to idle load as much as possible.

Settings 1 and 2 give you finer control over idle loading, and limit it if necessary. I wouldn't think you'd want to limit it unless you knew it was interfering with something else. So, otherwise, put that baby on 3 and let 'er rip.

the `idleLoadPeriod`

You also can set the number of ticks that Director waits before trying to do an idle load. For instance, the following statement tells Director to perform idle loads only every 15 ticks (1/4 second):

```
set the idleLoadPeriod = 15
```

Again, you would do this only if you had to eliminate conflict and problems, should the idle loading be preventing something else from working properly. Normally, you want to set `idleLoadPeriod` to 0 (the default) so that Director performs the idle loading without delay.

the `idleLoadTag`

Director enables you to create groups of items to be idle loaded. By establishing groups you can test to see when a particular group has completed, or you can compel a group to finish, or you can cancel the loading of a selected group without affecting the other preload requests you have in.

To identify groups, you can "tag" your requests. You do this with `the idleLoadTag` property. When Director receives a `preload` or `preloadMember` request, it attaches the current `idleLoadTag` to it. If you haven't specified a tag, your request will just have the default tag of zero (0) attached. You can, however, specify different tags for different requests, like so:

```
set the idleLoadTag =10
preloadMember "spaceship"
preloadMember "planet"
set the idleLoadTag =20
preloadMember "audio: space sound"
preloadMember "audio: rocket sound"
```

In this example, I set the tag to be 10 and then made requests to preload two cast members. Then, I changed the tag to 20, and made an additional two requests. The first two will be assigned the tag 10, and the next two will be assigned the tag 20.

The tag assigned must be a numeric value. Obviously, tags like 10 and 20 aren't very revealing about the requests they're associated

continues

continued

with. However, do you recall in chapter 10 on symbols how I said you could add zero to a symbol in order to reveal its true numeric value? At the time, it merely had curiosity value, but here's an instance where you can put it to use.

For instance, the previous example could have been done this way

```
set the idleLoadTag =#graphics + 0
preloadMember "spaceship"
preloadMember "planet"
set the idleLoadTag =#soundEffects + 0
preloadMember "audio: space sound"
preloadMember "audio: rocket sound"
```

Although a tag like `#graphics + 0` might look a little weird, it does evaluate to a numerical value, which lets you use it in place of numbers like 20 and 14, making for a far more readable program.

The tag that was in effect when the request was made is the tag that is associated with the request. Now that we have tags assigned, we can see how to use them.

idleLoadDone

Because idle loads take place during idle times, just having a request in doesn't necessarily mean that the loading has taken place. In fact, it might not have even started yet. For this reason it becomes necessary for you to check if the loading has completed. You can do this via the `idleLoadDone()` function. If the idle loading has completed, it will return TRUE.

The `idleLoadDone()` function takes a parameter specifying the tag group you want to check. For instance

```
if idleLoadDone(10) then
```

will only check the status of tag group 10. Likewise, you can use the tip I just mentioned on setting tags to check the status like this

```
if idleLoadDone(#soundEffects + 0) then
```

which, to my mind, is a bit more understandable than using some arbitrary number like 10 for a tag.

finishIdleLoad

Suppose you've requested that a certain series of members be preloaded in anticipation of the user clicking on a certain button. Once they've clicked on the button, however, you'll probably need to use those cast members.

This is where the `finishIdleLoad()` command comes in handy. Use it to tell Director to just go ahead and finish preloading the rest of the requested members—never mind waiting for idle cycles. Specify a tag to have it just finish loading that particular tag. For instance

```
finishIdleLoad(20)
```

will cause tag group 20 to finish loading right then and there. If you haven't been using tags then just do

```
finishIdleLoad()
```

to just finish loading all your outstanding requests.

cancelIdleLoad

Perhaps you've got some idle loading requests in, but the user has chosen to do something else, which now means you don't need that stuff preloaded any more. Using the `cancelIdleLoad()` command you can cancel your outstanding idle load requests. Used similar to `finishIdleLoad()`, it looks like

```
cancelIdleLoad()      -- If no tags were used
cancelIdleLoad(20)    -- To cancel tag group 20
```

You should note that this will not *unload* the stuff that was loaded, it just stops Director from loading any more.

the idleReadChunkSize

One very nice feature in Director is the capability to set the amount of data to load during an idle load. If you set the `idleReadChunkSize` to a certain size, when Director does an idle load it only attempts to preload that amount (maximum) during an idle load.

In other words, if you set the `idleReadChunkSize` to 32 KB, Director doesn't try to load more than 32 KB at any given time.

You might be tempted to set this as high as possible. Don't do it! If anything, you want to keep the number low, particularly if you have other idle events you want to keep up with.

For instance, as long as you have the `idleLoadMode` set to 3, to load as much as possible, and the `idleLoadPeriod` set to 0, to have no delay, you might as well keep the chunk size down around something like 4 KB or 16 KB. If you let the program load as often as possible, it just has to make multiple calls. The benefit is that the system doesn't get all tied up trying to do one large call. Do 4 KB, and if you have time, do another 4 KB. This still leaves plenty of reaction time for mouse clicks, rollovers, and whatever else you have going on. For example,

```
set the idleReadChunkSize to 4096
```

But experiment. You might find that using larger values enhances performance—as long as they're not *too* large.

Combining the Techniques

By allowing Director to preload as much as possible via the idle load mechanism and requesting that certain cast members be preloaded in anticipation of need, you should be able to greatly improve the performance of your program. If you request the most important preload items first, and then the lesser items next, Director attempts to service the idle queue and give you as many items as possible.

The more cast members you have in memory when you need them, the less Director must load on demand. Performance goes up, delays go down, and satisfaction increases all around.

Rollovers

I must be honest: I've never really liked the term *rollover*, but at the same time I've been at a loss to come up with a replacement term.

A *rollover* is what Macromedia calls the situation in which the mouse is over a sprite. The user has *rolled* the mouse *over* the sprite. Unfortunately, though, Director does not treat a rollover as an event so much as simply a condition. The sprite is rolled over or it's not.

As an event, you could have a situation in which a rollover would *occur*, and you could be notified of a rollover beginning, that is, when the mouse first goes over the sprite, and of a rollover ending (when the mouse moves off).

Alas, all Lingo provides is a way to tell whether a sprite is being rolled over. It doesn't even tell you *which* sprite is rolled over; you have to figure that out yourself.

Rollover()

The Lingo `Rollover()` function takes as a parameter the sprite you want to test to see if it's rolled over. In other words, a call to `Rollover(2)` would return `TRUE` if sprite 2 was rolled over.

At first glance, this might seem perfectly adequate for recreational use. You can set up something like this and stick it in your *idle* handler.

```
if rollover(2) then
  puppetSprite 2, TRUE
  set the memberNum of sprite 2 to the memberNum of "Glow"
else
  puppetSprite 2, FALSE
end if
```

In practice, though, this involves a few problems. For instance, whenever the mouse is on the sprite, it *always* changes the cast member of the sprite. You don't need to do it a million times, you only need to do it once! Consequently you have to start testing to see if you've done it yet. Likewise, when the sprite is *not* rolled over, you don't want to be unpuppeting the sprite *all* the darn time, just the once!

To make things worse, you can't directly tell what the current rollover is. As shown here, you have to specify a sprite and then see if that particular one is rolled over.

However, here's a routine to return the current rollover:

```
on getRollover
  if not the mouseCast then
    return(0)
  end if
  repeat with x = 48 down to 1
    if rollover(x) then
      return(x)
    end if
```

```
    end repeat
    return(0)
end
```

First, it checks to see if the mouseCast has a value. The mouseCast returns the cast number of the sprite that's under the cursor. If no sprite's there, it returns 0. Unfortunately there's no equivalent mouseSprite. Still, you can use the mouseCast to see if you're over *something*. If so, you then check to see which sprite it might be.

In 4.0, the mouseCast would return -1 if the mouse was not over a sprite. In 5.0 it returns 0 (zero). Needless to say, if you're converting a movie that depends on the return value of the mouseCast, this is something to watch out for.

I check backwards because the higher-numbered sprites overlay the lower-numbered ones, so this method starts with the topmost layer of sprites. When and if it finds a rolled-over sprite, it returns that sprite's number.

Keep in mind that the Rollover() function only checks the *bounding box* of the sprite. If you have a sprite that's shaped irregularly, like an oval, the Rollover() function still considers the sprite to be rolled over based on whether the cursor is within its bounding box (the imaginary rectangle that surrounds the irregularly shaped sprite) rather than over the actual sprite itself.

Simulating MouseEnter and MouseLeave Functions

So, now you've solved the problem of *which* sprite it is, but you're still stuck with the problem of telling whether you're entering that sprite for the first time.

For centuries, people have been clamoring to have mouseEnter and mouseLeave functions that let them know when the mouse has entered a sprite's personal space. You can reach a partial solution by using Lingo, but to reach a complete solution you really need a third-party xtra (see the next Tip).

In lieu of having the real thing, though, I'll give you a poor man's rollover detection system. I say it's a poor man's version because in our Lingo-only implementation you have to predeclare the commands you want to execute for each and every sprite. Further, you don't get the hierarchical event notification of the real xtra. As a result, it's a lot more troublesome, and limited, but hey, it's free.

Rollover Toolkit

One third-party xtra to make your life easier is the Rollover Toolkit, an author-mode version of which is provided on the CD-ROM that accompanies this book. Rather than a whole lot of involved Lingo, the Rollover Toolkit enables you to handle rollovers as easily as you would handle a mouse click.

I confess to feeling a little guilty about mentioning the Rollover Toolkit in the book, because my company puts it out, but I think I made up for it by giving you a poor man's rollover detection system of it here, even though the example here is more limited that the true Toolkit.

This book's CD-ROM contains Rollover Toolkit Xtras, documentation, and examples for Mac, Windows, and Windows 95. It is fully functional in authoring mode so you can try it out right away (but to run under a projector you must first register your copy of the xtra).

For more information, check out the README file on the CD-ROM. There's also more information in an ad in the back of this book.

The basic idea in this cheapo implementation is to keep a list of the handlers you want to execute for each sprite when the sprite is first entered or exited. Then when we see that a rollover change has occurred, the proper handler can be called. However, this entails first registering the handler you want to call, so our in-Lingo rollover system knows what to do.

By the way, you also need include the `getRollover()` function in the script, because this implementation uses it.

Initialization

It starts off by just initializing the lists:

```
on initRollovers
  global rolloverStartList
  global rolloverEndList

  set rolloverStartList =[]
  set rolloverEndList =[]
end
```

Registration

Unlike the *real* Rollover Toolkit, this cheap Lingo version requires you to declare ahead of time which Lingo command you want to execute for each of the sprites upon entering and exiting. Unfortunately, Lingo doesn't offer many ways around this.

These two functions allow you to declare a string, `whichCommand`, that it stores in a list for later retrieval in case the event occurs.

```
on registerRolloverStart whichSprite, whichCommand
  global rolloverStartList
  setAt(rolloverStartList, whichSprite, whichCommand)
end


on registerRolloverEnd whichSprite, whichCommand
  global rolloverEndList
  setAt(rolloverEndList, whichSprite, whichCommand)
end
```

The Actual Check

The `testForRollovers()` function is the part that does the dirty work. It needs to be called as often as possible, so put a call to it in your idle handler and maybe even an `exitFrame` or `enterFrame`.

The handler first gets the current rollover. If it turns out nothing has yet been rolled over, it sees if a prior rollover needs finishing up. If so, it calls the Lingo command stored for that previously (the do command executes a Lingo string).

If rollovers turn out to have changed (from one sprite to the next), this handler finishes up the old one and calls a start handler for the new one.

```
on testForRollovers
  global rolloverStartList
  global rolloverEndList
  global lastRollover

  set thisRollover =getRollover()
  if not thisRollover and lastRollover then
   do getAt(rolloverEndList, lastRollover)
   set lastRollover =0
   return
  end if

  if (thisRollover <> lastRollover) then
    if lastRollover then
      do getAt(rolloverEndList, lastRollover)
    end if
    do getAt(rolloverStartList, thisRollover)
    set lastRollover =thisRollover
  end if
end
```

Unfortunately, this doesn't address certain issues, such as sprites in adjacent frames with different cast members, different MIAWs, and other fun things like that. Further, it obligates you to perform a setup for each sprite you want to check, so it can be a bit of a pain. Still, it is serviceable.

Using the Lingo-Only Rollover Detection System

Using it requires that you put a call to initRollovers() in your startMovie handler and that you put a call to testForRollovers() in your idle handler.

Then, to register a sprite, you might do something like:

```
registerRolloverStart 2, "beginRollover(2)"
registerRolloverStart 2, "endRollover(2)"
```

where `beginRollover()` and `endRollover()` are handlers you've written to take a parameter of which sprite it is. Or, you can specify something like:

```
registerRolloverStart 2, "change2ToSmileyFace"
```

which calls that handler.

Alternatives

The alternative, as I mentioned, is the aforementioned Rollover Toolkit. It's provided on the CD-ROM that comes with this book, so you can try it out. It's fully functional in authoring mode (it just doesn't work in a projector until you register it).

I would actually suggest it, and not just from a mercenary point of view. The reason is that it allows you to use rollover functions in the very same manner that you attach `mouseUp` or `mouseDown` handlers to your sprites. If you want to be notified of a rollover event, just attach an `on startRollover` handler to your sprite, cast, frame, or movie, and the xtra automatically seeks it out and notifies it. All you have to do to handle a rollover is something like this:

```
on startRollover
  ... do your stuff here ...
end
```

No muss, no fuss! Anyway, it's provided and it *is* free for unlimited use in authoring mode, so it's worth a test drive, to say the least. Give it a shot.

Digital Video

* Playing video

* Positioning video

* Playing select part

* Using track information

Digital video in Director is usually either a QuickTime movie (Mac *or* Windows), or a Video for Windows (VfW) movie, also known as an AVI. The latter is available only on the Windows platform, thus making QuickTime the media of choice for cross-platform products.

As with everything else, you import digital video into a cast member, place that member in a sprite channel, and run the program. Unlike other cast members, digital video is always externally linked, due to the size and nature of the media.

Playing a Digital Video

Playing digital video is actually fairly simple. Each sprite can be placed in park, forward, or reverse. The property the movieRate of sprite controls this:

```
set the movieRate of sprite whichSprite to directionRate
```

The directionRate actually controls not only the direction, but the speed as well. 0 means don't play, a negative number means play in reverse, and a positive number means play forward. Normally the values you use for every-day playback are 0, 1, and –1; however, you can increase the playback speed in a given direction by using larger numbers. For instance, a fast-forward might look like this:

```
set the movieRate of sprite 12 to 2
```

Because 2 is positive, it goes forward, and because it's higher than one, it goes forward faster. The only problem is that you might see frames dropped as a result. Goodness knows computers still have enough trouble just keeping up with regular video—never mind fast-moving video.

Positioning Your Video

The video can be positioned to wherever you want it, at least on a time scale, by using ticks. That is, you can't directly say "put it on frame 15," but you could figure out where that would be in time. At 30 frames per second, frame 15 would be at a half-second position, or 30 ticks:

```
set the movieTime of sprite 12 to 15
```

You can get the expected length of the video by checking the duration property:

```
put the duration of member "homeVideo"
```

To position to the beginning is real easy:

```
set the movieTime of sprite 12 to 0
```

To position to the end would be:

```
set movieLength =the duration of member "homeVideo"
set the movieTime of sprite 12 to movieLength
```

Playing Specific Portions

To play specific portions of a digital video, you can set both the startTime and stopTime properties to be what you need them to be. For instance, to play the second minute of video:

```
set the startTime of sprite 12 to 2 * 60 * 60
set the stopTime of sprite 12 to 3 * 60 * 60
```

This will start at the two-minute point (2 * 60 seconds * 60 ticks per second) and stop at the three-minute point. If you had enabled looping, these would be the points around which it would loop.

Other Attributes

You can set all sorts of things with your video, depending on what you want as a result. With the controller of member property, for instance, you can indicate whether the video control panel appears so that the user can control the video. You may prefer to have it visible so that you don't have to manage it yourself, or you may prefer to have it hidden and control everything through custom buttons and Lingo.

You can make the video loop by setting the loop of member property to TRUE; you can indicate if it will be cropped when displayed in a smaller rectangle than it requires by setting the crop of member to TRUE; and so forth. All the various properties and commands are detailed in your Lingo manual.

Fun with Tracks

Because modern video now can support multiple tracks, Director now has support for multiple tracks built into Lingo, and can manipulate them individually.

The number of tracks can be checked easily, like so:

```
set numTracks =trackCount(sprite whichSprite)
```

Then, you can enumerate what kinds of tracks it has:

```
repeat with x=1 to numTracks
  set thisType =trackType(sprite whichSprite, x)
  put "Track "&x&": "& "&thisType
put
```

The possible types of supported tracks are #video, #sound, #text, and #music.

Incidentally, although this example checks a sprite, there are equivalent functions for checking members (when appropriate), such as trackType(member whichMember, x).

Using Tracks

You can control which tracks get used, like so:

```
on enableTrackType whichSprite, whichType, isEnabled
  set numTracks =trackCount(sprite whichSprite)
  repeat with x=1 to numTracks
    if trackType(sprite whichSprite, x) = whichType then
      set trackEnabled(sprite whichSprite, x, isEnabled)
    end if
  end repeat
end
```

This will go through and enable or disable all tracks of the specified type. To turn off all music tracks for the video in sprite channel 8, for instance, you would call it like this:

```
enableTrackType(8, #music, FALSE)
```

Retrieving Track Text

You can retrieve the text associated with a particular track—up to 32 KB worth—like so:

```
set videoText =trackText(sprite 8, 3)
put "The text for video channel 8 is "&videoText
```

In this example, track 3 is the text track. It might be that there's just one set of text for the whole video (perhaps it contains a description). Or, perhaps there's text appearing at different time points (lyrics, great for making a karaoke program!).

Keyframe Locations

Many videos use keyframing, and to get a good picture when you stop your video it's often necessary to stop on a keyframe. Keyframing is a compression method where, to conserve space, certain frames are retained in their entirety, and visual data in the intermediate frames is just the portion that has changed. If you stop a video on an intermediate frame, it's possible that it will appear incomplete. For this reason, you might want to ensure that you stop on a keyframe in order to get the best visual image available.

Using the track properties, you can see where the next or last keyframe location is (given in ticks):

```
set nextKey =trackNextKeyTime(sprite whichSprite, whichTrack)
set lastKey =trackPreviousKeyTime(sprite whichSprite, whichTrack)
```

Track Endpoints and Durations

The starting and ending times of tracks can be identified:

```
set trackStart =trackStartTime(sprite whichSprite, whichTrack)
set trackStop =trackStopTime(sprite whichSprite, whichTrack)
```

The duration is therefore easy to determine:

```
set trackDuration =trackStopTime - trackStartTime
```

Direct to Stage

On Windows, video plays direct-to-stage from the digital video driver. This means that you have to have your video in rectangular dimensions, and there's no animating on top of the video. You can put an MIAW on top, but that's about the extent of it, so plan accordingly.

Video, in general, still is not well-suited to the microcomputer environment, though it is getting better. Make sure you test accordingly, *particularly* off CD-ROM, because there can be a huge difference when running video from a hard disk and running it from CD-ROM. Video will benefit best from being transferred to the hard disk prior to playback; however, its size tends to preclude that. All you can do is cross your fingers, preload, and wait for the day that everyone has a 12X CD-ROM drive on their desktop. Sigh.

chapter 25

Audio

Although your program may seem perfectly fine without any audio, when you add sound you double the senses involved, from just sight to sight and hearing, and add another dimension to the user's experience. Whether it's background music, or just auditory clicks for when they press the mouse button, adding audio can really help establish the user's perception of your program as a high-quality, professional piece of work.

Adding audio in Director is actually relatively easy, as well it should be. Well, adding wavefile audio is relatively easy.

Understanding Wavefile Audio

Just as a quick review, *wavefiles* are recordings of waveforms. A *waveform* is a representation of sound as it appears to the listener. For instance, your favorite song on the radio is just one big waveform recording.

There are different levels of quality of wavefiles, depending on equipment and how important the quality is to you (vs. the tradeoff of size). The minimum sampling rate that is usually accepted by Director is 11.025 KHz (kilohertz), which means that one second of recording is represented by 11,025 bytes. That's 8 bits per byte (one channel). A 16-bit (2-byte) stereo (two channels) recording at the same frequency sucks up 44,100 bytes.

11.025 KHz is sort of the minimum for acceptable sound, and is better suited for voice. Many prefer 22.050 KHz for doing music, and some prefer 44.1 KHz for doing CD-quality music. At 44.1 KHz 16-bit stereo, one second of audio takes up 176,400 bytes. That's right—*one second.* That's why you have to think hard before deciding to do 44.1 KHz stereo sound for a 30-second sound clip. Such a sound clip can represent over 5 *megabytes* of space. However, it is true-life representation, as good as you're going to get. For most commercial products, though, 8-bit 22.050 KHz mono is a good quality/size compromise.

Wavefiles are stored in Windows as WAV files, and on the Mac as AIFF files (.AIF when stored on Windows). Director will play external AIF files on both platforms, whereas only Director for Windows can play WAV files, so that's something to keep in mind when doing your cross-platform planning.

Wavefile Playback

The first thing to understand about wavefile playback is that Director supports multiple sound channels. The number of channels supported depends on your equipment; however, you *usually* can safely plan on two channels, possibly more on the Mac (say, up to seven). For cross-platform general commercial development, I wouldn't count on having more than two channels available.

To verify that you have more than one channel available, you can check the multiSound property, as in:

```
if the multiSound then
  .. do something for two channels ..
else
  .. do something for one channel ..
end if
```

The default channel is channel 1. Sound will play in channel 1 unless you specify otherwise. You can have more than one channel playing at a time; for instance, you can loop a sound in channel 1 and then play a sound in channel 2. This is good for background music, say, with sound effects on top.

Director supports playback of wavefiles in two fashions: direct from disk, and from memory.

Direct from Disk

Playback direct from disk, or rather, direct from a disk file, is accomplished through the sound playFile command. Sound playfile takes the form:

```
sound playfile whichChannel, filename
```

The file name is assumed to be in the same directory as the movie. If it's not, you have to specify the full path to the file. For example:

```
sound playfile 1, the pathname & "intro"
```

where it will play whatever file it finds by that name.

To stop it, you issue the sound stop command:

```
sound stop 1
```

The benefit of sound playfile is that you can play audio recordings that are otherwise too large to fit into memory. Also, you can play recordings that are external to your movie, such as a recording that you made, or that the user had on disk.

Pitfall

Playing off disk can work either for you or against you. It can work against you because if you play off disk at the same time you're trying to load a movie or cast member off disk, you'll get conflict: a multiple contention for the same resource (the disk drive). If you plan to play audio at the same time that you want to load something, you should really have it in memory, or at least on another disk drive. Because the latter is trickier, you might just want to play from memory. To play from memory, you use `puppetSound`.

Playback from Memory

Playing wavefiles back from memory entails having the wavefiles loaded into memory, which restricts you to the smaller wavefiles. It's great for short sound effects, or even smaller wavefiles (say, 180 KB), but you're not going to easily squish a 2 MB wavefile into memory.

Playing back from memory is valuable for providing ongoing audio while you're doing disk activity, such as loading a movie or preloading other cast members.

You do so with the `puppetSound` command. It takes one of two forms:

```
puppetSound whichCastmember
puppetSound whichChannel, whichCastmember
```

If the channel isn't specified, it's assumed to be channel 1. The documented use is something like:

```
puppetSound 2, "click"
```

which will play a click sound in channel 2, but as you know from elsewhere in this book, looking up cast members by name is terribly slow. It's far better to look up the cast member once in advance and then just refer to it by number:

```
set clickSound =the number of member "click"
```

and then later (assuming `clickSound` is global):

```
puppetSound 2, clickSound
```

Lingo!

This isn't documented, but it works just fine, and is a tremendous performance booster. The only catch is that if you want to use this technique, then you *have* to specify the channel. Just doing `puppetSound clickSound` wouldn't work.

> There is a little-known difference between the two variations of the commands. It is commonly known that sounds played through the `puppetSound` command don't begin to play until the stage gets updated, so you usually are obligated to call an `updateStage` to get the sound to play. This is a common source of "Why isn't my sound playing?" questions.
>
> However, if you specify a channel, as in:
>
> `puppetSound 1, "mySound"`
>
> then the sound will begin to play right away; no `updateStage` is needed.

To cancel the sound playing, you tell it to play 0, as in:

`puppetSound 0`

or, for a specific channel (say, 2):

`puppetSound 2, 0`

Waiting for the Sound

Whether you're playing from disk or from memory, you may well want to wait for the sound to finish before moving on. This is necessary if you want to play more than one sound in a row, or simply if you want to play a sound and then go on with your program.

The way to do it is to check to see if the specified sound channel is busy, as in:

```
puppetSound 1, "intro"
repeat while soundBusy(1)
end repeat
```

This starts playing the sound and then loops around while the specified sound channel is busy.

Had a channel not been specified, as in:

```
puppetsound "intro"
repeat while soundBusy(1)
end repeat
```

the sound would not have started by the time we hit the repeat loop (because an updateStage was never issued—see last pitfall). Consequently we'd scoot right through the repeat loop. Later on, when the stage finally did get updated somewhere, the sound would start playing, leading one to think that the soundBusy() check wasn't working.

To remedy this situation, make sure you use an updateStage command if not specifying a sound channel, as in:

```
puppetsound "intro"
updateStage
repeat while soundBusy(1)
end repeat
```

Also remember that if you don't specify a channel when playing the sound, it will play by default in channel 1. You always need to specify the channel when checking to see if it's busy. There is no default to channel 1 for that. You *can* specify channel 0, but it means the same as channel 1, so all that referring to a channel 0 can do is be a point of confusion.

Disabling Wavefile Sound

Although you can use all sorts of methods to prevent sound from being heard, such as turning off the volume, the easiest is just to set Director's little internal flag, the soundEnabled, to FALSE. Director uses this to tell if sound may be played back on the machine. You can do so like this:

```
set the soundEnabled to FALSE
```

You can also treat the soundEnabled like a toggle switch, as in:

```
set the soundEnabled to not(the soundEnabled)
```

which will simply make the `soundEnabled` the reverse of whatever it was. If it was off, this will put it on, and vice versa.

Gradually Bringing In the Sound

Fading in the sound is a nice feature, and the `sound fadeIn` and `sound fadeOut` functions are great for this. They take the following forms:

```
sound fadeIn channel
sound fadeIn channel, ticks

sound fadeOut channel
sound fadeOut channel, ticks
```

If you specify *ticks*, the sound will fade in over that period of ticks. If you don't, Director will just do a default fade-in that usually works pretty well.

The fade-in command should be issued before you do the `updateStage` to start the sound, as in:

```
on playIntro
  puppetSound "intro"
  sound fadeIn 1
  updateStage
end
```

When you issue the `sound fadeOut` command, the sound immediately starts fading out, which means that you can't really "schedule" the sound to fade out; you can just make it do so. An example of the two would be:

```
on doit
  puppetsound "intro"
  sound fadein 1
  updatestage
end

on stopit
  sound fadeout 1
end
```

Pitfall

Don't try to wait for the sound to end if it's a looped sound and you just faded it out; you'll be waiting for a long time.

Setting Sound Volume

You can set the relative volume of sound for any specific channel by using the `volume of sound` property, like so:

```
set the volume of sound whichChannel to whichVolume
```

where `whichChannel` is the sound channel you want to set it for and `whichVolume` is a number between 0 (silence) and 255 (full volume). For instance:

```
set the volume of sound 1 to 128
```

which puts it at half-volume. Not only does this let you decrease the volume of a sound if you need to, but it also lets you control the relative volume between two or more channels. For instance, you may want the background music looping in channel 1 to be soft, but the sound effects or voice-over in channel 2 to be full volume.

If you don't have a special need to set the volume you should probably just leave it alone at regular (full) volume, as the user will usually have their computer set the way they want it anyway.

Understanding MIDI

MIDI is actually a specification that allows MIDI-conforming equipment to talk to each other. It actually stands for, if my memory serves me right, *Musical Instrument Digital Interface*. Instruments such as electronic pianos can support MIDI, computers can support MIDI, and if you plug your MIDI piano into a MIDI card on a computer and run your MIDI software, you can get a MIDI file out of the deal.

The drawback of MIDI is also one of its strengths. You can configure MIDI playback instruments and such and tailor the playback to your needs. Unfortunately it's sort of an arcane art. The drawback is that you can't be guaranteed that if you record a MIDI file on machine *x* that it will sound correctly when played back on machine *y*, because the two machines might have different playback configurations.

The flip side is that because it *is* such an arcane art, most people don't fiddle with their MIDI settings because most users don't understand what are called the MIDI patch tables. As a result, most everybody has the same default settings (unless they've run a program that changed it on them), and so most files usually *do* sound okay anyway.

The benefit of MIDI is its size. Whereas a wavefile is an exact representation of an audio waveform, within the limits of how it was recorded, a MIDI file is more like instructions on how to produce sound—sort of like a program. Whereas you can expend plenty of megabytes on your wavefile, MIDI files may be just a few KB, or maybe just a few 10 KB, for minutes of sound.

You can't put vocals on MIDI, or use nonstandard instrumentation easily, but that doesn't stop MIDI's popularity, because you can loop it and it makes great ongoing background music.

Understanding MCI

MCI stands for *Media Control Interface,* and it was Windows' attempt to abstract and standardize a way of playing many and varied media devices on Windows through a standard interface. In reality it actually works quite well, though it takes a little getting used to.

Not everything can be played through MCI, but many things can. I'm not even going to try to cover the MCI command set here; plenty of reference books and tutorials discuss the command set in depth. I almost would be willing to, except for one problem: MCI is not cross-platform.

Lingo Breakdown

The thing to remember is that Director only supports MCI calls on Windows. On the Mac, the calls are just ignored. This is the primary drawback of MCI. It's not a fault of Director—Director is just passing the message along. It's just the way things are, unfortunately.

On the Mac you need to use the XCMDs supplied with Director. The net effect is that there's no cross-platform solution available. The benefit is that each platform does have *a* solution. That's the tradeoff: individual solutions, but no cross-platform solution. At least it's better than having *no* solution.

Still, MCI is very useful for Windows. Although I'm sure people use it in Director to control some of the more exotic devices, the majority who use MCI probably use it to play MIDI files. The next most common use of it is to control CD audio (that is, play certain tracks on the CD with it). Both of these uses are discussed later in the chapter.

Using MCI

Using MCI is fairly simple, at least from the Lingo point of view. The syntax is:

```
MCI commandString
```

as in:

```
MCI "open myfile.wav"
```

The *commandString* part, though, is what will send you scurrying to the reference books. There's quite a little hierarchy of commands, options, extensions, and the like, and what you use depends on what you want to do. The best place to look, if you can get your fingers on one, is the *Multimedia Programmer's Reference* in the Windows SDK. This reference may also be sold separately in bookstores. In it you'll find the whole MCI command-string syntax and documentation.

MCI will return a result back to the caller. You can pick this up in the result, which you may know as the predefined place to return errors in Lingo. The result always has the result of the last Lingo call made. In the case of an MCI call, it has the result that is passed back from MCI. This may just be a handle or some other success code, or it may be an error string. If things don't seem to be working for you, make sure you put the result in the message window.

Playing MIDI Files

MIDI isn't directly supported by Director—too slippery a target. Instead you have to use MCI when on Windows, and use the MIDI Xtra for Mac on the

Macintosh (documentation describes how). All of Director's audio support is really only for wavefiles.

It has always seemed to me that one glaring omission of Director is its lack of built-in support for MIDI in the current versions (it once was available, but taken out). One reason seems to be the absolute variability of MIDI itself, in terms of patches, instrumentation, and whatever else. Still, the MCI interface makes it pretty easy.

Although some people go through the individual steps of opening up a MIDI device and all sorts of stuff, all you really need to do is just tell MCI to play the file:

```
mci "play test.mid"
```

and to stop it, just tell MCI to stop:

```
mci "stop test.mid"
```

Because you haven't specified the device type to handle the request, MCI will look at the file extension and noodle it out for itself. In this case MCI will treat the file as a MIDI file as a result of the .MID extension.

You can go ahead and play a file using this method. When it's done playing, you can just play another. The only thing is that if a file is still playing when you want to start another, then you need to explicitly stop the first one before playing the second. But that's probably good practice anyway.

Playing CD Audio Using MCI

Playing CD audio is almost as simple as playing MIDI. At a minimum you simply need to tell MCI to play the CD audio device (there needs to be one in Windows—your CD drive is assumed to be it):

```
mci "play cdaudio"
```

This will start playing the CD audio player from whatever position MCI thinks the player is at. You most likely would like some semblance of control over playback, so you probably want to be a bit more explicit. First, tell MCI that you want to refer to stuff in the TMSF format (tracks:minutes:seconds:frames), so that you can refer to track 12, time 2:05:11.

```
mci "set cdaudio time format tmsf"
```

This makes sure that your later requests to play a certain track are interpreted as just that, and not as requests to play a certain minute or second.

Then, specify which tracks you want to play. For example:

```
mci "play cdaudio from 7 to 7"
```

will play only track 7, but

```
mci "play cdaudio from 1 to 4"
```

will play tracks 1–4.

If you want to play the whole CD, you can just do mci "play cdaudio" like we covered already, but you'll probably want to position the CD player to the start of the disk first:

```
mci "seek cdaudio to start"
mci "play cdaudio"
```

And that should play from the beginning.

Getting CD Audio Information

Using the result, you can get information about the CD audio player and the disk in it. To do this, you make a status request and then look at the return value. For instance, this is how you get the number of tracks on the CD:

```
mci "status cdaudio number of tracks"
set numCDTracks =value(the result)
```

This example takes the result and stores it in the variable numCDTracks. If you're expecting a numeric result, it's necessary to run it through the value function because you need to remember that the result, as returned from

MCI, is a string. `Value` is a standard Lingo function to convert strings to numbers.

There's lots of other information you might want to get, but in particular you might be interested in the actual status of the player itself:

```
mci "status cdaudio mode"
```

And the result will be one of "not ready", "open", "paused", "playing", "seeking", or "stopped".

For the rest of the functions you should really dig up a manual on MCI from your local bookstore. You can also find information about MCI commands on the CD-ROM that comes with this book.

Duration of Playback

Director 5.0 includes new Lingo properties you can use to find out attributes of certain cast members, such as: their recording frequency (sample rate) via the `sampleRate of member` *whichMember*; the sample size (usually 8 bit or 16 bit) via the `sampleSize of member`; and whether the audio's in mono or stereo or, I guess, quadraphonic stereo, via the `channelCount of member`.

Although at first glance this information may not look particularly useful, you can put it together to determine how long your audio will play. What you do is find out how many bytes per second it takes to represent the sound, given the way that it was recorded. If you know that it takes so many bytes per second, and you know how big the recording is, you can just divide to figure out how many seconds it represents:

```
on getSoundLength whichSound
  set numChannels =the channelCount of member whichSound
  set numBits =the sampleSize of member whichSound
  set sampleRate =the sampleRate of member whichSound

  set bytesPerSecond =(numBits / 8) * sampleRate * numChannels

  set waveSize =the size of member whichSound
  set numSeconds =waveSize / float(bytesPerSecond)
  return(numSeconds)
end
```

The sample rate is how many times per second you've sampled the recording. An 8-bit sample has a 1:1 ratio of bytes to frequency, because there are 8 bits to 1 byte. If you sampled 16 bits each time, then it'd be 2 bytes per sample, so a 22,050 samples-per-second recording would consist of 44,100 bytes per second. That's *per channel*. You need to see how many channels there are.

Once you've determined the number of bytes per second in your recording, divide it into the wave size to figure out how many seconds of recording your wavefile represents. I use the float() function when I do the division, so as to get a more precise number; say, 5.83 seconds instead of just 5 without the float.

Although you should use soundBusy() for seeing if the sound is done, figuring out how long it will take lets you then figure out how many ticks that will be (just multiply by 60). In the example, if you could have ended like this:

```
set numTicks =numSeconds * 60
return(numTicks)
```

that would have returned the duration in ticks. If you know the ticks, you can then make a little progress bar or graph showing the progress through the audio, or you can schedule an animation, or prepare for your fade-out. Why, the mind just reels with the possibilities! Well, maybe not, but it's still pretty useful, and it's good to know it's there if you need it.

Animation Alternatives

Animation, at least in the score, isn't that hard to do. Through Lingo, however, you have to do a bit more work.

Depending on your background, however, you may prefer to animate through Lingo. A lot of your choice depends on how you've structured your program. Is it all done in Lingo, with nothing in the score? If so, you don't have a choice but to do your own animation. Or do you?

Doing Your Own Animation

There are many ways to animate in Lingo. At the most basic level is taking a sprite, repositioning it, changing its `memberNum` if necessary, and repeating as needed to achieve the animation.

If you're ambitious you may want to make an animation engine of sorts, a generic animation object. The only reason I didn't include one in this book is that I'm still making the perfect one; I haven't yet distilled what I want for animation services into an engine I consider done—it keeps changing, improving, mutating, and occasionally transmogrifying each time I work on it. When I'm 80 I'll probably just be finishing up and starting to write the documentation.

Actually, though, my experiences with my own engines and many others I've worked with lead me to recognize that there's no one single way of animating. Each engine is driven by the needs dictated by the application it's handling the animation for. Try to make the engine too general and it's either slow or it transforms all the way into being an animation programming language, which puts you right back where you started from!

With writing your own animations, one benefit is that you can work on techniques for synchronizing the animation with timer ticks so that it can match up with some music, voice, or sound that you might want to play. The drawback is that this is a pain to do, but it is certainly doable, and many people do their synchronization this way. Unfortunately, it's just not terribly simple.

Film Loops

But there are alternatives to writing an animation engine that you should be aware of. First, for simple animations, or even most animations, you should consider a film loop. I ignored them for the longest time but have recently become a convert and, frankly, I'm a little annoyed at having ignored them for so long. They've also greatly improved in terms of performance and usability over what they were in 4.0.

You can look up in your manuals the specifics of how to create film loops, but in general what you do is lay out in the score a sequence of frames representing your animation sequence. You then mark them off and convert them to a film loop cast member using the Create Film Loop command from the Insert menu. You can then remove the cells from the score so that they're not cluttering up your pristine work area and it doesn't have to look as though you've been using the score. What you're left with is the original cast members (the animation components) and a film loop cast member.

Stick the film loop cast member on the stage like any other cast member, and let the movie rip. It's auto-animating. It really makes things incredibly easy because you don't have to waste any time animating it yourself.

Imagine you have a button that, when clicked, will cause a different sprite on the screen to start animating. Using a film loop to do the animation, the script would look like this:

```
on mouseDown
  puppetSprite 14, TRUE
  set the membernum of sprite 14 to 20
end
```

In real life, of course, you're not going to want to do things like using literal numbers such as 14 and 20, but instead you'll want to use variables or cast member names or whatnot. (I just feel compelled to mention this every once in a while, so you don't think my programs all look like this!)

Now, if you're looping around in your frame or whatever, the sprite will automatically animate the way you laid it out in your film loop. Animation in this way becomes really easy from Lingo's point of view. Just change the member number! Because the film loop is stored in the cast, not the score, you can just treat it like any other cast member.

You can also, if you're quick on your toes, change from one film loop to another, to tie together a bunch of animated film loops. For instance, let's say you wanted to have an animation of someone walking, but by pressing a button you would make them run. To do so with film loops, make a "walking" animation loop, and a "running" animation loop, and to change from one to the other, just change the cast member of the sprite you're using.

To get the effect of moving across the screen, just keep increasing the `locH` of the sprite as you go along.

Explore film loops for all they're worth. They're simple, yet powerful in their simplicity (like all good tools). The only real drawback that comes to mind is that film loops are trickier to coordinate with audio and timer ticks. Sigh.

QuickTime Animation

The third option is to not do the animation in Director at all, but externally in something like QuickTime. The big advantage here is that audio and video synchronization is an absolute breeze. QuickTime takes care of all that for you, and does what's necessary (and what you request) to maintain that synchronization.

There are no small amount of drawbacks, though. First is that you have to actually have a way to create QuickTime animation. This means creating frames in some program and exporting them into a QuickTime movie.

Assuming you have that capability, you will find on the PC that QuickTime draws directly to the screen (through Windows). Normally you wouldn't be aware of this, but you have to be aware of it in regards to Director. By drawing directly and skipping Director's composite buffer, Director can't lay any sprites on top of the QuickTime animation or make the video background transparent.

This means that, first of all, any animation you put up will have to be rectangular. Second, the background of the video is the background that will appear on screen. Because you can't set the video sprite to be background transparent, you'll have to incorporate any screen background into the animation image when you make it. This is the part that truly sucks and also pretty much prevents you from using QuickTime for sprite animation. It effectively limits you to in-place animations.

But it's just as well, I guess, because the third problem is that QuickTime will just suck up every available CPU tick it can find. This'll drag your frame rate right into the ground for anything else going on, including moving the QuickTime video frame around. This is why, when I note that QuickTime isn't much good for sprite animation, it doesn't really matter anyway, because the performance would be awful even if QuickTime was great for sprite animation.

On the bright side, QuickTime does do a great job of synchronizing your audio and video!

I think the point to keep in mind is that QuickTime is good for what it's best at. If using it for animation, use it for your opening logo or any other standing animation where there's not a lot of other activity going on and where up-to-the-second mouse reaction isn't incredibly critical.

Of course, the same lesson can apply to any tool. Use the most appropriate one for the job, and use tools only for what they're best at.

Performance

Speed, it seems to me, provides the one genuinely modern pleasure.
Aldous Huxley (1894–1963)

In all the things we do with Director, should the speed be poor, the result will be criticized no matter how wondrous the software is otherwise, no matter how useful or technically innovative, or how beautiful the art.

In other words, if you're going to take the time to make a program, better make it fast or no one's going to bother with it.

That may be a little harsh, but it is true that slow programs win no accolades. Director has long had a reputation for being slow. I don't think it's so much that Director's slow as just the applications that have been written with it. You may consider the two to be the same, but they're not. Director is just a tool; what you do with it is up to you.

Doing something in C or assembly is no guarantee of speed either, I'll assure you. There were plenty of slow programs long before Director showed up on the scene, and there will be plenty written without the benefit of Director.

How can you avoid writing one of the slow applications? Your manuals and books cover many of the common speed issues; here we'll look at some of the less common techniques and learn how to cut some corners, or at least take them at high speed.

Preloading

Preload the heck out of everything, and crank up idle loading. Chapter 22 demonstrates this stuff; make use of it. Preloading is probably the single most effective thing you can do to speed up your program, particularly when running off of CD-ROM.

Name Indexing vs. Name Lookups

In version 4.0, any time you reference a cast member by name, such as "clickSound", Director has to look up that name in the cast tables. This happens at runtime, while your user is sitting there looking at the screen.

Now if you only have a handful of cast members in your program you may not care—but if you have hundreds or thousands?

Whenever you specify a name for a cast member, Director has to look it up and translate it to an index number *anyway*. Might as well save it some time. If there's a variation of the function that will accept the member *number*, by all means give it the number.

Director 5.0 seems to have taken some steps to resolve this problem. When you look up a cast member, Director records their locations for posterity because it has to scan through all the member names that precede the one you're looking for. That way, future references to one of those cast members will have practically the same speed as referring to them by number.

If you're so inclined, you can take advantage of this feature by making some reference to the last member in your cast. For instance, you might want to make a text field or something, call it "last member", and put it in, say, location 999 in your cast. Then, in your startMovie handler make a reference to it, as in:

```
set lastOne =the number of member "last member"
```

In the process of looking up this member, Director will have gone through all the preceding members and cached their locations. The only drawback to this technique is that it might cause a performance hit at startup time. On the other hand, everything else should just fly.

There is one good reason, however, to continue to use variables in place of the name string, and that is to make things easier for you in case you need to change the names of the cast members. By having the name assigned to a variable, you would only need to change the name in the one place where it appeared in the string (that is, where you first assigned it to a variable). If you weren't assigning it to a variable you'd have to physically change the name string in each and every place that it appeared.

That doesn't mean that you have to go around sticking little 2s and 24s in your program. Gosh, no. Although in this book I may use numbers such as:

```
set the memberNum of sprite 2 to 14
```

there's no way in real life I'd do that. You look at that 10 minutes later or 10 years later and there's no way to remember what the heck's so special about sprite 2 or what member 14 is supposed to be.

So what *do* you do? Why, you find out the member number and then assign it to a variable. Like so:

```
set clickSound =the number of member "clickSound"
```

Director will look up the item by name, which is good (absolves you from using absolute values for cast members), but assigns it to a variable (which will most likely be global if you intend to use it in more than one place). The result is the speed of indexing but the convenience and abstraction of naming.

Keep Your Media Size Down

Do you *really* need a 44 KHz, 16-bit stereo audio file? Will your users know or care, or would they be just as happy with 8-bit 11 KHz or 22 KHz?

I can appreciate the desire for quality, and suggest you go for it as long as overall performance isn't impacted. However, if you're going to start getting terrible performance just because you (or your client) insists on 44 KHz stereo, then you should seriously reevaluate your need to have that sort of quality. I can assure you that your user is going to opt for acceptable speed every time.

A program that cranks and has acceptable 22 KHz 8-bit mono audio will be praised far higher than a program that drags because it has 44 KHz 16-bit stereo audio. Before you decide to use 44 KHz 16-bit stereo, ask yourself if it is really worth making your load time eight times greater. Does that change the perception from being one of acceptable speed to unacceptable slowness?

The same applies for other media. Don't have a huge sprite where 90 percent of it is background transparent. There's no point insisting that the computer calculate more than it needs to!

The overall rule is *to keep things as small as possible while still remaining effective.* The smaller the files, the better the performance.

Another way to keep your size requirements down is to avoid bitmaps altogether and use 1-bit graphics with the `forecolor` and `backcolor` set. Creative use of Director's fill patterns can provide variety while consuming very little space internally.

Calculate What You Can in Advance

This goes hand-in-hand with the name-indexing suggestion. Calculate what you can in advance. No point doing it while you're trying to get something else accomplished.

Even something like this:

```
repeat with x=1 to count(myList)
  .. do your stuff ..
end repeat
```

It looks pretty innocuous, right? But that `count(myList)` function is getting called every time that loop cycles around. If it is critical that the loop run as fast as possible, then you don't need to be recalculating something you already know. Consider this as an alternative:

```
set numEntries =count(mylist)
repeat with x=1 to numEntries
  .. do your stuff ..
end repeat
```

Just figure it out once. If the size of the list isn't going to be changing on you, why keep asking for it?

The same applies with the name indexing. If you're going to use name indexing many times and in many instances throughout the course of the program, then do it once, stick the answer in a global variable, and refer to that from then on.

do Parsing

Lingo supports a do function, which will take a string and execute it. For instance, do `"go to the frame"` will execute the command go to the frame. Of course, people don't really use it like this; they have the string in a variable or they build it referencing variables, as in:

```
do "go to frame" & nextFrame
```

or even just:

```
do nextCommand
```

Be wary, though, of using do in time-critical functions. The command needs to be parsed and evaluated and executed. String operations take time. The less of them in critical situations, the better. If you can find an alternative, you should consider it.

Know Your Bottlenecks

Although video cards and disk drives and CD-ROM drives have improved greatly over the years, CD-ROM drives and video cards persist in being the two biggest bottlenecks you'll encounter.

Before CD-ROM was available, I would have said that your three biggest bottlenecks were video, video, and video. By video, I don't mean digital video such as QuickTime (though goodness knows that doesn't win any awards for speed either), but simply video output. If it's going to the screen, it takes time. 640×480 takes more time than 320×240, and larger animations take more time than smaller ones.

It all comes down to pixels, pixels, pixels. Actually, the video mode has a lot to do with the performance impact too, but because Director works mainly in 256-color mode we don't have to worry about the impact of the video mode so much, because 256-color mode is pretty fast.

Other video modes (like 16-color mode, or 24-bit color mode) can drag down the system in their own subtle ways. 24-bit color mode can drag things down by simple virtue of the fact that it's got three times as much data involved (versus 256-color's 8 bits). 16-color mode, on the other hand, has much less data, but because of the internal representation of the data, and the way that data has to be provided to the video card, makes it much less popular than it ought to be. Of course, this lack of popularity isn't helped by the fact that the 16-bit palette is fairly unchangeable.

256-color mode, on the other hand, is a very easy and fast video mode to program (internally; nothing you have to worry about as a user of Director). It provides reasonable results in an uncomplicated fashion, which is why Macromedia chose it as the primary video mode for Director.

Still, the difference between animating a 100×200 image or a 200×200 image is 20,000 pixels. Shooting for 30 frames per second, that's 600,000 bytes of difference. If your CD-ROM moves 320,000 bytes per second, you can start to see a problem.

Compression and other such things make this not such an even equation, but you can see how you can run up against some real limitations of hardware.

Nowadays I'd say CD-ROM beats video for the slowness prize. It can be 10–30 times slower than your hard drive. That's why it's *so* important to get your fingers on a CD-ROM burner and test your program on it. You might be shocked at the difference.

Using CD-ROM is where preloading becomes so important, as does keeping the media size down. When I was talking about the tradeoff between 22 KHz 8-bit mono and 44 KHz 16-bit stereo, I wasn't kidding. There's 8 times the difference in file sizes between the two. A 200,000-byte 22 KHz mono wavefile will take 1,600,000 bytes if recorded at 44 KHz 16-bit stereo (twice the frequency *and* twice the sample size *and* twice the channels). 200,000 or 1,600,000—who cares? The CD-ROM has plenty of room.

Well, *you* should care. The CD-ROM *does* have plenty of room, but the transfer bus does not. If a 2X CD-ROM transfers at 320 KB bytes per second, the difference between a 200,000 byte transfer and a 1,600,000 byte transfer is the difference between less than one second of response time or five seconds to do the same thing. That can be the dividing line between the perception of acceptability and the perception of unacceptable slowness.

Of course, you probably won't be preloading a 1.6 MB sound file, but even if you're using smaller sizes, the ratio and concerns remain the same.

Choose Your Media Judiciously

Think hard about how much room you truly can afford to spend on the CD-ROM. Remember, *what goes on must come off.* The CD-ROM is your friend in terms of space, your enemy in terms of speed.

Even if you're not producing on CD-ROM the same considerations hold true for network development, Internet development, and just plain old hard disk development. The scales and impact may vary, but good development practices are always valuable.

part V

Extending Director

chapter 28

Extending Director with Third-Party Externals

As mentioned in the beginning of this book, one feature that makes Director useful as a development tool is that you aren't restricted only to the functionality that Macromedia implemented in Director. Director can tap into external DLLs and XCMDs written by third parties (those other than Macromedia). These are called *xtras* and, in a former life, *xobjects*.

The xobjects are what were used in Director versions 4.0 and previous. From 5.0 on, it's supposed to be just xtras, although you can still write xobjects.

Xobjects

With Director 5.0 being relatively new, there are only a handful of xtras available, most of which are distributed on the Director 5.0 CD-ROM. What *is* available, though, is a huge collection of xobjects written for Director 4.0.

Some of these are commercially available. Some you may have already. You may have projects that you're working on that use a particular xobject. You may have found a shareware or freeware xobject that does some little thing you need. So, even though they are technically "obsolete," it makes a lot of sense to review their use here.

Using a 4.0 Xobject

Using an xobject entails opening it up, creating an instance of it (just like an object), making calls to it, disposing of it when you're done, and then closing it.

I'll go through the steps of using a 4.0 xobject. For this example I'll use an xobject I wrote last year: GETDATE.DLL, which is included on the *Lingo! CD-ROM*. This is only for Windows, so you Mac users can just hum along. I'm not trying to be facetious; the same stuff applies regarding use, but I just never happened to have written a Mac version of GETDATE.

I'm using this particular xobject as an example, not only because it's useful, but because it's about as basic an xobject as you're going to find. It has a New and a Dispose function, and the actual call to do the work.

For all xobjects, obviously, you should read and follow the documentation that comes with them in order to use them properly.

Opening the Xobject

To open the xobject, you use the openxlib function. It's syntax is this:

```
openxlib filename
```

The file is assumed to be in the current directory. This isn't always a good assumption, so you might want to provide an explicit path name to the xobject.

If it's in the same directory as the projector, you can use the Lingo `the pathname` to help you:

```
openxlib the pathname & filename
```

Because the corollary of `openxlib` is `closexlib`, and you have to provide the path name for that as well, I find it's usually easier to just put the file name in a variable and then refer to *that:*

```
set getdateFileName =the pathname & "getdate"
openxlib getdateFileName
```

You can, and should, issue these from the message window, just to try it out.

You can see if the xobject opened by using `showxlib`, which will list all the open xobjects:

```
showxlib
-- XLibraries:
-- "e:\macromed\director\xobjs\getdate\getdate"
```

You may have other xobjects or xtras in this list as well, but the important thing is that the xobject that you asked for be in it. Actually, had Director not found it, it would have put up an error message, so you would have known there was a problem long before.

Initializing the Xobject

Using `openxlib` just physically opens the file. It doesn't make the routines available to you *just* yet. For that, you need to initialize it, or make an instance of it, just like we talked about with the regular objects.

To do this, you need to call the `mNew` routine in the object. You should know, however, that certain xobjects will accept or require parameters for `mNew`, so you need to check the xobject's documentation for examples and information.

Calling `mNew` takes the form:

```
set xobjVariable =xobjName(mNew)
```

where *xobjName* is the file name (not the whole path, just the file name) of the xobject, and the *xobjVariable* is where you want to save the object ID, as described in Chapter 12, "Objects." For instance, use the following to initialize GetDate:

```
set getdateObj =getdate(mNew)
```

I usually name my object ID variables as *something*Obj, but that's just my preference. If you plan to use it outside of the present handler, though, you should make sure it's a global variable or a property or something.

Calling the Xobject

At this point you're ready to call whatever function the xobject has that you're interested in. I can't help you too much here except to show you the general process—you need to consult the documentation for the xobject to see what's available. The general syntax, however, is:

```
set returnVariable =xobjVariable(mFunction, optionalParams)
```

For instance, use this to get the date from GetDate:

```
set currentDate =getdateObj(mGetDate)
```

In case you're wondering, GetDate returns the current date in the form YYYYMMDD, which is useful for applications that are used in more than one country when you need to be able to get the date back out in some standard format. If your program tests for a short date of, say "12/31/96", in U.S. format, it wouldn't be very successful in Europe where the month and day are reversed ("31/12/96"). For this reason it's better to convert to a standard format and check *that*, which is where GetDate comes in.

Anyway, it's pretty straightforward. The one thing to note is that when called, you use xobjVariable(mFunction). The xobjVariable is the object ID gotten back from the call to mNew.

mNew is one of only two times that we use the file name to make the call. The only other time is mDescribe. The rest of the calls, including mDispose, use the object ID variable.

Listing the Xobject's Functions

If you lost, or just want to verify, the documentation, you can check the function table of the xobject. This tells you what the xobject offers in the way of function calls, though the documentation within it varies with the xobjects. Some may be thorough, some nonexistent. Let's look at GetDate's:

```
getdate(mDescribe)
-- Penworks XObject Utilities
GetDate
I       mNew            --Creates a new instance of the XObject
X       mDispose        --Disposes of XObject instance
I       mGetDate        --Returns a long numeric date (YYYYMMDD)
```

The top command (`getdate(mDescribe)`) was issued, and the rest is output from the call. It provides a comment at the top, that it is one of Penworks Corporation's XObject utilities, then provides the name of the xobject (GetDate) and lists the function.

To the left of the functions is a list of return value types. "I" means that it returns an integer, "X" means no return value. Others you might see are "S" for string, "P" for a picture handle, "O" for an object handle, and "V" for a variable amount of variables.

If there were more than one letter listed, such as "IISI", the remainder to the right would be the types of parameters it accepted. "IISI" means a return value of integer, and accepting three parameters, an integer, a string, and finally another integer.

Disposing of the Xobject

Disposing of your xobject instance is simple. The format is:

```
xobjVariable(mDispose)
```

For instance, use the following to dispose of GetDate:

```
getdateObj(mDispose)
```

Always, *always,* make sure you dispose of the xobject. If your program stops in authoring mode, dispose of it from the message window, but make sure you get rid of it. Failing to dispose of the xobject might crash your system, depending on what the xobject does, and opening up the same one multiple times during testing without ever disposing of any will at least chew up memory until finally Director itself crashes.

Closing the Xobject

Finally, when done, you need to close the file. This is like `openxlib`, but in reverse. Give the same file name that you did to `openxlib`. If you used a variable, you can just supply that:

```
closexlib getdateFileName
```

Developing a 4.0 Xobject

Any future development should really be done with xtras. Because 5.0 *accepts* xobjects, however, you might get a hankering to *develop* xobjects.

To do so you'll need the xobject Developers Kit. The Windows version was included on the Director 4.0 CD-ROM. I don't think you'll be able to acquire it anymore unless you find a copy of 4.0 or someone who will part with their xobject Developers Kit. The Mac one had to be ordered separately from Macromedia. The kits are not anything like each other.

Each kit has some documentation. Beyond that, the only other writing I'm aware of regarding the kits has been in the *Lingo User's Journal,* which has run articles at various times about developing with each of the kits. You can order the back issues if you need them; more info on the *Journal* is in an ad in the back of this book.

However, as mentioned, you should really look to use the 5.0 xtras. No point in pursuing obviously obsolete technology if you can avoid it.

Xtras

Xtras are new to Director in 5.0. Internally they share a common programming interface (much more common, that is, than the 4.0 xobjects did), and they are much more likely to be cross-platform than xobjects ever were. They *cannot* be run from 4.0, however, so keep that in mind.

There are different kinds of xtras, and they do widely different things. Some are *Tool Xtras* that become author-time tools. Some are *Sprite Xtras* that become usable custom-behaving sprites. Some are *Transition Xtras* that provide custom transitions. Finally some, like the Rollover Toolkit for detecting rollovers, extend the Lingo language and are called *Lingo Xtras*.

Further, some may be usable on more Macromedia products than just Director. For instance, a Transition Xtra might be usable in Director *and* in Authorware.

Using a 5.0 Xtra

Installing xtras is very easy, and directions come with the xtras, but installation usually just involves placing the xtra in the XTRAS subdirectory or folder under the Macromedia directory. Then, when you next open Director, that xtra will be available. Some, such as Tool Xtras, are available from the xtras pull-down menu. Others, such as Lingo Xtras, can have their commands always available, once installed. You can see the loaded xtras by using the showXlib command as described earlier in the section "Opening the xobject."

Using xtras usually requires no extra work on your part. Many Lingo Xtras automatically make the Lingo extensions part of Director. Use the new Lingo commands like any other. The only thing is that they may not show up in the help system, so you'll just have to be mentally aware of what's a Director Lingo command and what came from an xtra.

The only reason you have to keep track of which aren't Director commands is that if you get too used to xtras, you'll think they are part of the language. You don't want to make a projector and ship it and forget that you needed to ship the xtra along with it.

Some xtras have separate versions for authoring mode and projectors, and some have to be specifically purchased only for projectors. Others, such as the Rollover Toolkit, can be used in either, but require a special key file before they'll function in a projector. Make sure you have all the necessary files before you ship a project that uses an xtra.

Some Lingo xtras may have to be opened in the manner of xobjects, that is, using `openxlib`, so you may want to read the xobject part of this chapter in case you happened to have skipped over it. Most, however, will probably just incorporate their commands into Lingo automatically, so you won't have to worry about opening them specifically. The extended Lingo'll just appear to be like part of the original Lingo language.

There *ought* to be documentation with the xtra describing its use, so look for it. More often than not your biggest problem might be expecting it to be installed when in reality you might not have it in the proper xtras subdirectory. That's about the extent of it. They're really easy to use.

Developing a 5.0 Xtra

Now, developing is a totally different story altogether. Writing your own xtra is not a task for the squeamish. To begin with, you should have your C/C++ programming up to date.

4.0 Windows xobjects were really just glorified DLLs. You had to conform to a particular calling convention and lay out your resource file in a particular way, but that was about the extent of it.

The 5.0 xtra, in order to achieve a cross-platformish, multiple-product sort of existence, utilizes the new Macromedia Open Architecture (MOA), which is an *application programming interface*, or really more of a programming framework.

Not only won't I cover MOA development in depth here, I won't even attempt to cover it in shallow. There's a huge amount of documentation that goes with it when you get the XDK, which is available on the Director 5.0 CD-ROM.

You can write Lingo Xtras, Tool Xtras, Sprite Xtras, and Transition Xtras with it; I described these briefly earlier. There's quite a learning curve that goes with using MOA, and it might look fairly formidable when you first crack open the documentation, but it is worth it to you to persist.

If you've written 4.0 xobjects, all I can say is that 5.0 xtras are just on a whole other plane. It's more akin to working with, say, Microsoft's MFC for the first time, though not quite as extensive. The best thing to do is to get the XDK and read through the documentation, then take the sample xtras and try changing them around. Chances are that you can find one that's close enough to what you want to do that you can modify it to meet your needs without having to go through the whole development process from scratch.

Useful Third-Party Xtras

At the time of this writing, which is just about the same time as the release of 5.0, there were but a few 5.0 xtras available. This is mainly because only a limited handful of developers had early releases of 5.0 in order to do advance work on xtras for commercial release.

With the release of 5.0, however, and the unleashing of xtra technology on the masses of developers, we should see many more xtras come onto the market. Also, the advance developers had the xtra development kit for only a few months. Some xtras simply required more time than that to create and weren't available for release at the time of Director 5.0's ship date, but should be available shortly after the release of Director 5.0.

All the xtras mentioned here are available on the Director 5.0 CD-ROM, so you may already have them in your possession. They may require that you register or license them for distribution, so be sure to read the documentation that goes with them.

Database Xtra

FileFlex, from Component Software, lets you read and write dBASE files. Whatever database you use, chances are that there's a feature or a utility available to get it into dBASE format and, if so, you can access it from within Director using FileFlex.

FileFlex has been around for some time, so it has quite a bit of a track record to go with it. For complete information on FileFlex and Component (they keep busy over there), visit Component Software's Web site at `http://www.component-net.com`.

Printing Xtra

The printing xtra of choice is PrintOMatic, which makes up for all of Director's failings in printing. Allowing you to print text, graphics, and most any cast member, it even has features allowing print previews.

Again, this is a product that was around prior to 5.0 and is pretty well tested and fleshed out. There are some more limited printing xobjects that are around, notably EZPrint, but to my knowledge they're not yet ported to xtras, whereas PrintOMatic is. PrintOMatic can be ordered from gray matter design, which you can reach at `http://www.gmatter.com`.

Rollover Xtra

Rollovers, long the bane of Director developers, are now as easy to use as checking for mouse clicks. The Rollover Toolkit from Penworks Corporation lets you stick on `startRollover` handlers on any sprite or cast member (or frame, etc.) and be notified of rollover events. Likewise there's one for on `endRollover`, and other useful rollover functions as well.

Unlike the other two xtras, this is new to 5.0 mainly because it simply wasn't possible to do this sort of thing before the advent of MOA. Penworks Corporation, however, has been around since 1991, and isn't planning on disappearing anytime soon.

All versions (Windows, Windows 95, and Macintosh) are on the CD-ROM for this book. The Mac version didn't quite make it in time for the Director 5.0 CD-ROM, but because it's included on the CD here, you're in luck. You can also always download the current versions from the Penworks web site at `http://www.penworks.com`, or from the Macromedia forum on CompuServe.

MPEG Xtra

MpegXtra lets you play full-screen MPEG video on Windows in Director. Available from Tabuleiro da Baiana Multimedia in Brazil, it too is a new-for-5.0 xtra.

You can check out the TBM web site at `http://www.tbaiana.com` for more information.

Sound Xtra

Sound Xtra lets you play *and* record sounds to and from disk from within Director. *Very* cool. You can do AIFF files on the Mac and WAV files under Windows, in everything from 8-bit 11 KHz mono to 16-bit 44 KHz stereo. Further, it's asynchronous, meaning that the world doesn't stop while this stuff is going on (meaning, you can run a meter, or animate, or respond to clicks while it's working).

Sound Xtra can be ordered from Gray Matter Design, which you can reach at `http://www.gmatter.com`.

All Available on the Director CD-ROM

As I mentioned, all these are available on the Director 5.0 CD-ROM, either under Xtras or the Partners directories, as are some others not mentioned here. You should definitely go exploring; there's a lot of neat add-ons in there!

Extending Your Audience with Shockwave

The final frontier for Director movies nowadays is the Internet's World Wide Web. The Director technology for playing back movies on the Web is called *Shockwave.* This new technology incorporates a runtime engine for Director into your favorite browser. The result is multimedia on the Web, replete with audio and animation.

Shockwave is available as a plug-in for Netscape 2.0, and it is also scheduled to be incorporated into other browsers, such as Microsoft Internet Explorer, CompuServe's CIMs, AOL/NaviSoft, and SGI WebForce. The latest plug-ins are available for free at Macromedia's Shockwave page (`http://www.macromedia.com/Tools/Shockwave`).

With the appropriate plug-in installed, you just need to visit any page that offers Shockwave content, and the Web will never seem quite the same again.

How Shockwave Works

To play a Director movie outside of Director itself, the movie first needs to be bound to a runtime engine. When you create a projector, you're really incorporating the movie into a file along with the runtime engine.

Although creating a projector automatically adds some 600 KB to the final product (because of the runtime engine), you know that the size of a .DIR file itself varies with the amount of media that you incorporate. It can range anywhere from a few KB to many megabytes.

Shockwave is pretty ingenious in its simplicity. What Macromedia did was create a plug-in version of the runtime engine. In other words, with the Shockwave plug-in, Netscape now becomes the Director runtime engine. When you go to a Web page with a Director movie on it, the movie is automatically downloaded to your hard drive (it resides in the Netscape cache), and is then executed automatically by the plugged-in runtime engine. With Netscape running the movie on your desktop, you have effectively achieved multimedia on the Web.

By making the runtime engine a separate plug-in, only the movie has to be downloaded to get Shockwave to work. Macromedia actually went further and created *Afterburner*, which is a compression utility for Director files. What you put up on the Web is not a raw Director file, but an "afterburned" one. Depending on the type of media included (graphics, audio, etc.), you can, in some cases, reduce the size of the Director movie by as much as 60 percent. The Shockwave plug-in will automatically decompress the movie to play it.

Powers and Limitations

Most of your Director programs can be moved to Shockwave with little or no changes. It's important to keep the *size* of the file down so that it will transfer quickly, but *technically* there's no reason why most Director programs won't play as they are. As a result, most anything you can do in Director you can do on the Web.

For security reasons, however, some things are not available in Shockwave. For instance, Shockwave will let you use an xobject or xtra only if it already has been installed on your hard drive. This is to prevent some deviant developer with a warped sense of entertainment from spaghetti-izing someone's file system. If your Shockwave Web page requires the use of a particular xobject or xtra, then you'll just have to make a link or something to let the user download and install the file first. I suspect most users won't want to do this unless you have a particularly compelling Web site, so xobject and xtra use will probably end up being kept to a minimum.

At the time of this writing, Shockwave for Director 5.0 was not yet available, although it might be by the time you read this. It's possible that some of these limitations have been lifted, so be sure to visit Macromedia's site at `http://www.macromedia.com/Tools/Shockwave` for the latest developer's version of Shockwave.

Also, Shockwave does *not* support MIAWs (Movies In A Window). You can still chain from one movie to another, though.

Linked media and QuickTime are also not available, although future versions of Shockwave are expected to support them.

Creating a Shockwave Program

Although it's relatively easy to create a Shockwave application, the hard part is to create a *small* one. More than anything else, it's important that the user not experience an untoward delay when going to display your Web page.

Between eliminating the need to download the runtime engine, and compressing the original movie itself, Shockwave files (.DCR files) can be as small as 2 KB or 4 KB—if you're very conservative in what you do. Full programs are best if kept to under 100 KB, and small utilities (launchers, logos, and so on) are better if kept to under 20 KB, because most people are still working through 14.4 or 28.8 modems.

Of course, what's optimal and what's typical aren't necessarily the same thing. There are plenty of 300 KB, 600 KB, even 900 KB Shockwave programs out there. There must be a strong perceived value, however, before a user on a 14.4 modem is going to sit still for a 900 KB download.

Let's defer the subject of creating small applications for the moment, though, and just look at the mechanics of developing the Shockwave application. First, become familiar with the Shockwave section at the Macromedia Web site (`http://www.macromedia.com/Tools/Shockwave`). From there you can read tech notes, see demos, and download the developer tools such as Afterburner.

As mentioned earlier, xobjects and xtras are verboten, so you'll have to make do without them. After you get your Director movie built and tested, you need to create the compressed (afterburned) version of it. To do so, you first need to download the Afterburner utility from the Macromedia Web site. It's a self-extracting executable, so run it in a temporary directory, because it will create the setup program files, including setup.exe, which you then run to do the actual installation.

When Afterburner is run, it simply puts up a filespec dialog box to let you pick the Director .DIR file that you want to compress. Select your file, and Afterburner will compress it and place the compressed .DCR version in the same directory as the .DIR file. The .DCR file is what you will be wanting to put up on your Web site.

Posting a Shockwave Program

Now that you have a .DCR file, you need to incorporate it into your Web page somehow. You do this by means of an HTML <EMBED> tag. The general format is `<EMBED WIDTH=x  HEIGHT=y  SRC="myfile.dcr">`. The width and height specifications are the sizes that you specified for your movie in the Movie Info dialog box.

One problem with embedding Shockwave files in this manner is that not everyone has a Netscape browser, or one that recognizes the <EMBED> tag.

Some users may have an older version of Netscape that interprets <EMBED> differently from Netscape 2.0. (In older versions of Netscape, <EMBED> specified an OLE link.) Also, some users might have Netscape 2.0 but not the Shockwave plug-in.

Browsers not supporting <EMBED> will simply ignore it, so that's not a serious problem, apart from the fact that for those users the Shockwave program won't work. For the other problems, some workaround needs to be achieved. The current technique is to stick the <EMBED> tag inside a LiveScript (the Netscape Navigator 2.0 programming language) routine. Further, using a <NOEMBED> tag gives a consolation image to those not fortunate enough to have the latest in Netscape technology. The overall result looks like this:

```
<SCRIPT LANGUAGE="LiveScript">
<!-- Hide from unenabled browsers.
document.write( '<EMBED WIDTH=150 HEIGHT=150 SRC="myapp.dcr">');
<!-- Done hiding -->
</SCRIPT>

<NOEMBED>
<IMG WIDTH=80 HEIGHT=80 SRC="toobad.jpg">
</NOEMBED>
```

With this method, users properly equipped will see your Shockwave application. Those with Netscape 2.0 but not the plug-in will see a "broken" icon, and all others will see the alternative image specified in the <NOEMBED> tags.

Configuring Your Server for Shockwave

In order for Shockwave to operate properly on your server, your server must be properly configured to handle the MIME types. There are a variety of ways to do this, depending on the type of server you have, but the general thrust of it is to set a BINARY action for files of suffix .DCR (compressed Director movie), .DIR (uncompressed Director movie), and .DXR (uncompressed, but protected, Director movie). The MIME type for these should be *application/x-director*. More information on configuring specific server types is available from the Macromedia Web site.

In some ways, this may be the most frustrating part of working with Shockwave, because it may be the only portion that's out of your control. Should you have your own server on site, you can do your own configuration, so it shouldn't be a problem, but if you have to rely on an Internet Service Provider to manage access to your Web site, you may find yourself at their mercy. If your Internet service provider is unresponsive, it's possible you may have trouble getting your changes made. On the other hand, as more and more people develop for Shockwave, this should become less and less of a problem, because the server might be set up to handle Shockwave already.

Upload Your Shockwave Movie and Try It

Of course, the next thing is to upload your movie and take it for a spin. If you have broken icons, the most likely reason is that you yourself don't have the Shockwave plug-in. (Don't forget that!) Also, make sure that you have the <EMBED> tags correct. If the file's coming down as text, make sure your server has the MIME types set properly.

Because not everyone has Netscape 2.0 or the Shockwave plug-ins, it might be nice to include hot-buttons to the Netscape and Macromedia Shockwave sites, making it easy for your users to download the stuff themselves. Many developers also create Shockwave-specific pages, to minimize the unintentional visits by non-Shockwave users. However, in time, even this might be unnecessary.

Lingo Extensions

Lingo has a few new commands to support Shockwave. These are typically asynchronous commands. *Asynchronous commands* request that an operation be performed, and then they return without waiting for the operation to complete. When the call returns, the operation may not have completed yet—in fact, it may not have even begun. You have to check the status yourself later through one or more mechanisms. Asynchronous commands are commonly used in multitasking environments where you can't expect every task to drop what it's doing just to respond to you. In short, put in your request and check back later to see if it's done.

Checking status under Shockwave Lingo is done via the netDone() function. This will return FALSE if there is an operation in progress. At first glance, it may seem that this limits you to only one operation at a time. However, you can also have Lingo return a value that is an ID number for the last operation started, and you can use that ID at any point to check if that particular operation has completed. That function is getLatestNetID().

For example:

```
... start operation A
set firstStatusID =getLatestNetID()
... start operation B
set secondStatusID =getLatestNetID()

repeat while not netDone(firstStatusID)
-- twiddle thumbs
end repeat
-- At this point the first one has completed,
-- but not necessarily the second one.
```

So, let's look at these operations we're starting. Lingo lets you do this:

```
getNetText uri
```

This requests the retrieval of a text resource from a *URI* (universal resource indicator, as in an http: address). You have to use netDone() to monitor for completion, at which point the text can be retrieved via the netTextResult() call, like this:

```
getNetText "http://www.myserver.com/mytext.txt"
repeat while not netDone()
end repeat
put netTextResult into field "info field"
```

When you begin a new operation, Director discards any existing netTextResult() for space reasons, so you should retrieve whatever text you're expecting before starting a new operation. (That is, do it as soon as you find that the call to netDone() succeeds.)

The Lingo `preloadNetThing(uri)` function invokes a Netscape preload to drag the `uri` item off the Net and stick it in the disk cache. This is good for downloading movies, graphics, or audio ahead of time, as it'll get the stuff onto the hard disk for quick operation. You have to use `netDone()` to monitor for completion. Keep in mind that the user's cache may be very small (or nonexistent), and that it can be purged at any time.

For example:

```
preloadNetThing "http://www.myserver.com/nextmovie.dxr"
```

Through the `gotoNetMovie(uri)` function you can chain off to another Director movie somewhere else on the net. The current program will continue until it's had a chance to retrieve and start the new program. Issuing more than one request (that is, for a different movie) will cancel the previous request and begin work on the new one.

Some people have used this function to create a Shockwave launcher that takes you to other Shockwave movies on the Net. Those launchers have names and URLs of other movies in them, and they use `gotoNetMovie()` to invoke them.

If you have a large Shockwave application you want to run, another good use is to create a tiny movie of the same dimensions as the real one and put *that* up on the Net. You can then provide some initial feedback to the user, keeping them entertained while you use `gotoNetMovie()` to launch the big one.

The `gotoNetPage(uri)` command will switch you over to a different Web page. Actually, it'll open up any URI, Web page or other MIME type. This is good for making your own little surf-cruiser. Many people use this to serve as a dispatcher on their home page (using the interactivity of Director to take them to another page at the same site).

Not only will `gotoNetMovie()` load a Shockwave movie elsewhere on the Web, but it has the added benefit of retaining all the internal global variable values and properties, and lets those values carry over into the new movie. `gotoNetPage()` does not work this way,

> however. When you go to a new page, it's like starting fresh, and there's no such persistence of variables over to the new page.
>
> One feature that's conspicuously absent, but highly requested, is the capability to write data out, so that information can be saved and then retrieved at the next visit. Although currently unavailable, it's high on Macromedia's list to implement soon in one fashion or another.

You can use `netError()` to check for the status of your operation requests. It returns an empty string while the operation is in progress, an `"OK"` string if it succeeded, or the error message if not. Also, if you've not put in any asynchronous operations yet, it'll return the string `"none"`.

Backward Compatibility with Director 4.0

Because the Lingo functions I just described aren't in Director 4.0, you'll need to use a shared cast file that emulates them. Such a file is available on the CD-ROM with this book.

It is a SHARED.DIR, which is how Director 4.0 incorporated shared cast members. You use this for testing locally, but do not upload it to your site, as it will override the true functions that are present in the plug-in runtime playback engine.

Lingo Restrictions

You're not allowed to use the following commands under Shockwave (for the most part, these are all disabled for security restrictions, as opposed to technical limitations):

- ♣ `openResFile`, `closeResFile`. You can't open external resource files.

- ♣ `open window`, `close window`. You can't open MIAW windows. This ability was eliminated for technical reasons rather than security reasons, I suspect, because it involves child windows.

- ✣ `importFileInto`. You can't import text into and therefore change the movie.

- ✣ `saveMovie`. You can't save the movie back out.

- ✣ `printFrom`. You can't print the contents of the stage, or a range of stage frames.

- ✣ `open`. You can't run external applications.

- ✣ `quit`, `restart`, `shutdown`. You can't reboot your machine, and so on.

- ✣ `mci`. You can't issue MCI commands. Note that this prevents you from using MIDI (which is done through MCI) or anything else you have that might rely on MCI.

Various other file functions are unavailable as well, to reduce the danger of meddling.

Creating Shockwave-Sized Movies

Now that you know how to make a Shockwave movie, the trick is to make a *good* one. I won't presume to discuss visual design here, but I will talk about size and performance.

The first equation is that, as far as downloading is concerned, the smaller the file, the shorter the transfer time. When making a Shockwave application, don't think CD-ROM—think floppy. In fact, think single-sided, single-density floppy. Get that critter down in size—*way* down. Test it through a 14.4 modem and see how acceptable performance is.

Use all the tricks mentioned in Chapter 27, "Performance." In addition, keep sound to a minimum (get small samples and loop them), use 1-bit bitmaps if any at all, make use of fills and patterns, and set the forecolor and backcolor through Lingo rather than having colors in the bitmap.

Finally, keep the stage size down. If you're using bitmaps, see how small you can get the playback window and still have it look acceptable, and then try to get it smaller still. Do you really need a 640×480 screen? Most of it probably can't be seen anyway, because Netscape itself takes up a good chunk of the user screen. How about 320×240? If you can live with 320×240, can you live with 160×120? That's one-fourth the original size. Every pixel counts, so do your best to be conservative.

As mentioned earlier, one trick is to make a small-sized movie (that is, small in size to download, *not* in terms of screen dimensions) to keep the user entertained while the larger one loads in the background. This is highly recommended if you must have something of larger-than-desired download size. Another trick that some people use is to split up their work into parts and time the duration of doing a preload of a Web resource via `preloadNetThing()`. If it takes over a certain amount of time, you might choose to forego certain features with the understanding that the user has a slow modem or machine. Of course, regular network delays may affect your results, so keep that in mind too.

Index

G

H

handlers, 62-66
of ancestors (objects), 169-171
calling
in objects, 159-160
for rollovers, 284-285
event, 34-35, 62-63
cast members, 36
debugging scripts, 40-41
frames, 37
movie scripts, 37-38, 43-45
multiple movie scripts, 43-45
overriding hierarchy, 38-40
score scripts, 41-42
sprites, 35-36
objects, 150-156
personal, 63
predefined, 45
subroutines, 63-66
variables
global, 56-60
local, 55-56
handles (objects), 156
hard drives, performance, 320
**hierarchies, overriding event handling,
38-40**
hypertext, stacks overview, 246-247

I-J

idle loading cast members, 274-278
cancelIdleLoad( ) function, 277
finishIdleLoad( ) function, 277
idleLoadDone( ) function, 276-277
idleLoadMode property, 274
idleLoadPeriod property, 275
idleLoadTag property, 275-276
idleReadChunkSize property, 277-278
idleLoadDone( ) function, 276-277
idleLoadMode property, 274
idleLoadPeriod property, 275
idleLoadTag property, 275-276

idleReadChunkSize property, 277-278
idles, 195-196
cycles
availability, 198-199
limiting, 199-200
performance, impact on, 197
uses, 197-198
infinite loops, 96
initializing
arrays, 258-259
lists, 139
property, 144, 249
rollover, 283
xobjects, 325-326
**Insert menu commands (Create Film
Loop), 309**
installing xtras, 329-330
installMenu( ) function, 217
instantiation, 156
Internet
performance, 320
programming considerations, 22-23
Shockwave, 335-336
*backward compatibility with
Director 4.0, 343*
configuring servers for, 339-340
creating applications, 337-338
*embedding applications in Web pages,
338-339*
Lingo command restrictions, 343-344
Lingo functions, 340-343
overview, 336
performance/size, 344-345
security limitations, 336-337
uploading/testing movies, 340
items in lists, 138

K-L

keyframes, 291

**Lingo versus scores, programming consid-
erations, 25-27**

mouseLeave function, simulating, 281-283
   calling handlers, 284-285
   initializing lists, 283
   registering commands, 283
   Rollover Toolkit, 282, 285
   testForRollovers( ) function, 283-284
movie in a window, *see* **MIAW**
movie scripts, 43-45
   event handling, 37-38
movies, *see* **MIAW**
MpegXtra, 332
multi-platform capabilities, advantages of Director, 16
multiple casts, programming considerations, 29
multiple channels, wavefile playback, 294-295
multiple movie scripts, 43-45
multiple movies, programming considerations, 27-28
multiple parameters, 69-71
multiple stacks (property lists), 248-249
   closeStacks( ) function, 251
   error checking, 252
   initializing, 249
   pop( ) function, 250-251
   push( ) function, 249-250
   testing, 251-252
multiple tracks, digital video, 290-292
Musical Instrument Digital Interface, *see* **MIDI**

N

name constants, symbols, 129-130
name indexing versus name lookups, performance, 314-316
naming
   cast members, 156-157
   submenu items, 213-214
   variables, 51-52, 54
nested loops, 96-97
   two-dimensional arrays, 263-264
netDone( ) function, 341

netError( ) function, 343
netTextResult( ) function, 341
networks, performance, 320
new( ) function
   arrays, 258-259
   random lists, 241
NOT expressions, 81
null strings, 203
numbers
   random
      generating, 234-235
      nonrepeating, 239-243
      randomSeed, testing with, 238-239
      range, determining, 236-238
      uses, 234
   variables, naming, 52
   working within property lists, 146
numToChar( ) function, 203

O

objects
   anatomy, 155
   ancestors, 163-164
      handlers, 169-171
      properties, 167-169
      uses, 164-166
   arrays
      creating, 256-261
      testing, 261-263
   birthing, 156
   calling handlers, 159-160
   creating, 156-159
      parameters, 158-159
   descriptions, 149-155
   handlers, 150-156
   handles, 156
   ID numbers, 155-156
   instantiation, 156
   parameters, position dependency, 160
   pointers, 156
   reference counts, 161-162
   releasing, 160

scripts, 150-156
  parent, 151-154
  as tools, 162-163
  see also xobjects
one-frame movies, programming considerations, 26-27
opening
  xobjects, 324-325
  xtras, 329-330
openxlib function, 324
operators in expressions, 79
optimizing
  compilers, 50
  loops, 92-93
or operator in expressions, 79
overriding event handling hierarchy, 38-40

P

palettes, programming considerations, 24-25
parameters, 66-75
  multiple, 69-71
  objects, creating, 158-159
  parentheses, wrapping in, 74-75
  position dependence, 70-71
    in objects, 160
  values, returning, 71-74
parent scripts (objects), 151-154
parentheses
  expressions, 82
  wrapping parameters, 74-75
partial windows, 176-177
patents, advantages of Director, 15-16
Penworks Corporation, 332
performance, 313-314
  bottlenecks, 318-320
  calculations, 317
  CD-ROM drives, 318-320
  do functions, parsing, 318
  hard drives, 320
  idles, impact of, 197
  Internet, 320
  loading cast members from CD-ROM, 267-269

media size, 316-317
name indexing versus name lookups, 314-316
networks, 320
preloading, 314
programming considerations
  CD-ROMs, 20-22
  Lingo versus scores, 25-27
  movies, protected, 25
  multiple casts, 29
  multiple movies, 27-28
  one-frame movies, 26-27
  palettes, 24-25
  platforms, 23
  projectors, 23-24
  World Wide Web, 22-23
  xtras, 29-30
  Shockwave applications, 344-345
  video cards, 318-320
personal handlers, 63
platforms, programming considerations, 23
playing
  audio, duration of playback, 305-306
  CD audio via MCI, 303-305
  digital video, 288
    playing portions of, 289
  MIDI files, 302-303
  wavefiles, 294-300
    direct from disk, 295-296
    disabling, 298-299
    fading in/out, 299
    from memory, 296-297
    multiple channels, 294-295
    soundBusy( ) function, 297-298
    volume, 300
plug-in modules, xtras, 30
pointers (objects), 156
pop( ) function, 250-251
position dependence, parameters, 70-71
positioning digital video, 288-289
predefined handlers, 45
preloadEventAbort property (cast members), 270

preloading
cast members, 269-270, 278
idle loading, 274-278
return values, 271-272
performance, 314
preloadMember( ) function (cast members), 271
preloadMovie( ) function (cast members), 271
preloadNetThing( ) function, 342
preloadRAM property (cast members), 271
PrintOMatic, 332
program flow, 61-62
programming, event-driven, 61-62
programming considerations
casts, multiple, 29
CD-ROMs, 20-22
Lingo versus scores, 25-27
movies
multiple, 27-28
one-frame, 26-27
protected, 25
palettes, 24-25
platforms, 23
projectors, 23-24
World Wide Web, 22-23
xtras, 29-30
projectors, programming considerations, 23-24
CD-ROMs, 20-21
properties
of ancestors (objects), 167-169
arrays, 258
idleLoadMode, 274
idleLoadPeriod, 275
idleLoadTag, 275-276
idleReadChunkSize, 277-278
locH (sprites), 125
locV (sprites), 125
preloadEventAbort (cast members), 270
preloadRAM (cast members), 271
puppet (sprites), 123-124
multiple channels, 127

setting (sprites), 125
testing (sprites), 125
property lists, 143-144, 248-249
accessing, 145-146
closeStacks( ) function, 251
error checking, 252
initializing, 144, 249
numbers, working with, 146
pop( ) function, 250-251
push( ) function, 249-250
sorting, 146-147
testing, 251-252
protected movies, programming considerations, 25
puppet property (sprites), 123-124
multiple channels, 127
puppets, 121
commands, 126
puppetSound command, 296-297
purging cast members, 272-273
push( ) function, 249-250
put command, message window, 103-105

Q-R

quality of wavefiles, 294
QuickTime animation, 310-311

random list functions, 241-243
random numbers
generating, 234-235
nonrepeating, 239-243
randomSeed, testing with, 238-239
range, determining, 236-238
uses, 234
real-time operations, disadvantages of debugger, 116
recording sessions, modifying score, 190-191
reference counts (objects), 161-162
registering rollover commands, 283
releasing objects, 160
repeat while... loops, 88-90
repeat with... loops, 90-93
variations, 95

**software patents, advantages of Director,
15-17**

sort( ) list function, 137

sorting lists, 146-147

sound playFile command, 295-296

sound

duration of playback, 305-306

MCI (Media Control Interface), 301-302

commands, 302

playing CD audio, 303-305

MIDI (Musical Instrument Digital
Interface), 300-301

playing files, 302-303

programming considerations,
CD-ROMs, 21-22

sample rates, 306

size/performance, 316-317

sound effects, creating, 66

wavefiles

playback, 294-300

quality, 294

Sound Xtra, 333

**soundBusy( ) function (wavefile playback),
297-298**

sprites, 121-124

adding to scores, 191

animating with film loops, 308-310

event handling, 35-36

properties

locH, 125

locV, 125

puppet, 123-124, 127

setting, 125

testing, 125

puppeting multiple channels, 127

rollovers, 279-280

Rollover( ) function, 280-281

*simulating mouseEnter/mouseLeave
functions, 281-285*

stacks

creating routines for, 248

overview, 246-247

property lists, 248-249

closeStacks( ) function, 251

error checking, 252

initializing, 249

pop( ) function, 250-251

push( ) function, 249-250

testing, 251-252

status messages, put command, 103-105

stepping through programs (debugger), 108

strings, 201-205

changing case, 204-205

displaying text, 205-206

encryption, 202-204

naming variables, 52

versus symbols, 132-134

submenu items, changing, 213-214

subroutines, 63-66

subwindows, 176-177

symbols

advantages, 134

characteristics, 132-134

declaring, 130-132

as name constants, 129-130

versus strings, 132-134

T

Tabuleiro da Baiana Multimedia, 332

tags, <EMBED> HTML tag, 338-339

tandem lists, 141-143

tell command (MIAW), 184-185

test conditions in loops, 87

testForRollovers( ) function, 283-284

testing

arrays, 261-263

properties (sprites), 125

Shockwave movies, 340

stack routines, 251-252

text

displaying, 205-206

fields, 206-208

colors, setting, 207-208

fonts, 206

setting text in, 207

text

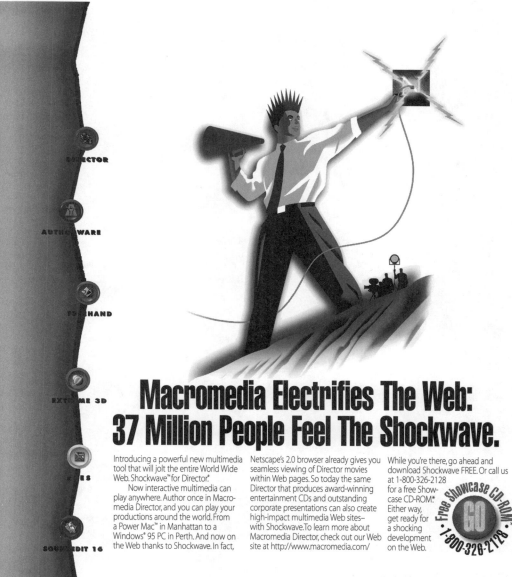

Macromedia Electrifies The Web:
37 Million People Feel The Shockwave.

Introducing a powerful new multimedia tool that will jolt the entire World Wide Web. Shockwave™ for Director.®

Now interactive multimedia can play anywhere. Author once in Macromedia Director, and you can play your productions around the world. From a Power Mac™ in Manhattan to a Windows® 95 PC in Perth. And now on the Web thanks to Shockwave. In fact,

Netscape's 2.0 browser already gives you seamless viewing of Director movies within Web pages. So today the same Director that produces award-winning entertainment CDs and outstanding corporate presentations can also create high-impact multimedia Web sites– with Shockwave. To learn more about Macromedia Director, check out our Web site at http://www.macromedia.com/

While you're there, go ahead and download Shockwave FREE. Or call us at 1-800-326-2128 for a free Show-case CD-ROM.* Either way, get ready for a shocking development on the Web.

Free Showcase CD-ROM.* GO 1-800-326-2128

MACROMEDIA®
Tools To Power Your Ideas

The Lingo developer's secret *(is the Lingo User's Journal)*

Did you learn anything from this book? You can get more of it *every month*. Tab Julius, author of *Lingo!*, also publishes the popular newsletter, the *Lingo User's Journal*, and there's a special offer for *Lingo!*'s readers!

The Lingo User's Journal covers topics *far beyond* the scope of this book. Beginners can keep up on their basics, and intermediates and advanced users will find a treasure trove of articles, tips, secrets and code.

Special Offer!
To readers of this book - get **sixteen issues** *for the price of twelve* by sending in this order form with your payment!

---

1. Fill it out - Please print clearly and include all information
2. Fax it out - *For fastest service*, fax to 1-800-PW-FAXNUm (+1 603-968-3341 intl.)
3. *Or*, Send it out - *Mail to:* Lingo User's Journal • PO Box 531 • Holderness, NH • 03245-0531

I'll take 16 issues for the price of 12! Payment by Visa, MasterCard, American Express, Check or Money Order (US funds only). *Special Rate*: $42 for 16 issues to US/Canada/Mexico, $64 for 16 issues for all other addresses when this form is returned with your payment.

Name _____

Company _____

Address _____

City, State, Zip, _____
etc.

Email address _____

credit card number _____

_____ / _____
expires on

signature _____

telephone _____

___Mac ___PC ___Web   ___Beginner ___Intermediate ___Advanced

---

The Lingo User's Journal has readers in over thirty countries: Don't be left out - *learn the latest Lingo secrets!*

China • India • Israel • Pakistan • South Africa • Canada • Austria • Belgium • Denmark • Finland • France • Great Britain
Germany • Greece • Ireland • Italy • Netherlands • Northern Ireland • Norway • Portugal • Scotland • Spain • Sweden • Switzerland
Australia • Hong Kong • Japan • Malaysia • New Zealand • Singapore • Taiwan • United States • Argentina • Brazil

Lingo User's Journal • Penworks Publishing • Penworks Corporation • PO Box 531 • Holderness, NH • 03245
International: Tel +1 603.968.3341 Facsimile +1 603.968.3361
admin@penworks.com • http://www.penworks.com • Tel 1-800-PENWORX • Fax to 1-800-PW-FAXNUm

Rollover Toolkit™ *Xtra for Director 5.0*

The single most valuable Xtra you can get!

Director users have long asked for **the legendary mouseEnter and mouseLeave functions** - and now they're finally here: in the Rollover Toolkit from Penworks Corporation. StartRollover and EndRollover handlers can be attached to any sprite, cast member, frame or movie - it's no harder than checking for a mouse click!

It's free to use in authoring mode - you don't have to register until you want to use it in projectors. You have the Xtra already - it's on the CD-ROM that comes with this book! (documentation and sample movie too)

Special Offer! To readers of this book - get **all three platforms** *for the price of two* by sending in this order form with your payment!

It's definitely worth it! Payment by Visa, MasterCard, American Express, Check or Money Order.

1. Fill it out - Please print clearly and include all information

2. Fax it out - *For fastest service*, fax to 1-800-PW-FAXNUm (+1 603-968-3341 intl.)

3. *Or*, Send it out - *Mail to:* Penworks Corporation • PO Box 531 • Holderness, NH • 03245-0531

Special Rate: All three projector platforms for the price of two. $25/platform. Disk delivery extra $5 each.

___Macintosh ___Win 3.x ___Win '95   Choose: ___platforms @$25 each (email delivery) *or*
___*all three* for $50 total (email delivery)

___ I want it on disk! $5 additional per platform (or $10 additional for all three)

Name _____

Company _____

Address _____

City, State, Zip, _____
etc.

Email address _____

credit card number _____

___/___
expires on

_____
signature

_____
telephone

Now rollovers are no harder than checking for a mouse click, thanks to the Rollover Toolkit!

Always up to date - you can always download the latest version and stay current. Minor version upgrades are free; author-test the major versions before you buy! **Try it now** - it's on the CD-ROM that came with this book!
Special Offer - get all three platforms for the price of just two! Unlimited projectors, and **No Royalties!**

Penworks Corporation • PO Box 531 • Holderness, NH • 03245
International: Tel +1 603.968.3341 Facsimile +1 603.968.3361
admin@penworks.com • http://www.penworks.com • Tel 1-800-PENWORX • Fax to 1-800-PW-FAXNUm